ADOBE®
PHOTOSHOP CS

THE ART OF
PHOTOGRAPHING
WOMEN

ADOBE®
PHOTOSHOP CS

THE ART OF
PHOTOGRAPHING
WOMEN

KEVIN AMES

WILEY

Wiley Publishing, Inc.

Photoshop® CS: The Art of Photographing Women

Published by
Wiley Publishing, Inc.
111 River Street
Hoboken, N.J. 07030
www.wiley.com

Published by Wiley Publishing, Inc., Indianapolis, Indiana
Published simultaneously in Canada

Library of Congress Control Number: 2004100901

ISBN: 0-7645-4318-0

Manufactured in the United States of America

10 9 8 7 6 5 4 3 2 1

1K/RS/QT/QU/IN

For general information on our other products and services or to obtain technical support, please contact our Customer Care Department within the U.S. at (800) 762-2974, outside the U.S. at (317) 572-3993 or fax (317) 572-4002.

Wiley also publishes its books in a variety of electronic formats. Some content that appears in print may not be available in electronic books.

For Little Bear

Credits

Acquisitions Editor
Tom Heine

Project Editor
Katharine Dvorak

Technical Editor
Joan Sherwood

Copy Editor
Paula Lowell

Editorial Manager
Robyn B. Siesky

Vice President & Executive Group Publisher
Richard Swadley

Vice President and Publisher
Barry Pruett

Project Coordinator
Maridee Ennis

Graphics and Production Specialists
Clint Lahnen, Shelley Lea, Brent Savage

Quality Control Technician
Charles Spencer

Book Designer
Daniela Richardson and Marie Kristine Parial-Leonardo

Proofreading and Indexing
Ethel M. Winslow, Sherry Massey

Cover Image
"Rachel" photograph © 2003 Kevin Ames

Cover Designer
Anthony Bunyan

Foreword

Back in 1984, Aldus PageMaker (the first postscript page-layout application) was introduced and, although it did a lot to astound people, it also did a lot to anger people. Well, one group in particular — typographers (people who set type for a living). They mocked PageMaker. They laughed at it. Most totally dismissed it and continued to do so until PageMaker, and another page-layout application, QuarkXPress, put them right out of a job. Getting these people to change — to give up the way they had been setting type for years (which was tedious, inefficient, and costly) — and join the desktop publishing revolution wasn't easy. Even though it could be proven that desktop publishing was faster, easier, and a whole lot more fun, getting people to give up their "comfortable old way" and try a revolutionary new way was one tough battle.

Now it's 2004 and we're right smack dab in the middle of another technological revolution — the digital photography revolution. Even if you're not yet shooting with a digital camera, you're working with Adobe Photoshop, a digital darkroom that does for photography what PageMaker did for page layout — it makes the process faster, easier, and a whole lot more fun. When Photoshop was first introduced, photographers mocked it. They laughed at it. Most totally dismissed it. But they don't any more.

Today you can watch similar battles brewing between photographers shooting traditional film and photographers who now strictly shoot digitally. Stop by your local camera store and it'll take you all of about 30 seconds to get into a "film is better/digital is better" debate. Even though the revolution is well underway, not everybody has come aboard. For example, Photoshop is more than 12 years old, yet you'll still find a few photographers with traditional darkrooms. Digital photography isn't quite that old yet, and you'll find photographers, even some professionals, still shooting with traditional film. But every day, more and more of these film photographers are going digital, and they aren't looking back. It's a one-way trip. Just like using Photoshop. Once you start really using it, it's hard to go back to mixing chemicals in the dark.

This digital photography revolution didn't happen overnight. The Photoshop revolution took 12 years and counting. And the digital photography revolution that asks professional photographers to give up their darkroom for Photoshop, and their Nikon F-5 for a Nikon D1x digital SLR, has been one tough battle.

That's why revolutions need strong leaders. Evangelists. Trainers. Educators. People who care so passionately about what they've found, and how it's changed their lives for the better, that they're driven with a burning desire to share those ideas with others. And that's why you and I are so lucky. We both found Kevin Ames, the author of the book you're holding in your hands right now.

Kevin is a digital revolutionary in every sense of the word. He's an artist, educator, a craftsman, a passionate evangelist and most important — a leader. He's exactly the person you want to be learning Photoshop techniques from. I should know. I'm one of his students. And every time I hear him speak, read his articles, or spend time with him one-on-one, I learn something new, despite the fact that I'm fairly handy with Photoshop and not a total hack of a photographer.

I was first introduced to Kevin through a mutual friend, digital photography guru Jim DiVitale. As conference technical chair for the PhotoshopWorld Conference and Expo, I was putting together an after-hours session called "The Creative Side of Digital Photography" and I had asked Jim to moderate the session. Jim told me "You've got to get Kevin Ames on this panel. This guy is doing cutting-edge stuff, he's a great public speaker, and a hell of a photographer." Jim is one of the most respected names in digital imaging and photography, and if Jim says you're good — you're good. So I contacted Kevin, he agreed to be on the panel, and as you might expect, he was a huge hit. So the next year, I asked Kevin to not only be a part of the late night session, but to do a regular conference session. He rocked the house. Now Kevin is a fixture at PhotoshopWorld, doing live fashion shoots, panels, retouching sessions, and basically doing what he does best — educating and evangelizing. Kevin gets you excited about Photoshop. Excited about digital photography. Excited about what the two can do together, and he always gives you a look into what's coming down the road. He knows, because he's out there blazing the trail.

I've been encouraging Kevin to do a book for some time for two reasons: First, Kevin is doing things with digital photography and Photoshop that no one else out there is doing; and second, he's a gifted trainer who's willing to share everything. If he knows it — he shares it. He doesn't hold anything back.

That's why I'm so excited about *Photoshop CS: The Art of Photographing Women*. Very few books have the power to change the way you work, impact your career, and suddenly change everything. This is one of those books. It opens doors. It challenges old ideas and introduces new ones. And perhaps best of all it introduces you to a truly talented, gifted, and giving educator who really just wants one thing. To show you the way and share with you how it's done.

You're going to love learning from Kevin. Welcome to the club.

Scott Kelby
Editor, *Photoshop User* magazine
President, National Association of Photoshop Professionals

Preface

Photoshop CS: The Art of Photographing Women is about passion — passion for photography and passion for photographing women. There is an art to photographing women. And the art has changed. Those changes are what the book you hold in your hands is all about.

Digital capture revolutionized the act of recording light with a camera and how images are processed after being taken. Lighting, composition, and exposure are for the most part the same as they have always been. The revolution is that now the ability to realize an idea onto a print can rest with the originator of the image: the photographer.

Digital tools, especially Adobe Photoshop CS, are as integral to the modern photographer as the darkroom was at the turn of the last century. Back then a photographer had to develop film or glass plates and make a print to view the work. Now photographers must have a working, although not necessarily an in-depth, knowledge of Photoshop. The days of handing film to a client and getting paid are just about gone. Clients want digital files for their brochures, advertisements, catalogs, and Web sites. Clients often don't (and some will not) deal with multiple vendors to prepare files for output. They look to the photographer for these services.

The first part of *Photoshop CS: The Art of Photographing Women* is about the processes of digital photography. It begins with background into the ways that digital capture has changed how a photograph is made. Photography is now very similar to making a movie. As in movie production, there is shooting and postproduction work. This book approaches postproduction as part of the planning of a photograph. Every shot begins with the questions "What is best done in the camera?" and "How does postproduction add to improving the resulting photography?" It is not at all about "fixing things in Photoshop."

The new processes of photography include color and exposure correction. In one chapter I focus specifically on lighting. *Photo* means light. It is the first word of both photography and Photoshop. Understanding some of how light works makes working postproduction in Photoshop much more rewarding. In other chapters I show step-by-step how to archive photographic files, ways to view a shoot and even post entire takes on the Internet, as well as how to edit photographs non-destructively so they can be revised anytime later.

The second part is all about photographing women and the postproduction in Photoshop that makes prints of them beautiful. Here, too, I take a step-by-step approach to each project. I include lots of illustrations, notes, and tips on how things work and why.

The goal of this book is to help you understand how similar techniques are applied to achieve results in differing situations. The old saying "Give a man a fish and he'll eat for a day, teach him to fish and he'll eat for a lifetime" seems the best way to describe how I wrote this book. It is not a tips and tricks book. Now don't get me wrong, I love tips and tricks. They are fun, interesting, and often useful. This book is project- and process-oriented. Each step builds the foundation for the next one. Each project builds skills for the ones that follow. By the time you have worked through the examples in the second part, you will have a working knowledge of how photography relates to postproduction and how to do it for yourself. More importantly you will understand the reasoning behind the postproduction from the photographer's point of view.

I shot every photograph in this book. Okay, I didn't shoot the photo of me in the pool (Chapter 14) or my portrait by my good friend and amazing digital photographer Jim DiVitale. This is important because I can share what I was thinking at the time of the shoot and the photographic decisions that were made on set or location and how the images would be finished in Photoshop. Then I take you through the steps of post-producing the photographs.

I am hopeful that after you've worked through the projects in this book you'll come away with a feel for how photography and Photoshop are intertwined. And that you'll develop a sense of when to move from the camera and into Photoshop. Remember, great Photoshop begins with great photography.

Kevin Ames
November 27, 2003
Atlanta, Georgia

Acknowledgments

These are all of the wonderful and amazing friends, teachers, writers, and photographers who have made a contribution either directly or otherwise to the writing of *Photoshop CS: The Art of Photographing Women*. What you are about to read is similar to the list of credits that roll at the end of a movie that so few in the audience stay to watch. Please don't leave the theater early; take a couple of minutes to acknowledge them with me.

For support and understanding above and beyond the call, I extend my heartfelt thanks and love to Starr Moore. I truly could not have written this book without you.

To David Chapman, manager of Professional Photo Resources in Atlanta, who has counseled me and countless others about digital cameras, lenses, equipment and life, and who kept those early Macs running with selfless caring and love, thank you.

Thanks and love to Jim DiVitale, my brother in digital photography, teaching, concerts, long walks in Dublin, Ireland, and in Piedmont Park discussing everything and solving some of it. The way of the fast retreat and much artistic inspiration are his.

Special appreciation of the heartfelt kind to Linda Adams, stylist and art director extraordinaire; to Lois Thigpen, Kitty Bundy, Victoria Duruh, and Rodney Harris of Elite Models/Atlanta for booking so many fabulous models; and to Justin Larose, the best digital and photographic assistant any photographer could dream of working with.

Thank you, thank you, thank you to my editor from Wiley, Katharine Dvorak, for encouragement, advice, good grammar, and humor; and to my technical editor, Joan Sherwood, who's secret identity is that of technology editor for *Photo>Electronic Imaging* magazine. To Barry Pruett, my publisher, and Tom Heine, my acquisitions editor, for the courage to go to bat for the important things.

Deep and everlasting gratitude goes to my friend from way before computers, Eddie Tapp, who was my first Photoshop guru and studio mate in the early years of this digital craziness.

Thanks and kudos, too, go to everyone affiliated with Photoshop World and *Photoshop User* magazine. Especially to Scott Kelby, president of NAPP, Editor in Chief of *Photoshop User*, and all around good guy and friend. I would be remiss to leave out Jim Workman, Dave Moser, Jeff Kelby, Felix Nelson, Dave Cross, Kathy Siler, and my editors at *Photoshop User*, Chris Main and Barbara Thompson, and all of the wonderful folks at KW Computer Training. The members of the Photoshop World Dream Team, who have shared tips ideas, encouragement, and insight into the book-writing process, also deserve high praise and commendation, especially Jack Davis, Ben Willmore, Joe Glyda, Burt Monroy, Julianne Kost, Daniel Brown, Vincent Versace, Deke McClelland, Taz Talley, Russell Brown, and Peter Bauer, all of whom have contributed graciously to my knowledge.

Acknowledgments

For always asking, "how's your book coming along?" and not to mention great meals, thanks to all at Everybody's Pizza in Virginia Highlands and Java Jive on Ponce de Leon Avenue in Atlanta. Aurora Coffee is my official purveyor of extraordinary coffee to start the day and add that extra kick to afternoons.

To Rob Carr, master retoucher, and Katrin Eismann, Photoshop Diva, for their special insights and kindnesses.

To M.O.M. in Boise, thanks for everything, especially your love.

To Beth, Tucker, and Tali at *Jezebel* magazine, Karen Morrione at Working Media Marketing, Joe Gottlieb at Hassett & Cohen, and Joe Alcober of Alcober Design.

To my dear friend and fabulous fashion photographer, Lisa Sciascia, for sharing her ideas and the passionate discussions on concepts, light, and style.

Dean Collins taught me lighting, the importance of giving back by teaching others, and gave me the opportunity to become one of Software Cinema's authors. Thanks, Dean.

Last and certainly not least, thanks to you for spending your time to read the credits. I truly appreciate you. It is my sincere hope you'll have a lot of fun working through *Photoshop CS: The Art of Photgraphing Women* and that it will help you get the ideas that may have been stuck in your head on to a photographic print.

About the Author

Kevin Ames began his photographic career at the age of 12, when he sold pictures of a class field trip to his schoolmates for a tidy profit. From this entrepreneurial and creative beginning, Kevin has become a recognized leader in the fast-evolving world of commercial digital photography.

"Whenever I'm using a camera, I'm not so much concerned with it, as I am with the light," Kevin says of his creative philosophy and process. "I love to control and model and make light work on whatever I'm photographing. It's my passion when I'm behind the camera."

His company, Ames Photographic Illustration, Inc. (www.amesphoto.com), is based in Atlanta, Georgia, and serves clients on location or in the studio. Ames specializes in creating evocative images that promote its customers' products, services, and ideals.

Photograph copyright © 2004 by Jim DiVitale.

"Making photographs for people being my own boss . . . I am doing what I've always wanted to do, since I was a child watching my parents develop photographs in their bathroom/darkroom. I always knew I wanted to be a photographer, and so every day that I'm making photographs and creating is a perfect day."

Kevin is much in demand as a teacher and speaker. He is a Photoshop World Dream Team instructor at the semi-annual Photoshop World conference. Kevin is also a software cinema author and presenter at Dean Collins' Photoshop Training Camp Live! events across the country and is author of the Dean Collins' *Fashion Basics* and *Fashion Advanced* Photoshop training CDs. He has taught classes at art schools and conferences around the world, including Fotographia Orvieto in Orvieto, Italy; Arthouse in Dublin, Ireland; and at the Commercial and Industrial Photographers of New England conference in Boston as well as in other major cities across the United States.

Kevin also teaches advanced digital photography at the Creative Circus in Atlanta, Georgia. Subjects of his classes and lectures include *Making the Digital Transition, Digital Asset Management, Digital Fashion Photography and Post-Production, Digital Negatives—the Case for Shooting Raw, Fashion Shoot Live!, Retouching Beauty,* and *Putting Your Portfolio Online.*

"I hope to teach the new way of thinking that digital offers," notes Ames. "When I'm helping people learn the possibilities of digital, my main concern is to show the problem-solving abilities that are the underlying power of the tips and tricks. I want students to learn how to apply techniques creatively to get the visions in their heads out for others to see."

Kevin writes the "Digital Photographer's Notebook" column for *Photoshop User* magazine. His articles and reviews have appeared in *Studio Photography & Design*, *Photo>Electronic Imaging*, and *Digital Output* magazines.

His credentials include being a Certified Professional Photographer, Certified Electronic Imager, Photographic Craftsman, and an Approved Photographic Instructor. He has served as Co-Chairman of the Digital Imaging and Advanced Imaging Technology Committee and Chairman of the Commercial Advertising Group for the Professional Photographers of America.

Kevin can be reached at kevin@amesphoto.com.

Contents

Contents

part 1

Workflow: From Capture to Digital Postproduction

Chapter One

Bit Depth: The Key to Quality Files and Photographs

A beautiful photograph begins in a photographer's mind. The journey to capture an image and turn it into a work of art for the wall, book, or client hinges on careful planning and execution of the details — casting, props, wardrobe, hair, makeup, and sets — either in the studio or on location.

One step in planning a photograph is determining what tasks can be accomplished in the camera and what will be finished in digital post-production. Learning to see what is happening at the camera and whether to change it on set or refine it in postproduction is a skill that comes only with practice, and lots of it. It is also a skill that is critical to learn in a world where a photograph is not finished with the click of the shutter and a trip to the lab.

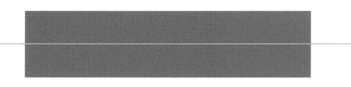

Lighting and capturing the image are the underpinnings of a successful photograph. Recognizing, understanding, and deconstructing the photograph into its components for editing in Adobe Photoshop CS prior to shooting are also important steps in the process. The work that comes after the image is recorded on film or digital media contributes to the ultimate success of the image.

Sometimes circumstances prevent perfection at the camera. A working knowledge of the capabilities of Photoshop and how to apply them is invaluable when work at the camera falls short.

Let's begin at the beginning, which is always a good place to start. This chapter explains what *bit depth* is and presents the important differences between 16- and 8-bit images. An exercise in this chapter demonstrates these differences and why they are important to the success of a final print. This chapter also illustrates a technique for seamlessly burning in highlights using 16-bit files. This technique is useful for producing an optimum file for digital output. It also helps build a foundation for working in 16-bit — one of the keystone features of Photoshop CS.

Bit Depth In Depth

Bit depth is the number of tones represented by each pixel in an image. A 1-bit image is black and white with no grays at all. A 2-bit image has four total tones: black, white, and two gray tones. No matter what bit depth is involved, two of the tones are always black and white. The progression doubles the number of tones for every single increment of bits (2^8). The higher the number of bits a camera or scanner is able to record, the more tones available to each pixel.

Black-and-white digital photographs are most often 8-bit files: black, white, and 254 grays for a total of 256 tones. The value 0 always equals black. The value 255 always equals white. Color digital photographs have three 8-bit channels — red, green, and blue (RGB) — making what is sometimes referred to as *24-bit color* (that is, 3 channels of color times 8 bits per channel equals 24-bit color). An 8-bit RGB file carries the possibility of over 16 million colors. (For the math whizzes in the audience: 256 red tones times 256 green tones times 256 blue tones equals 16,777,216 colors.) This is more than enough information as the finest digital printers and printing presses can only reproduce a few thousand distinct colors. The 8-bit format is also the standard for the vast majority of output devices, including inkjet, dye-sublimation, LED, and four-color printing presses. And because 8-bit files are easily damaged in postproduction, a high bit depth workflow is desirable.

Photoshop CS enables the user to work in the very high quality16-bit mode. Layers, layer masks, vector masks, adjustment layers, and gradients are now fully supported in 16-bit mode. Photoshop now also supports files up to three hundred thousand (300,000) pixels in any dimension as well as files larger than 2 gigabytes (GB).

Certain creative filters are still reserved for the 8-bit mode. In a typical Photoshop editing session, you would work in 16-bit mode non-destructively for highest quality. (Chapter 6 discusses non-destructive Photoshop in detail.) A duplicate of the file would be converted to 8-bit for the application of the Artistic, Brush Stroke, Distort, Pixelate, Render, Sketch, and Texture filter suites now available in the *Filter Gallery*. The special filter tools — Extract, Liquify, Lens Blur and Pattern Maker — are also 8-bit only.

Where Do 16-bit Files Come From?

You make 16-bit files from film by setting the scanner's software to 16-bit and dragging the highlight and shadow sliders all the way to the left and right, respectively. The preview will look very flat. This technique ensures that the resulting file has all the information the scanner can capture. From digital captures, 16-bit files result by converting raw camera files in either Photoshop's Camera Raw, by using a third-party conversion package, or by relying on the software that comes with the camera. Camera Raw in Photoshop allows the output to be in either 8- or 16-bit. It also provides a superior method of increasing the resolution of the file created from the linear raw data. Unless the image is only going on a Web site, I strongly recommend that you only build out raw files to 16-bit TIFs. Most camera manufacturer's software will make 16-bit TIFs from their version of raw files.

File degradation is cumulative. Working in 16-bit up to the point of Liquifying a photograph or applying a creative filter ensures that the highest quality file is available for output.

Digital Negatives

So what's the big deal about 16-bit anyway? The sensors in digital cameras and scanners capture in bit depths that are significantly higher than 8-bit. Some new digital camera backs already capture actual 16-bit files.

Cameras set to save images in JPEG or TIF formats throw away data that isn't needed to make an 8-bit file. The data is gone. It is lost forever. Think about it like this: Imagine dropping off a roll of film at a non-professional lab. When it is finished, you pick up the prints and without looking at them you throw away the negatives. No photographer would consider having her or his precious film processed and printed at a less than top-grade lab! (And every frame we shoot is potentially precious, isn't it?) There are times when this choice has to be made, especially when traveling overseas with the difficulties of getting unprocessed film through airport security without damage from overzealous x-ray machines. The negatives can always be reprinted. No one would ever knowingly throw them away, especially without even looking at the prints. Yet that is exactly what happens digitally when a photographer chooses camera-based conversions to 8-bit JPEG files or TIFs over saving as a raw file.

A capture saved as a raw file contains all the information that the camera's sensor chip is able to capture. There is a lot more data than even the monitor can show. The data is available to bring back blown-out skies and for any other tonal and color corrections that would severely challenge (damage) an 8-bit capture. As mentioned earlier, much higher resolutions than originally captured can be generated from the linear raw file with no discernable quality loss. Additionally, a raw file can be built out to a 16-bit file, giving Photoshop the data with which to make changes so great they would ruin an 8-bit file, resulting in banding or posterization in the final output. These adjustments include correction for over- and underexposure, color shifts, and the ability to interpolate the file to a much larger size beyond the larger sizes available in Camera Raw. You can make all of these changes without degrading the resulting 8-bit files. Here's why it works and how to do it yourself.

A 16-bit file has 65,534 tones of gray plus black and white for a total of 65,536 tones per channel. This is an incredible amount of information to

Most pro-sumer digital cameras can capture photographs in the raw format. This is the format of choice for producing files that will be output with the highest-quality reproduction. Some professional digital cameras only save in raw. Some offer the choice of raw, raw and JPG, or (and this is where, in my opinion, the camera becomes rank amateur) JPG or TIF. Files saved in raw have all the information that the image sensor saw, every bit of it (pun intended).

A couple of raw file traits exist that might seem to be drawbacks to this option. First, raw files have more data so they take up more space on the storage device in the camera. Second, because raw files are bigger, they limit the *burst rate,* or number of frames the camera can save without pausing. I like to think of this pause as when I would be changing the film in my camera back in the bad old, er, I mean film days. After the shoot is over, the Compact Flash card, Microdrive, or whatever media is in vogue at the moment is downloaded to the computer and backed up onto a CD or DVD.

Take care of these raw files. They are your digital negatives after all. Raw files, like their film analogs, are not affected when you output them to a working JPEG file or TIF. Changes made in either Photoshop's Camera Raw or the camera software only tell the computer what effects to apply to the resulting JPEG file or TIF. The raw file never changes. All the original data remains pristine. (In Chapter 4, I discuss how to make bulletproof archives of your digital negatives.)

What Are Raw Files Anyway and Why Are They Complicating My Life?

sample down to the 256 tones per channel of an 8-bit file. The following exercise demonstrates the effects of tonal (exposure) changes in 16- and 8-bit files. It includes a technique for combining different versions of the same image to bring down an overexposed highlight.

You can download the sample 16-bit file used in this exercise from www.amesphoto.com/learning. Click the link for "Photoshop CS: The Art of Photographing Women" and then click "Chapter One." The photograph is a digital image captured in black and white with a Leaf DCB II digital back on a Fuji GX-680 II without the filter wheel.

Step ⁄ : **In Photoshop CS open the File Browser (⌘/Control+Shift+O). Navigate to the folder for Chapter 1 and double-click the "16-bit.tif" thumbnail to open it.**
Information about the image is displayed at the bottom of the document window (Mac) or application window (Win).

Step 2: **Set the display to Document Sizes by selecting it in the fly-out menu** (1.1).

The file size is 8MB. In order to learn how to make corrections "by the numbers," the file must first be converted to RGB. Color and tone corrections are discussed in Chapter 2.

Step 3: **Choose Image➡Mode➡RGB Color to convert the file to RGB.**

Notice that there is a check mark next to 16 Bits/Channel. The file size is now 24MB. Three 8MB channels — one each for red, green, and blue — equals 24MB. The document size now reads "Doc: 24M/24M."

Step 4: **Make a copy of the file by choosing Image➡ Duplicate.**

Rename the file "8-bit.tif" (1.3). This file is used in the final composite of this exercise and to demonstrate what happens to an 8-bit file when it undergoes exposure changes in Photoshop.

1.1

The document size of an image in Photoshop is displayed in the bottom of the document window. In this example the document size is displayed as Doc: 62.6M/184.7M (1.2).The first number is the size of the flattened image. The second

Document Size

is the size of the image with layers. If the size isn't displayed, there is a fly-out menu for getting the size and other information about the image. Another way to see the file size and dimensions is to choose Image➡Canvas Size. The Canvas Size dialog box will not only display the file size and show the dimensions, but it also enables you to resize the image canvas.

1.2

Duplicate Image

Duplicate: 03-1898-055_172.16bit.TIF   OK

As: 8-bit.tif   Cancel

☐ Duplicate Merged Layers Only

1.3

Step 5: Convert "8-bit.tif" to 8-bit by choosing Image➡Mode➡8 Bits/Channel.
Notice that the file size is now 12MB, half the size of "16-bit.tif" (1.4). A 16-bit file has 256 times more tones per channel as an 8-bit file (256 x 256 = 65,536 tones per channel). It is also twice the size in megabytes.

After converting the file to 8-bit, the photograph still has good overall exposure yet the model's shirt is overexposed. It has lost some detail and is bright enough to draw the eye away from the model's face. It is difficult to see the water droplets on her arm. Let's set up the files needed to fix this problem while learning the advantage to working in 16-bit. The numbers tell the story.

Step 6: Display the Info palette (Window➡Info).
A check mark indicates it is visible.

1.4

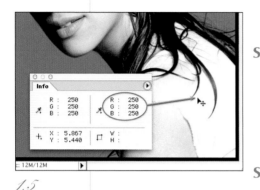

1.5

Step 7: Make "16-bit.tif" active by clicking inside the image or on its header bar and then bring up the Levels dialog box by pressing ⌘/Control+L.

To use the mouse for this step, choose Image➡Adjustments➡Levels.

Step 8: Hold down the Option/Alt key and then click and hold the highlight slider (the white triangle on the right). The image displayed goes black. Move the highlight slider to the left.

The areas that appear first are the brightest highlights. Make a mental note of the area displayed, in this case her shoulder.

Step 9: Release the Option/Alt key and the screen returns to normal. Click Cancel in the Levels dialog box (or press Esc on the keyboard) to close it without applying changes. Move the cursor over the area revealed as the brightest highlights.

Look at the Info palette. It shows the values as R: 250 G: 250 B: 250. Because 255 is pure white, we know from the numbers that probably no printable detail is there (1.5). (For more on what the numbers mean, check out the nearby sidebar, "Steps, Tones, and the Meaning of Life.") Onwards. . . .

Steps, Tones, and the Meaning of Life

The top section in this figure is a gradient of the continuous tones of black to white – 0 to 255 (1.6). These are the steps that make up a photograph on the monitor, on an inkjet or photographic print, or even on the printed page. Below that gradient is a 21-step chart showing blocks of values. The steps are helpful when visualizing the values between groups of tones. Shadow detail starts at around 25. 18% gray is right where you would expect it at 127. And yes, I know what you are thinking, "128 is the middle of 256." And yes it is. When you run the cursor over middle gray in Photoshop it reads 127. Why? Because 127 is the middle value for the 254 tones of gray in a 256 step 8-bit image that includes a step each for pure black and pure white. About the highest number where white with detail will reproduce is 242. When a reading moves into the high 240s and the 250s, highlight detail is lost rapidly. At these readings some detail might appear on the monitor. It will not reproduce on a print or on the printed page. Depending on the output device (printer, and so on) values below 25–29 will have no detail in the shadows.

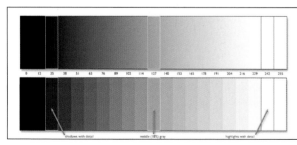

1.6

Step *10*: **Choose the Color Sampler tool from the fly-out menu of the Eyedropper tool** (1.7) **and set the Sample Size to 3 by 3 Average in the Color Sampler tool Options bar.**

Move the cursor around the highlighted area of the model's shirt until each of the RGB values read 250. (Refer to Figure 1.5 for the location.) Click to set Sampler #1 there. Now look at the Info palette. It has increased in size adding an area for Sampler #1.

Step *11*: **Open the Levels dialog box by clicking ⌘/Control+L, and move the gamma (midtone) slider to the right to darken the highlights.**

Continue moving the slider until the middle Input Levels box reads 0.45 (1.8). The overall photograph is very dark. The Color Sampler now shows that the highlights have lowered, as well, from 250 to 245.

Step *12*: **Look at Sampler #1. It shows 250/245, indicating a move from 250 to 245. Click OK.**

Sampler #1 now reads 245, the changes made by the Levels adjustment.

All the work has been done in 16 bit. Here's why.

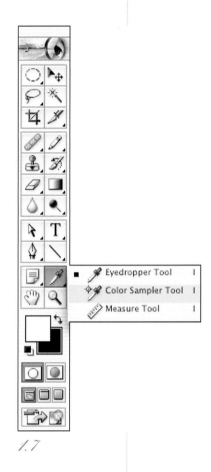

1.7

Step *13*: **Click on "8-bit.tif" to activate it and then press ⌘/Control+Option/Alt+L on the keyboard.**

Adding the Option/Alt key tells Photoshop to apply the settings used last for Levels. The Levels dialog box appears, displaying the exact adjustments in the midtone Input Levels box (0.45) as in Step Twelve. Click OK to accept the settings. "8-bit.tif" has received the same adjustment as "16-bit.tif." Now it gets interesting.

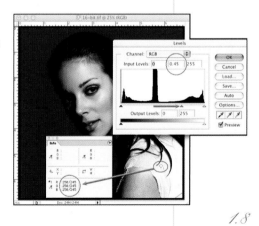

1.8

Tip

{ The keyboard shortcut for the Eyedropper is i+Shift+i. }

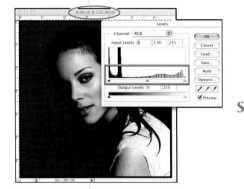

1.9

1.10

Step 14: Open the Levels dialog box again and look at the histogram.

The dropouts in the histogram are areas where data has been lost (1.9). This effect is called *combing* because the remapping of pixels creates gaps making the histogram resemble a comb. The lost data in this 8-bit file can result in banding or posterization when it is printed.

Step 15: Click Cancel or press Esc on the keyboard to close the Levels dialog box.

Because "8-bit.tif" will be used in another step without the Levels adjustment, press ⌘/Control+Z to undo Levels. The image reverts to the brighter version.

Step 16: Double-click "16-bit.tif" to make it active and then open the Levels dialog box.

Notice that this histogram, which represents exactly the same changes made to "8-bit.tif," is solid and shows no evidence of combing (1.10). It works because there are a huge number of additional tones (65,536 per channel in 16-bit and only 256 in 8-bit) to use in making the tonal adjustment. This means that fairly massive changes can be made in a 16-bit file without data loss when it is converted to 8-bit. When you've finished checking out the histogram, click Cancel or press the escape (Esc) key to close the Levels dialog box.

Now, I know what you're thinking: "Okay. If I have an 8-bit file that really, really needs a big exposure adjustment, I can convert it to 16-bit, fix it, and convert it back to 8-bit." Good try. This is one of these something-from-nothing scenarios that look great in theory and even seem to work in Photoshop and winds up looking not quite as good as complete and total garbage when printed. This won't work, so don't even *bother*. And remember: To achieve the highest quality, *always* begin post-production in 16-bit.

Step 17: Duplicate the darker version of "16-bit.tif" by choosing Image→Duplicate and name the new file "8-bit Burn.tif."

Step 18: Convert the new file to an 8-bit image by choosing Mode→8 Bits/Channel, and then close "16-bit.tif" without saving it.

Step 19: **Activate "8-bit burn.tif" by clicking on it and then select the Move tool by pressing V on the keyboard.**

Hold down the Shift key and drag "8-bit Burn.tif" onto "8-bit.tif." The Shift key centers an image in the file it is dragged to using the Move tool. If the files are exactly the same size they will be in perfect pixel-to-pixel registration with each other. Look at the Layers palette. "8-bit burn.tif" has become Layer 1. The whole image is dark. Close "8-bit burn.tif" without saving.

1.11

Step 20: **Double-click on the words "Layer 1" in the Layers palette and rename the layer "Burn."**

Go to the bottom of the Layers palette. Hold down the Option/Alt key and click the Add Layer Mask icon (1.11). The dark image disappears. A black layer mask is added to the Burn layer. A Layer Mask icon is displayed to the right of the eyeball and a light border appears around the mask indicating that it is ready to edit.

Step 21: **Press ⌘/Control+Option/Alt+0 to zoom to 100% and press B on the keyboard (or click on the Brush icon on the Tool palette) to select the paint brush.**

In the Brush Options bar, choose a 200-pixel soft-edged brush from the Brush Preset Picker and set the Opacity to 100% or press 0 on the keyboard (1.12).

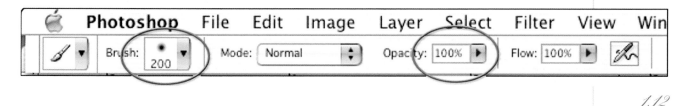

1.12

Step 22: **With the foreground color set to white and the Burn layer active, click the layer mask to activate it. Brush over the model's shirt and arm.**

You are burning in the washed-out highlights by revealing darker areas from the Burn layer when you paint white on the layer mask.

Step 23: **Look at the Layer Mask icon** (1.13).

The area just painted appears white, allowing the darkened shirt and arm to blend with the brighter version below. If an unwanted dark area appears where your brush moved onto the background around her arm or back, switch the foreground color to black (X on the keyboard) and paint it out.

Step 24: **Change the opacity of the layer to fine-tune the effect** (1.14) **and then save the image to your hard drive. It will be useful for practicing retouching flyaway hair and skin smoothing later in the book.**

1.13

1.14

Understanding Colorcast

Colorcast is the appearance of one or more colors dominating the highlights, midtones, and/or shadows within an image. Let's use another image to look at a pure example of how colorcast works and what a neutral color balance is.

Step 1: **Open the 8-bit file "Christina.tif."**

Step 2: **Display the Info palette by choosing Window→Info.**
A check mark by the word *Info* indicates the Info palette is visible. If you don't see it, look for the Info tab. It is docked with the Navigator tab by default. Click on the Info tab to activate the palette.

Step 3: **Choose the Color Sampler tool from the Tool palette or press Shift+I on the keyboard.**

Step 4: **In the Color Sampler tool Options bar, set the Sample Size to 3 by 3 Average and then click on the model's cheek to set Sampler #1. Set Sampler #2 on her jacket and Sampler #3 on a midtone on her jeans** (1.15).

Step 5: **Look at the Info palette. Notice the additional readouts numbered 1, 2, and 3.**
These correspond to the color samplers you just placed. Make sure your placements read as close as possible to the values in the sample Info palette shown in Figure 1.15. To move a sample, hold down the ⌘/Control key and click and drag it to a new location. The Color Sampler tool allows you to place up to four sample pickers on an image.

Step 6: **Look at the numbers** (1.16). **Your samples may be slightly different than those shown here.**
The number in each sample is the tonal value of that color on a scale of 0 to 255. Sampler #1 in the Info palette shows equal tonal values for the red, green, and blue channels, which in this case is 250. This means that the value of that sample is a highlight with very little detail. Remember that 255 is pure white. Sampler #2 samples the shadow area of her jacket and reads 24 for each of the color channels. The last sampler, #3, shows an almost perfect middle gray with an RGB reading of 126.

1.15

Step 7: Press ⌘/Control+L to open the Levels dialog box.
At the top of the display is a drop-down menu labeled
Channel. By default, the composite of all three channels —
RGB — is displayed. Click on the drop-down arrows. The
four choices are composite RGB, Red channel, Green channel,
and Blue channel. The keyboard shortcuts are
displayed, too.

**Step 8: Choose the Green channel and then click on the
gamma (midtone) slider (the gray triangle in the
middle) and move it to the right until the middle
box of the Input Levels is 0.65.**
Look at the image on the screen. It has a magenta cast (1.17).
Green is the complement of magenta. By reducing the amount
of green, magenta becomes dominant. In the Info palette, a
second set of numbers has generated. The readings to the left
of the slash are the original readings, and the right-hand numbers show the changes. The green channel now reads 247, 86,
7. The Red and Blue channels remain at 250, 126, 24. The
sampler numbers indicate more Red and Blue and less Green.
Red and Blue in equal amounts make magenta.

Tip

When the highlight and
shadow samplers display
equal values of RGB,
those tones in the image
are neutral, having no
colorcast.

1.16

Step 9: **Press ⌘/Control+3 to make the Blue channel active and move the gamma slider to the right until the middle box of Input Levels reads 0.65.**

Take a look at the Info palette. Now the Green and Blue channels read 247, 86, 7, while the Red channel stays at 250, 126, 24. The image has taken on a red colorcast. There is more red (3 points in the highlights, 40 points in the midtones, and 17 points in the shadows) than green and blue, hence the overall red color (1.18). Click OK in the Levels dialog box to accept the changes.

Step 10: **Reopen the Levels dialog box (⌘/Control+L).**

Notice the combing in the histogram. There isn't much damage. (Remember, the effects are cumulative.) This concept is also useful to know when toning black-and-white images in Photoshop. More effective and less damaging ways of toning exist, which I explore later in this book in Chapter 11 and in Chapter 16.

Step 11: Click Cancel to close Levels without applying the changes.

You have experienced the quality of 16-bit files and have an understanding of colorcast. In Chapter 2 I use the same tools on a 16-bit file to neutralize the color and introduce Curves to remove colorcast.

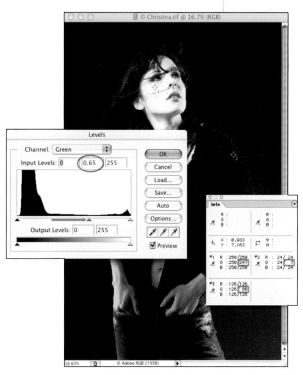

1.17

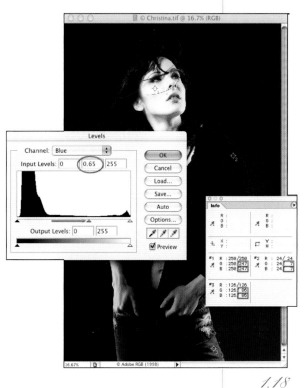

1.18

Chapter Two

Color Correction: Color by Numbers

T his chapter looks at tonal (exposure) and color control in separate exercises so that you can see the techniques individually and how and why they work. The exercises are then combined to begin developing a digital workflow. Three more workflow-related subjects are explored: initial sharpening, color aliasing reduction, and copyright protection. The chapter also includes an introduction to Photoshop Actions and how this feature can speed up production on numbers of images. Workflow can be daunting or even boring. Once it is set up, it can be highly automated. Don't be intimidated. It's all good.

Color Correction

In Chapter 1, finding highlights, midtones, and shadows wasn't hard to sample in our image, as the black-and-white image was composed of nothing but neutral tones. Finding highlights, midtones, and shadows in color photography is much more difficult. Unless there are highlight and shadow values that you know are neutral, accurately color balancing an image is difficult. Often, finding neutral values in a color photograph is nothing more than a SWAG (also known as a *Scientific Wild A** Guess*). Therefore, having a neutral reference in the first photograph of each lighting setup is important.

A photograph made during magic hour — that incredible time shortly before the sun sets when the light is golden and the sun is low in the sky — will often be too warm. It has too much orange in it. I know what you're thinking . . . "Orange! What combination of RGB makes um, well, 'O'? And how in the world do I fix that?" That is *exactly* the question. When a photograph contains colors that aren't intuitive, making them neutral becomes guesswork. That's why photographing a neutral reference in the first frame of each new lighting situation is critical. "Why the first frame?" you might ask. Because doing so is more likely to become a habit if you always do it first. Otherwise you can easily get caught up in the shoot and completely forget to make one. A photograph with the GretagMacbeth ColorChecker Chart or their new ColorChecker Gray Balance Card is an essential tool for good color. This exercise uses a combination of the techniques discussed in Chapter 1 to correct the color and fine-tune the exposure at the same time. Steps One through Five get the color accurate to about 90% most of the time. Steps Six and Seven are for color fanatics who want to work on the midtones as well as the highlights and shadows.

2.1

Step 1: **Go to www.amesphoto.com/learning and download the folder for Chapter 2. Navigate to the 16-bit file "colorchecker.tif" and open it in Photoshop CS.**
At first glance the model's skin tones look great (2.1). A closer look reveals a colorcast so orange that it looks as if Christina had a very bad out-of-the-bottle-bronzing kind of day. Look closely at the gray swatch. Notice it is very orangish in its overall colorcast.

The digital world is pervaded by acronyms. Most, not all, have three letters. Some have four or more not including hyphens. When acronym use is unavoidable or I make one up (as I am about to do), I'll point it out with the new acronym, TLA (for *three-* or *two-letter acronym*).

Acronyms

2.2

Step 2: **Select the Color Sampler tool by pressing i + Shift + i. Check the Options bar to be sure the Sample Size is set to 3 by 3 Average. Place Sampler #1 on the white patch, Sampler #2 on the black patch, and Sampler #3 on the gray patch that is two to the left of the white patch** (2.2).

This is backwards from the way the samples appear on the ColorCheckers. It is in the order of making the correction: highlights, shadows, and midtones.

Step 3: **Display the Info palette (Window➡Info).**

The Info palette is expanded to display the readings for Samplers #1, #2, and #3. The readings show the color bias for each of the three tones (2.3). Sampler #1 shows highlights

Note
The placement of the color samplers is some-what arbitrary. Your numbers might not exactly match the ones in the book. It is all right to use the ones you choose. The techniques are the same.

[21]

with detail, R: 245, G: 240, and B: 194. Red is the dominant color because it has the highest value. The image has a red colorcast in the highlights. Sampler #2 displays shadow values of R: 34, G: 34, and B: 28. This time red and green dominate with the highest value indicating that the colorcast in the shadow is red-green. Remember that a neutral tone is one whose RGB numbers are equal. Driving the lower values up to the brightest one, in this case red, neutralizes highlights. It works the opposite way in the shadows — you drive the brighter values down to the lowest one.

Step 4: **Open the Levels dialog box (⌘/Control+L or Image➡Adjustments➡Levels) and choose the Green channel from the Channels drop-down menu or by pressing ⌘/Control+2 on the keyboard.**

Step 5: **Click on the highlight slider and drag it to the left while watching the numbers in the Info palette.** Notice that the Info palette now displays two sets of numbers separated by a slash. The numbers on the left represent the starting point. The numbers to the right are the changes that have been made with the adjustment. When the Green channel reading to the right of the slash on Sampler #1 reaches 245, release the mouse. You select the slider by clicking it with the mouse. No shadow adjustments are needed because red and green both read 34.

Step 6: **Press ⌘/Control+3 to select the Blue channel and then click and drag the highlight slider to the left until Sampler #1 (the highlight) reads 245.** Use the up and down arrows on the keyboard to make fine adjustments. Going from 194 to 245 is a big change. Look at Sampler #2. The Blue channel shadow value has changed to 36.

Step 7: **Click on the shadow slider and drag it to the right until it reads 34.** The highlights read R: 245, G: 245, B: 245 and are neutral because they are equal. The shadows are neutral, too, reading R: 34, G: 34, B: 34. Color balancing of the highlights and shadows is complete (2.4). Notice that the midtones are not neutral with readings of R: 184, G: 182, B: 168. We'll use another tool in a later step to balance the midtones. While the Levels dialog box is still open, we'll fine-tune the exposure.

2.3

Step 8: **Press ⌘/Control+~ to activate the composite RGB channel and then click on the highlight slider and drag it to the left until the highlights (#1 Info field) read R: 249, G: 249, B: 249.**

The white tile on the Color Checker chart has no detail. Boosting it into the very high 240s or even 250–252 is all right for the upper exposure (tonal) values.

Step 9: **Now click on and move the shadow slider to the right until the shadows (#2 Info field) read R: 28, G: 28, B: 28 (2.5).**

Again, there is no detail in the black tile. Increasing the shadow numbers into the high 20s increases the overall contrast. These changes may result in one channel being a point off. You can correct this by going into the channel that is not equal to the other two and either boosting it in the highlights or dropping it in the shadows. Sometimes the values fall in between and getting the numbers exactly the same is not possible. If they are within a point or two, the image will still be very close to being neutral. Two and a half points represent less than a 1 percent difference.

Step 10: **Click the Save button in the Levels dialog box and name the file "Levels.alv."**

Step 11: **Click Save and then click OK in the Levels dialog box.**

The highlights and shadows are now neutral and have had their exposures tweaked. The settings have been saved so they can be used to correct files shot under the same light without the Color Checker chart.

Note

The tilde (~) key is under the Esc key on both Macintosh and Windows keyboards.

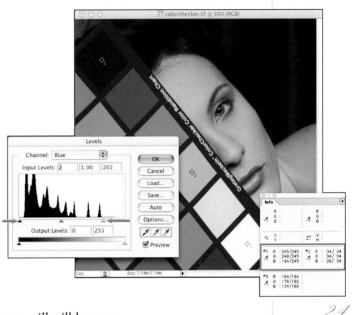

2.4

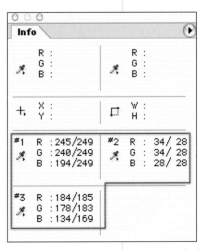

2.5

Here's the part of the process that needs finesse. Look at Sampler #3 in Figure 2.5. The midtones (#3 Info field) read R: 185, G: 183, B: 169. These colors are not neutral — not even close. Midtone colorcast happens when the camera itself is not neutralized for the lighting situation that exists at the time of making the exposure. (See the sidebar "Color Balancing the Camera" later in this chapter.) You might think that you could fix highlights and shadows by moving the gamma (midtone) slider and balancing to the middle value. Unfortunately, using the Levels dialog box causes changes across the entire tonal range, which means that a shift of a color in the midtones also affects the shadows and highlights. Try neutralizing with the gamma slider in the Levels dialog box and see what happens. Afterwards, press Esc to cancel the change.

Correcting the midtones is not difficult with different adjustment tools: the Curves dialog box and a calculator. Here's how it works:

Step *1*: **Press ⌘/Control+M on the keyboard or choose Image➡Adjustments➡Curves to bring up the Curves dialog box.**

Step *2*: **Set the grid to fine in the Curves window by pressing Option/Alt and clicking in the window.**
The diagonal line that cuts the box in half from lower left to upper right is the same as the histogram in the Levels dialog box. The lower-left portion represents shadows; the middle, midtones; and the upper right, highlights. I superimposed a histogram to give you the idea (2.6). (Don't look for it in the Curves window because it isn't there. There is now a floating histogram palette in Photoshop CS that you can watch as you make changes.) Levels is a linear correction across the entire range of tones in a channel. Curves is more selective and a truly versatile and elegant tool. You can set a point to move the whole curve or sections of it. In the case of the midtones, you are going to isolate then change the middle part of the curve. Because the colorcast is in the midtones, the neutralization is made to the average of those RGB values (R: 185 + G: 183 + B: 169 = 537 divided by 3 channels = 179).

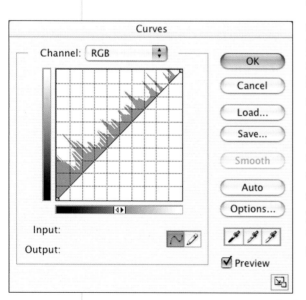

2.6

Let's get back to work.

Step 3: **Press ⌘/Control+1 to choose the Red channel.**

Count one box up and over from the lower-left corner along the line and click to set a point. Count one box down and one box over on the line from the upper-right corner and click to set a second point (2.7). These points isolate the midsection that controls the midtones we want to neutralize.

Step 4: **Click in the middle of the curve and enter the Red value, 185, in the Input box.**

The line changes into a curve and the color goes way cyan. Don't panic.

Step 5: **In the Output box enter the average of the RGB values: 179.**

The curve softens and the colors become more balanced.

Step 6: **Now press ⌘/Control/+2 to bring up the Green channel and set the constraining points the same way you did in the Red channel.**

Click in the middle of the line to set a point. Enter the green value, **183**, in the Input box. The image is very magenta when the output is at 127 (2.8). Press the Tab key and enter the RGB average, 179, over the high-lighted 127 in the Output box. The image looks better now.

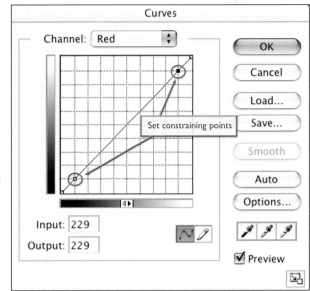

2.7

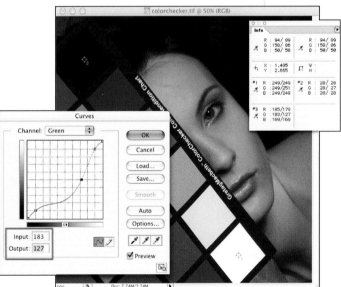

2.8

Step 7: **Finally, press ⌘/Control+3 for the Blue channel and again set the restraining points on the curve.**
Click on the middle of the curve to set the point for the adjustment. Enter **169** in the Input box and the RGB average **179** in the Output box. Look at the Info palette (2.9). The midtones are neutral and so are the highlights and shadows.

Step 8: **Save this setting by clicking the Save button in the Curves dialog box, and name the file "Curves.alc."**
Click OK and close "colorchecker.tif" without saving it.

Color Balancing the Camera

Compare the two photographs in this figure: 2062-B-0026.tif and 2062-B-0059.tif (2.10). They are almost identical with the exception that 2062-B-0059.tif has been "color balanced" in the camera at the time of photography. Take a look at the numbers in 0059. There is only a 6-point spread (less than 2 percent) in the highlights, a 2-point difference (less than 1 percent) in the shadows, and a 3-point spread (just above 1 percent) in the midtones. There really is no colorcast in the image. The postproduction here is minimal. If you want to color balance it and bump the exposure, here are the steps:

1. **Step 1:** From the File Browser (⌘/Control+Shift+O), open the file 2062-B-0059.tif. Select the Color Sampler from the Tool palette or press i + shift + i. Set Sampler #1 on the white swatch. Set Sampler #2 on the black swatch, and Sampler #3 on the gray swatch, second to the left of the white. Display the Info palette (Window➡Info).

2. **Step 2:** Color balance the image. Open the Levels dialog box by choosing Image➡Adjustments➡Levels or pressing ⌘/Control+L on the keyboard. Make the Green channel active from the Channel drop-down menu or press ⌘/Control+2. Drag the highlight slider to the left until #1 G: reads 236/237. Drag the shadow slider to the right until #2 G: reads 32/31. Activate the Blue channel (⌘/Control+3). Drag the highlight slider to the left until #1 B: reads 231/237. Drag the shadow slider to the right until #2 B: reads 33/31. The midtones are still 5 points apart. This is not a printable difference, being right at 2 percent.

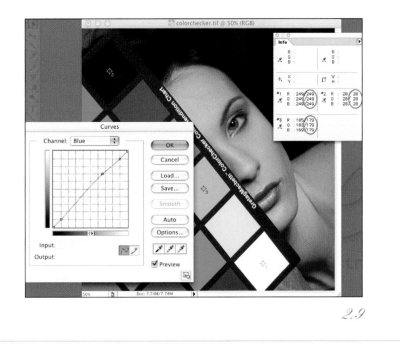

2.9

3. **Step 3**: Adjust the exposure. Choose the RGB composite channel by choosing ⌘/Control+~. Drag the highlight slider to the left until #1 reads RGB: 249. Drag the shadow slider to the right until #2 reads RGB: 28. Click Save and name this file "Levels1.alv." Click Cancel and close the file without saving.

This method is by far the preferred one to color balance a photograph. It saves a lot of postproduction work and certainly yields a less stressed file and an absolutely less stressed photographer. Check the manual that comes with your camera to find out how to make it neutral under different lighting conditions. Not all cameras have this feature, so knowing how to correct even the worst color in Photoshop is important.

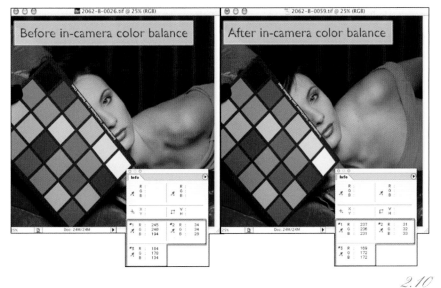

2.10

2.11

2.12

Automation

The previous exercise is a lot of work. It would be mind numbing if all of those steps had to be repeated manually for every photograph we make. Fortunately, Photoshop has a very postproduction-friendly feature called *Actions*. Simply put, Actions are scripts that Photoshop records while you do a process once for playback later on other files that require the same corrections. To write an Action to automate the color and tonal corrections from the last exercise, follow these steps:

Step 1: Double-click "colorchecker.tif" in the File Browser to open it.

Because you didn't save it in the previous exercise, it should still be orangish. If you saved over the original by mistake, download another copy from www.amesphoto.com/learning.

Step 2: Display the Actions palette by choosing Window➡Actions.

Step 3: From the bottom of the Actions palette, click the Create New Set icon (2.11).

The New Set dialog box appears. Name the new set "Postproduction" and click OK. The new set appears in the Actions palette.

Step 4: Again from the bottom of the Actions palette, click the Create New Action icon (2.12).

The New Action dialog box appears and prompts for a name for the Action. You can also start a New Action by clicking on the fly-out arrow in the upper-right hand corner of the Actions palette and choosing New Action.

Step 5: In the New Action dialog box, type "color and tone correction" in the Name field, select F12 for the Function Key, and then click Record (2.13).

The bottom of the Actions palette displays the controls of a tape recorder. The Record button is red, indicating that an Action is being recorded.

New Action		
Name: color and tone correction		Record
Set: Postproduction		Cancel
Function Key: F12 ☐ Shift ☐ Command		
Color: ☐ None		

2.13

Now go through the steps of the color and tonal correction exercise again except use the saved corrections for each dialog box.

Step *6*: **Open the Levels dialog box (⌘/Control+L) and click Load** (2.15). Choose Levels.alv, click Load, and then click OK (2.14).

Step *7*: **Open the Curves dialog box (⌘/Control+M) and click Load.** Choose Curves.acv, click Load, then click OK (2.15).

Step *8*: **On the Actions palette, either click the Stop Playing/Recording icon at the bottom or click the fly-out menu and choose Stop Recording** (2.16). The Action is complete.

Step *9*: **Close colorchecker.tif without saving it and then open it again.** It is now back in the uncorrected state.

Step *10*: **Press the F12 function key on the keyboard.** The Action plays and makes all the corrections without further prompting. And it is very fast. It can also be played back from the Actions palette by clicking on color and tone correction in the Postproduction set and clicking the Play button at the bottom of the palette or by selecting Play from the fly-out menu.

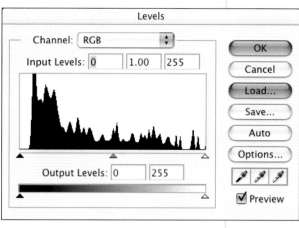

2.14

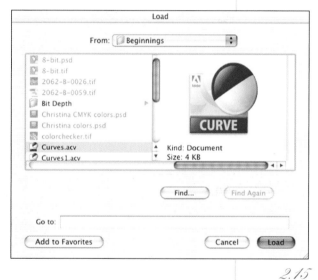

2.15

2.16

Actions: Helpful Stuff You Really Want to Know

Actions are one of the most productivity-enhancing features of Photoshop. They are versatile and literal – they do *exactly* and *only* what they are told to do. The color and tone correction Action you wrote in the previous exercise also works for any corrections you do later as long as you save the corrections as Levels.alv and Curves.alc. In the sidebar "Info – Color Balancing the Camera," you use Levels to correct the color and tone of an image that didn't need the Curves correction. When you color balance a file with Levels alone, open Curves and save it as Curves.acv without making any modifications. The Levels corrections were saved as Levels1.alv. To use the corrections with this Action, change the name of Levels.alv to ~Levels.alv. Change the name Levels1.alv to Levels.alv. As long as the corrections are in the same folder (directory), the Action will load them up and apply them.

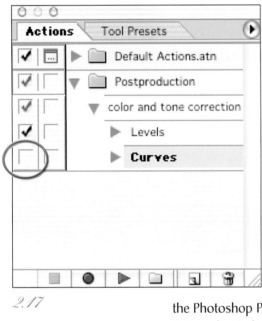

2.17

Another way to tell the Action to skip a command is to uncheck the box next to step in the Action itself. In the example shown here, the step for Curves is deactivated (2.17). When making changes to Actions, make certain that the Actions are doing what you want them to by testing them on the same file used to make them in the first place.

One last thing – newly created Actions live in memory. Quitting and restarting Photoshop will preserve new Actions as long as the Photoshop Preferences file on your computer is intact. Save the set the Actions live in by choosing Save Actions from the Actions palette fly-out menu.

Sharpening

I like to think of color and tone corrections and the rest of the file preparation as pre-postproduction steps. You might think of them as developing film or just as plain old pains in the neck or . . . whatever. They still have to be done.

Digital images, whether scanned from film or captured directly to a file, are inherently soft. They are not sharp. It isn't fair. There is no reasonable (as in without a lot of useless theory and math) explanation for it. They aren't sharp. And you aren't going to let your friends or clients see soft photographs now are you? So there is work to be done. Before we get on with it, it is important to address a myth of Photoshop lore that says "You mustn't *ever* sharpen an image more than once." The reality is that you better not *oversharpen* it *ever*. A little judicious sharpening in the pre-postproduction stage never hurt anyone or any image for that matter.

To get an idea of what this is all about, compare the two sides of this figure (2.18). The images on the left (labeled original image) have had color and tone corrections made whereas the images on the right (unsharp mask) have had the Unsharp Mask filter run on them as well. The difference in sharpness is pronounced. The following steps will be combined with the next section to develop an Action that is run on all image files prior to working in postproduction.

Step **/**: **Download Eye.tif from www.amesphoto.com/ learning.**
The file has already been corrected for color and tone.

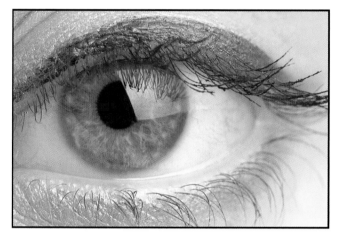
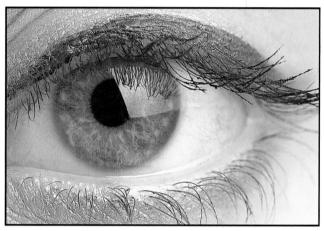

original image   unsharp mask

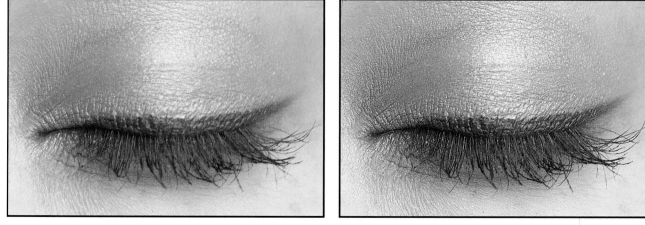

2.18

Step 2: Convert the 16-bit image to an 8-bit file (Image➡Mode➡8 Bits/Channel).

Step 3: Zoom in to 100% by pressing ⌘/Control+ Option/Alt+0.

Step 4: Go to Filter➡Sharpen➡Unsharp Mask to open the Unsharp Mask dialog box.

Here are the settings — Amount: 100%, Radius: 1 pixel, Threshold: 0 Levels.

Step 5: Drag the Unsharp Mask dialog box until it is positioned like the view shown here (2.19) and then move the cursor into the preview pane. Click and drag until the preview pane is similar to the one shown in Figure 2.19.

Step 6: Click on the image in the preview pane.

The sharpening effect is turned off in the preview pane as long as you hold down the mouse button. Look at the image. It is still sharp. When viewing at 100%, comparing images before and after unsharp masking is easy.

Step 7: Release the mouse button and the preview image becomes sharp. Click on the Preview check box to turn the sharpening on and off on the image.

Note

When applying the Unsharp Mask filter to a file going to final output, viewing the image at a magnification of 50% is desirable. This magnification gives you a much better idea of how the image will actually look in print. Click OK to apply the filter.

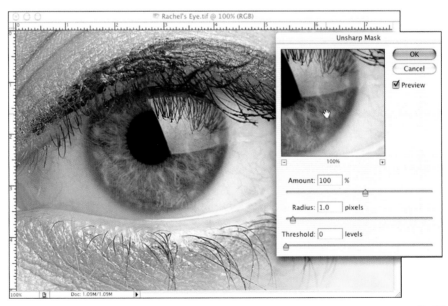

2.19

Step 8: **Go to the Edit menu and choose Fade Unsharp Mask Edit➡Fade Unsharp Mask.**

Leave the Opacity at 100% and change the Mode to Luminosity from the drop-down menu. Click OK. This step applies the sharpening effect to the grayscale tonal values and not the colors. Sharpening is concerned with making the image sharp, not the colors. Close Eye.tif without saving the changes.

Anti-Aliasing Color

Only two more pre-postproduction steps are left to do. One reduces the effects of color aliasing and the other copyrights the image. Take a look at this figure (2.20). It is a close-up of the pixels from colorchecker.tif. The areas where white transitions into black and black transitions into gray exhibit color aliasing.

2.20

Color aliasing happens most often in situations like these where the algorithm that determines what color to assign where gets confused because the tones black, white, and gray have no color in them. Look at the skin tone transition at the top edge of the chart. There is no color aliasing because there is color in the skin. This is one of those really obsessive things photographers fix for two reasons: one because we can, and two, because this aliasing isn't supposed to be there in the first place. The following exercise goes through the steps for fixing the problem.

Step 1: **Open colorchecker.tif and press F12 to run the color and tonal corrections Action.**

Step 2: **Zoom in to 600% on the word Color by pressing ⌘/Control+Option/Alt+0 and then ⌘/Control++ (plus sign) five times.**
Above 100% (actual pixels) this keyboard shortcut increases the size in 100% increments. ⌘/Control+– reduces the size in 100% steps down to 100%. Another way

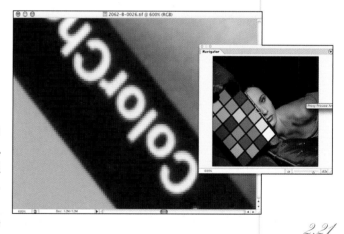

2.21

to zoom in is to center the box in the Navigator palette and click the large mountain icon until the view readout gets to 600%. You can also type 600 in the view readout and press Enter. Drag the box until the word *Color* displays in the document window (2.21).

Step 3: **Choose Filter→Blur→Gaussian Blur. In the dialog box enter 1.3 pixels in the Radius window.**
Clicking and dragging in the preview pane of the dialog box moves the view. Holding down the mouse button cancels the effect in the preview pane. Checking the Preview button toggles the effect in the document window. Clicking on the minus (–) or plus (+) signs zooms the preview pane out or in. The percentage of the view is displayed between the signs.

Step 4: **Click OK to accept the blur.**
The image becomes soft. Don't worry: the next step takes care of it.

Step 5: **Choose Edit→Fade Gaussian Blur or use the keyboard shortcut ⌘/Control+Shift+F to open the Fade Gaussian Blur dialog box. Leave the Opacity setting at 100% and change the Mode to Color. Click OK.**
The image is sharp and most importantly the color aliasing has been significantly reduced (2.22).

This operation only affects color aliasing. The cleanup it provides without affecting any other portion of the image makes it perfect to run on all files headed for postproduction. There is one more technique to explore. After that you'll put all three of them from this chapter together in an Action that will make pre-postproduction a breeze.

2.22

Copyright Protection for Your Photographs

Okay. This technique won't make your photograph better or more beautiful, but it will make it yours. Every photograph you take is yours by law. You own the copyright. And while this book is definitely not a tome on copyright law or even how to copyright your work, one of the important steps in the process is giving notice that your photograph is a copyrighted work. Photoshop CS makes this easy. You'll make a new file for this section.

Step 1: **From the File menu choose File➡New and press Return/Enter to create a new blank file.**
The settings in the dialog box don't matter.

Step 2: **Choose File➡File Info to open the dialog box. By default it opens on Description** (2.23).
From the Copyright Status drop-down menu choose Copyrighted. In the Copyright Notice section, type your copyright information. If you have a Web site, type in the address in the Copyright Info URL box, and then click Advanced.

Step 3: **Click Save at the bottom of the Advanced pane and name the file (c)2004.xmp. Click OK. Click OK again to accept the changes to the File Info dialog box.**

Tip

The format for a legal copyright notice is as follows: © year first name last name (for example, © 2004 Kevin Ames). On the Mac press Option+G for the © symbol. On Windows use parentheses around the letter c.

Untitled-1		Untitled-1

Description
Camera Data 1
Camera Data 2
Categories
History
Origin
Advanced

Description

Document Title:
Author:
Description:

Description Writer:
Keywords:

! Commas can be used to separate keywords

Copyright Status: Copyrighted
Copyright Notice: ©2004 Kevin Ames / kevin@amesphoto.com
Copyright Info URL: www.amesphoto.com
Go To URL...

Powered By
xmp

Created: 10/25/03   Application:
Modified: 10/25/03   Format:
Cancel   OK

Description
Camera Data 1
Camera Data 2
Categories
History
Origin
Advanced

Advanced

▶ PDF Properties (pdf, http://ns.adobe.com/pdf/1.3/)
▶ Adobe Photoshop Properties (phot...//ns.adobe.com/photoshop/1.
▶ TIFF Properties (tiff, http://ns.adobe.com/tiff/1.0/)
▶ XMP Core Properties (xmp, http://ns.adobe.com/xap/1.0/)
▶ XMP Media Management Propertie...tp://ns.adobe.com/xap/1.0/mi
▶ XMP Rights Management Propertie...://ns.adobe.com/xap/1.0/righ
▶ Dublin Core Properties (dc, http://purl.org/dc/elements/1.1/)

Powered By
xmp

Replace...   Append...   Save...   Delete
Cancel   OK

2.23

Step 4: Choose File→Close. When prompted, choose Don't Save.

Nobody said that the work that goes into getting files ready for postproduction is by any means insignificant, easy, or fun. Color and tonal corrections, basic sharpening, and color aliasing reduction are most important for the success of the final photograph. These steps along with copyrighting the image form the beginning of a postproduction workflow.

The next section of this chapter shows how to put all the previous steps of sharpening, color alias reduction, and protecting your copyright together into a single Action that will speed the workflow leading into postproduction at the click of a mouse or the stroke of a function key.

Speed Up with Actions

Step 1: Create a new document by pressing ⌘/Control+N on the keyboard.

From the dialog box choose 4 x 6. Leave it named Untitled-1 because it will be closed after the Action is finished. Make sure the Color Mode is RGB. Click OK.

Step 2: In the Actions palette, highlight the set Postproduction.

Click the Create New Action icon from the bottom of the palette or select New Action from the fly-out menu located at the palette's upper-righthand corner (2.24). Name the new Action USM -Alias (c). Set the Function Key to F13 and click Record (2.25).

2.24

2.25

Step 3: **Choose Filter➡Sharpen➡Unsharp Mask.**
Check to make sure the settings read Amount: 100%, Radius: 1.0 pixels, and Threshold: 0. Click OK. Choose Edit➡Fade Unsharp Mask and change the Mode to Luminosity. Leave the Opacity at 100%. Click OK.

Step 4: **Choose Filter➡Blur➡Gaussian Blur and check to make sure the blur is set to 1.3 pixels. Click OK.**

Step 5: **Press ⌘/Control+Shift+F to open the Fade Gaussian Blur dialog box. Leaving the Opacity at 100%, change the Mode to Color. Click OK.**

Step 6: **Choose File➡File Info. Click Advanced at the bottom of the listings in the lefthand pane. In the Advanced pane click Append. Navigate to the location of the saved 2004.xmp file. Click OK.**

Step 7: **At the bottom of the Actions palette click the Stop button** (2.26).

Step 8: **Click each rotating triangle open under the USM–Alias (c) Action. Compare each step to the one shown here** (2.27).
The only difference will be in the Set File Info of current document entry. It will contain your copyright information.

Note

Quitting Photoshop saves all the current settings including preferences, tool presets, styles, and more. If the computer crashes and closes Photoshop none of the settings are saved. Saving the Action set periodically, especially when developing Actions, is a good idea. Another good practice is to occasionally close and reopen Photoshop.

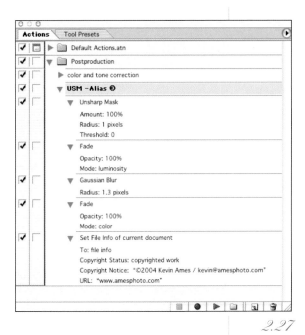

2.26

2.27

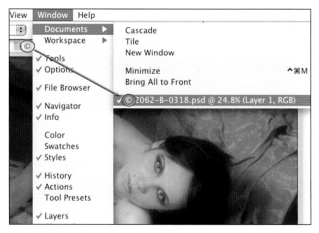

Tip

The © symbol means more than just protection of ownership in this workflow. Anytime the © appears also signifies that the pre-postproduction steps have been completed. Notice that this is the last part of the Action to run. The © also appears on open files listed in Window➡Documents (2.28).

2.28

Step 9: **Highlight the Postproduction Actions set by clicking on it.**

From the Actions fly-out menu choose Save Actions and enter the name **Postproduction.atn** in the dialog box. Click Save to save the set in the Photoshop Actions folder (the default location).

Whew! That's a lot of ground to cover in one chapter. And it is fruitful ground. You made it through with two very useful Actions, each assigned to its own function key. They are ready to help streamline your workflow.

Before testing the power of Actions, take a break from Photoshop and explore where images come from. The next chapter is a birds and the bees primer on lighting, how it works, exposure, and some other peeks under the photographic cabbage leaves. It details the steps of lighting a model and the scene. It explores what each light does, why it works the way it does, and how to set the exposure with a light meter and a color checker chart.

In Chapter 4 you'll use these photographs to go step-by-step through batch processing of files with your postproduction Actions. Chapter 5 demonstrates how to build custom galleries of images in Photoshop that clients can review with a Web browser on the Internet or off of a compact disc or DVD.

Workflow is the term used in digital enterprises to describe the steps an object goes through on its way from capture to output. Traditional photography's work-flow after the film was exposed was something like the following: Take the film to the lab. Make clip tests. Evaluate clip tests. Mark remaining film for push, pull, or normal processing. Process film. Pick up film from the lab. Cut film into strips. Sleeve film. Edit film. Cut heros from strips. Mount heros. Deliver heros to the client. Note that the heros are original film for which there is no exact duplicate. If lost, it is gone forever.

Workflow Defined

In digital photography your computer is the lab. A typical workflow is the follow-ing: Capture the image. Download raw image files to hard drive. Rename raw image files. Burn raw image files to disc. Edit raw image files for postproduction. Produce 16-bit tif files from raw selects, color and tonally balance, run basic sharpening and color aliasing reduction and copyright on 16-bit TIFs. Retouch. Archive retouched files. Prepare files for output. Output or deliver to client. (A big advantage to the digital workflow is that only copies of flattened files are deliv-ered to the client. The original raw capture files and the PSD files containing the layers used to produce the final image remain in the photographer's archives for self promotion and future sales.)

Many of these steps can be done in Photoshop using Actions to reduce time spent in front of the computer. Files shot under the same lighting conditions can be run automatically and unattended. The digital workflow offers the photogra-pher unprecedented control of and over her or his images.

The greater the number of files (photographs) involved in a shoot, the longer the workflow takes. It is important from a standpoint of time (it being money after all) to streamline the workflow. A workflow from capture to client proofs on the Internet is detailed in Chapter 4 and Chapter 5.

Chapter Three

Illuminating Light: How Light Works in Photography

After changes upon changes we are more or less the same.
Lyric from the "Boxer" by Simon & Garfunkel

Once upon a time, photographers concentrated on which lens offered the most lines of resolution and the best contrast. They debated which film had the tightest grain with the highest speed. There were discussions of the developer that produced the greatest number of zones and the paper/chemistry combination that reproduced the most tones. Which format was superior? Was it 8 x 10, 5 x 7, or 4 x 5? When portability was the issue, did you pack the medium format or the 35mm? What camera system had the best optics? Which one was the most durable? Whose shutter was more accurate? And what about films? Fujichrome, Kodachrome,

Ektachrome, Vericolor, Fujicolor, Agfa, GAF, Ilford, Fuji, Kodak, 3M, Konica . . . (the list goes on and on) were all hot topics of conversation on Saturday mornings at the local professional camera store.

A very short time ago (or a long time ago in computer years) the digital imaging thunderstorm burst through and rained down upon photographers. Some of us got wet. And the topics shifted. Tips and techniques for using Adobe Photoshop were shared. New acronyms and terminology popped into the language of photography – RAM, ROM, CCD, LCD, RGB, HSB, LAB, DPI, PPI, PSD, JPG, CMOS, Macs, PCs, megapixels, megabytes, gigabytes, dye-sub printers, ink sets, inkjet printers, papers . . . (as you can imagine or have already experienced this list, too, goes on and on) – and became subjects for heated debates in coffee houses and Internet chat rooms around the world. Everyone was now so concerned with recording and reproducing light that lighting itself has been left in the dark.

Light, Writing, Vision

Photography means *light writing*. That makes *light* literally the first word in photography. It is also the first word in Photoshop. Doesn't it seem slightly odd that most photographers concentrate on the *writing* part and pay little, if any attention at all to the light? It's important for a book on photography (Photoshop and postproduction aside) to pay the appropriate homage to photography's first word and in the processes shed some light on *light*.

Okay, I know you are thinking, "I already know all of this stuff." That's fine. Let me ask you one question and if you get it right, you can skip this chapter.

"Do you feel lucky?"

Oops. Wrong movie.

The question is *"As you get closer to a light, does it become harsher or softer?"*

No, I'm not going to tell you now. If you're curious, read on . . . .

Defined by the *Merriam-Webster Unabridged Dictionary*, light is, *1 a: something that makes vision possible.* How cool is that? Light makes vision *and photography* possible. Let's explore those possibilities. This chapter begins by looking at some of the properties of light and how to use them. Then it moves into how to measure light in a way that can be used to accurately render a subject digitally. (Deep-Dark-Never-Before-Revealed-Secret — this stuff works great with film, too. Gasp! I used the "f" word.)

Quality Versus Quantity

First, let's talk quality. One of the most difficult concepts to understand about lighting is the difference between quantities and qualities of light. Much of this confusion comes from thinking that bright light is harsh light. Bright light isn't necessarily harsh. And yet it can be. One of the most important principles of how light behaves is that *the larger the light source is in relation to the subject, the softer the quality of light.* That means that the closer the subject gets to the light source, the softer the quality of the light on the subject. (In other words, the source of light becomes larger in relation to the size of the subject as the subject gets *closer* to the light.)

At first this concept seems to make absolutely no sense at all. The light gets harsher, not softer, we say to ourselves. ("Look at how bright the light is!") Ah-hah!

Note

Soft light makes skin creamy, eyes liquid, and fabrics flowing. Women *love* soft light.

Figure 3.1 is a close-up of Laura without any makeup (3.1). The "Sunny" image is lit with harsh light as defined by the very sharp edged cast by her nose. Skin texture is revealed. Note the two beauty marks above her left eyebrow, the pores, and very fine hairs on her forehead. Also notice the specular highlights (mirror images of light source) on the left side, tip, and bridge of her nose caused by naturally occurring skin oils. Compare these light quality tipsters with the "Overcast" photograph. The only difference is the light source has been diffused (spread out into two dimensions) so that it is huge when compared to the size of the subject. The soft light quality minimizes the skin textures and oils by spreading out the shadow edge. Soft light makes textures almost disappear. Add makeup, and the retouching becomes a whole lot easier.

Desperately Seeking Soft Light

Sunny   Overcast

3.1

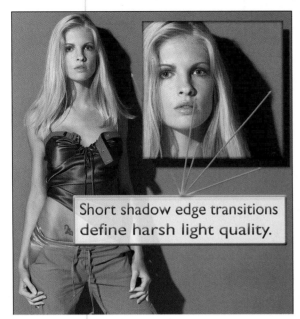

Short shadow edge transitions define harsh light quality.

3.2

Long shadow edge transitions define soft light quality.

3.3

What really happens is that as the subject moves closer to the light source, the light becomes both *brighter* and softer simultaneously. The actual problem is that almost every description of the quality of light is confused with the quantity instead. The harsher/softer description is really a quantity/quality issue. As the subject moves closer to the light source, the light in fact becomes brighter (quantity), while becoming softer (quality). The key to the harsher/softer question is the edge of the shadow cast by the subject.

Here is an everyday way to think of this concept. On a bright, clear, and cloudless sunny day the light source is the sun. The sun is 864,000 miles in diameter, give or take a mile or two. It is also 8.32 light minutes away from the camera and our subject. The sun is a high intensity light source about the size of a thumbnail held arm's length from the eye. In relationship to the subject, the sun is a very small light source indeed. It's bright, too. For example, in this figure our model, Laura, is lit by the sun (3.2). A shadow is cast on the wall behind her. Is it harsh or soft? Well of course we know it's harsh. Bright sunlight is harsh light. That is a true statement. We've heard this all our photographic lives. So how do we know it's true? The answer lies in the distinct, hard edge that demarks the dark shadow from the rest of the wall. The sharp edge of this transition is the visual clue that the light is harsh. This is called the *shadow edge transition*. A very short transition from highlight to shadow denotes harsh light.

The cause of confusion is the word *bright*. The more accurate statement is "*On a clear day sunlight is harsh light.*" Bright is a *quantity* term. Harsh is a *quality* term. During an eclipse the sun becomes very dim. Yet the shadows don't change. The contrast does. There will be more on contrast later in this chapter.

Continuing the example, look at Laura after clouds roll in front of the sun, making the sky overcast (3.3). Two things happen: The light source becomes larger in relationship to the subject, and the clouds diffuse (spread over a larger area) the light, so the quality of light becomes much softer. The quantity of light is reduced two ways: by the density of the cloud cover and by the spreading of light over a larger area dimensionally (the whole sky). Check it out. The shadow edge

Most women, even those who choose not to wear makeup on a daily basis, understand that it is a great help if not a necessity when being photographed. They welcome the makeup artist with open arms and often hugs. Men on the other hand, especially those who are not used to being photographed, might feel intimidated by the prospect of wearing it. It helps to assure them that unless they tell someone they have makeup on, no one will notice. They might hear comments of how good they look that day. And no one will ever say "(insert man's name here), I just love your makeup!"

I have found that the soft brushes used to apply a light amount of powder knocks down the shine on male skin by dulling its surface efficiency (shininess caused by oily skin). It also calms them down quite a bit. After making the first series of exposures, bring your male clients to the makeup counter and powder them down. They really have no clue about how a good makeup brush feels on their face. (If you are a male and reading this, put the book down right now and have someone — women usually have these things — run one of these brushes over your face; close your eyes first. You'll know immediately what I'm referring to. And ladies, if you haven't powdered your guy, what are you waiting for? You don't even have to add powder. Just brush lightly over his face. You know the drill!) Now you know why this is great for those uptight "real-men-don't-wear-makeup-types" before shooting, er . . . photographing them.

Make Up!

transition of the cast shadow on the wall widens over a much greater distance indicating a softer quality of light. Shadows cast on a very overcast day can be nonexistent because the light source is so incredibly large when compared to the size of the subject.

The sun is the *origin* of light in each example. On clear days it is both the origin and the *source* of light. On overcast days the cloud cover becomes the *source* of light. The sun remains the *origin* of light. A sharp shadow edge transition defines the light quality as *harsh*. A wide shadow edge transition defines the light quality as *soft*.

Note

Harsh light is ideal for revealing textures because of the sharp shadow edge transition that defines it visually. It is good for revealing weaves of fabric, strands of hair, and the makeup of a surface. Skin is a surface, too. Seeing texture in a woman's skin is not a good thing. (Texture in skin means wrinkles, lines, and pores.) Women really don't love harsh light.

Shedding Some Light on Light

Another concept that confuses what we think light is doing and what it actually is doing is *contrast*. *Contrast* is the difference between a highlight and a shadow measured in f/stops. Contrast is concerned with the quantities of light and their relative brightness and not its quality. High contrast situations are often considered to be harsh light even when the shadow edge transitions are wide, indicating soft light. In order to lower the contrast of a scene, light is added to the shadows. Lowering the contrast does not change the quality (harshness/softness) of light only the relative brightness within the image.

Compare these two images of Laura (3.4). The left image is sunlit with no fill. The right image is the same exposure with a reflector positioned to bounce some of sunlight back into the right side of the photograph. The added light brightens the shadow (and the highlights) *lowering* the contrast of the shadow in comparison to her skin. Look at the shadow edge. It is the same in both photographs. It's still a short transition. The quality of light is still harsh. The only difference is lower contrast. More detail is visible in the shadow. Compare the backgrounds. The one on the right that has light reflecting into it has a lighter background. The fill is not enough to change the exposure; it is enough to add a bit more life to the image. Controlling contrast is important especially when photographs are reproduced on web printing presses where shadows can load up with ink (dot gain) and lose detail.

One more concept to go: Light either hits a subject or bounces off of it. It is considered to be either *incident* or *reflective* depending on where it is in relation to eye, capture device (sensor chip), or film. *Incident* light falls onto the subject. *Reflective* light bounces off of the subject and is on its way to the camera or the eye.

INCIDENT LIGHT METERS

Incident light meters measure the light before it gets to the subject. An incident meter measures light that has not been influenced by the qualities of a subject. These qualities can include color, shape, and tonal efficiency of the surface. Because incident meters see only the quantity of light hitting the subject, they report an exposure that represents the true tone of the subject in a photograph. This is called the *diffused value*. The *diffused value* is the proper exposure for a photograph. The diffused value sets the aperture (f/stop) and shutter speed on the camera.

REFLECTIVE METERS

Reflective meters, like the ones built into cameras, measure the light after it has bounced off of the subject. Reflective meters are used to measure the relative brightness in f/stops (contrast) between the highlights and the shadows.

Note

Harsh light that is low in contrast is a compromise that reveals textures in fabrics without revealing too many flaws in skin, especially when a makeup artist is involved in enhancing the skin's natural beauty.

Note

Today's incident meters are all handheld. The better ones made by Minolta and Sekonic read the light in an environment (ambient or existing) with an electronic flash. An investment in a high-quality incident meter will last for many years. My studio uses Minolta Flashmeter IVs. One of them has been in service for fifteen years. That is a great return on an investment.

3.4

These readings are used to determine contrasts within a photograph. Contrast is subjective. It is one of the creative controls a photographer can use to establish mood or drama. Harsh and soft light qualities can be represented in situations of high, medium, or relatively low contrast.

Photoshop's measuring tools, the Eyedropper and Color Sampler, display reflective data on the Info palette. They can be used to measure the relative brightness between areas in an image. The advantage of using these tools is that they are much more accurate than a light meter. They read the actual reflectivity of objects in the captured image. In the traditional capture world it would be like using a densitometer to read reflectivity from developed photographs as they are made in the field — impossible with film, simple with a digital camera, laptop, and, of course, Photoshop! Remember that in photography, accuracy rules!

Lighting: "Great Photoshop Starts with Great Photography"

Three things are of concern when lighting a subject for photography: the quality of the light, the exposure for the diffused value, and the relative brightness between the highlight and shadow areas. These considerations are important because their interplay defines the quality of the image artistically and how well the image will reproduce on the printed page, on a photographic or inkjet print, or on the Web. Paying attention to these considerations can greatly reduce time-intensive postproduction services.

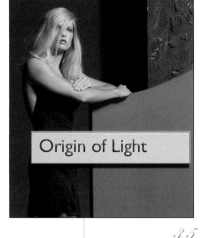

Photographs can have many quantities and qualities of light at the same time. Quantities of light are relative to each other. They are measured in relationship to the chosen exposure for the image. In the following fashion shot, I discuss how I set up the lighting and which incident controls I chose and why. I then discuss setting the *diffused value* — the exposure with both an incident meter and a Gretag Macbeth ColorChecker chart. One thing that might surprise you is how little time is actually spent working with the camera.

3.5

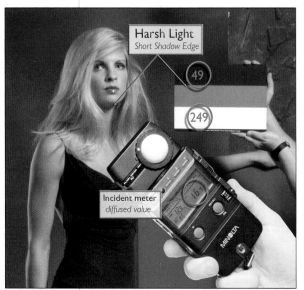

Laura Phillips from Elite Model Management/Atlanta is our model for this shoot. I start the session with one light on Laura. The origin of light in this case is a 22" "beauty dish" placed at a 45° angle above and to the right of the camera. This figure shows the effect of a single light (3.5). An incident meter in the scene reads the light falling on the subject (3.6). The diffused value is f/16.4. Examine the shadow edge transitions. They are short. The light on Laura is harsh. The aperture setting on the camera's lens for this image is f/16.4. The shutter speed for all the photographs in this section is 1/125th of a second.

As with light meters, lighting controls are either *reflective* or *incident*. *Reflective controls* deal with light after it has hit the subject and is on its way to the imager. Filters for color correction or soft focus and vignetters are reflective controls. They are mostly only used with film.

3.6

Modern incident and reflective light meters provide readings that are accurate to one-tenth of a stop. This causes confusion because some f/stops have decimal points in their names. By popular convention a reading of f/ five point six point three (f/5.6.3) means f/ five point six and a third (of an f/stop) instead of f/6.3 (which is really f/5.6 plus a third of an f/stop). The reading on the hard light image (Figure 3.6) reads f/ sixteen point four, telling the photographer that the correct exposure is f/16 and between a third and a half. Depending on personal preference, photographers round the tenth of a stop in this instance either up to a half (very slightly underexposed) or down to a third (very slightly overexposed). It is important to use tonal references such as a Gretag Macbeth ColorChecker Chart or their ColorChecker Gray Scale Balance Card used in the examples in this chapter.

Decimals and Thirds

Incident controls are devices that come between the origin of light and the subject. They do their work on the light before it strikes the subject. Diffusion panels, scrims, flags, and cookies are examples of incident lighting controls. Each one of these controls will be used in the shoot.

A *diffusion panel* made of translucent sailcloth fabric stretched on a Chimera 42 x 72-inch frame is placed in front of the origin of light and moved closer to Laura. The shadow edge becomes wider and the light quality softens (3.7). The panel spreads the light two dimensionally over a 21-square-foot area making the source much, much larger in relation to the size of her face (about half of a square foot). The panel is now the *source* of light and the beauty dish on the flash head is the *origin* of light.

Diffusion Panel

3.7

The diffusion panel also lowers the amount of light reaching Laura. Whenever the origin of light is modified, a new incident reading is taken. The diffused value is now f/11.4, or one stop darker than the harsh light exposure. The new exposure is set on the camera, allowing an additional stop of light to reach the sensor. The light panel reduces the amount of light reaching Laura by one f/stop. The exposure does not change even if the panel is moved closer to or farther away from the model.

The background areas become brighter because the exposure is now one stop more than before. Laura remains the same in both examples because the exposure has been adjusted to compensate for the diffusion panel. The ColorChecker in both images shows the same reflected brightness. These Photoshop readings are considered reflected because they show the relative brightness of the black and white patches on the card.

Note
The light in photographs made with flash is controlled by the aperture. A burst of light from an electronic flash travels at the speed of light. Shutters are not fast enough to control the amount of flash recorded at the camera.

Densitometry is the science of charting how much light causes an increase of the amount of silver retained on a negative after the film is developed. An f/stop of density measured from a black-and-white film negative is a logarithmic value of .3. A density change of .1 is the equivalent of one-third of an f/stop. In Photoshop, an opacity change of 13 points is, by general rule, a third of a stop (above 25) and is subject to what amounts to reciprocity in bright highlights (above 249) where more and more light is needed to drive the numbers up to 255.

Note

The names and placement of the lights and incident controls used in this lesson are shown in this figure (3.9). The effect of each one is labled on the corresponding photograph illustrating the building of the lighting. The flag in front of the strip light blocks its light from hitting the lens and causing flare.

The exposure as read from the ColorChecker shows that Laura will record with detail in her skin and hair (R, G, B: 249) and in her black dress (R, G, B: 49.) The shadows under the wrinkles around her waist read in the low 20s (3.8).

I use an incident control to lower the contrast by adding light to Laura's shadows. The bounce panel is a Chimera 42 x 72-inch frame covered with a white reflector panel. It is moved to the side opposite the source of light (the diffusion panel). Light bounces into the shadows on her hair and arm (3.10). Now details in these areas open up becoming more visible. Notice that her back is beginning to separate from the background. Notice, too, that even though the contrast is lower, the shadow edge transition did not change. The brightness or darkness of shadow areas is subjective. Contrast can be raised for a moody and dramatic look or lowered for a more open feeling.

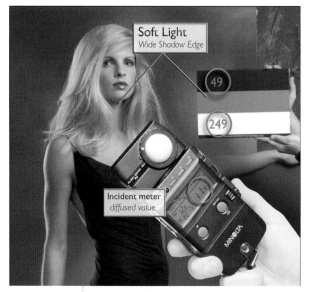

3.8

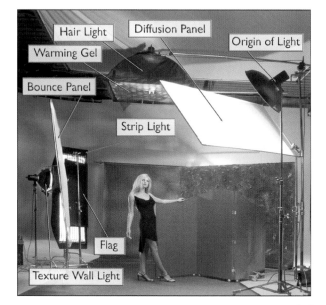

3.9

Laura's blond hair has very little life and it merges with the background. I add a Chimera medium soft box fitted with a fabric grid and a warming gel directly overhead. This separates her hair, shoulders, and arms from the background. The grid minimizes spill on the background. The warming gel (Rosco 3407) puts a golden glow in her hair and warms the color on her arms (3.11).

This light is fired independently of the other lights and measured with a reflective meter pointing at her hair. The power of the light is adjusted until it is about half a stop brighter than the diffused value.

Laura's back and dress still get lost in the background. A large Chimera strip light with a grid adds a beautiful highlight that separates them nicely. A reflective reading of the highlight is again about a half stop brighter than the diffused value (3.12).

Tip

When a diffusion panel is introduced to a lighting set, it affects the color of the light. It is important to shoot another Color Checker so that the color shift from the panel can be neutralized as was done in these examples.

Bounce Panel

3.10

Hair Light w/grid

3.11

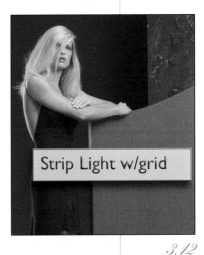

Strip Light w/grid

3.12

Contrast and Seeing

Controlling the quality of light and constraining it to a range that the camera can record and even more important, to one a printer can reproduce, is what lighting is all about. One of the biggest problems with recording images is that digital chips (CCD, CMOS) and film have limited contrast ranges they can capture. Our eyes are limited to about the same range except that we have brains. When we look at a high contrast situation our eyes "see" an image. What really happens is that first we view the bright areas and the brain remembers the details in the highlights. Then the iris of the eye instantly opens wider to see into the dark areas while the brain remembers the bright ones and integrates them into a single picture we refer to as *sight* or *vision*. Capture media has no brain. It can record a limited contrast range. Contrast must be controlled to allow the subject to be photographed with recordable detail in the highlights and shadows.

Ambience: Light existing in the surrounding or pervading environment.

Contrast: The difference in f/stops between the highlights and the shadows. Contrast that is too high will produce a photograph that has loss of detail in the highlights and/or the shadows. Adding light to the shadows reduces contrast.

Diffused value (or highlight): Represents the true brightness or tone of an object. The diffused value sets the exposure for a photograph.

Diffusion: A method of making an origin of light larger by spreading light two dimensionally (height and width).

Gobo: An incident lighting control that goes between the light source and the subject used to block light.

Incident controls: Modifies the origins of light before light strikes a subject to be recorded. This includes the choice of light, tungsten or electronic flash, the number of lights and their output as well as diffusion panels, gobos, and so on.

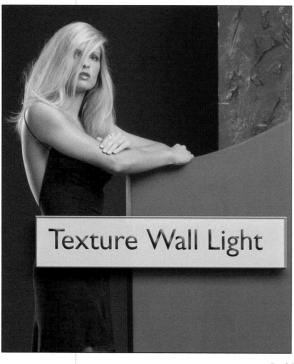

Texture Wall Light

3.13

The last part of the lighting scheme is to bring up the illumination on the background elements. They consist of a texture wall on the right and red background paper that runs from above the set down to and then along the floor. A light with a 16" reflector with a red Rosco #25 gel is aimed at the wall. Barndoors keep the light from spilling anywhere but the wall (3.13). The red background paper is still very dark. A bare bulb head is placed behind the texture wall. It shines through a four-foot square panel with leaf-shaped holes cut in it. This incident control is called a *cucoloris* or *cookie*. It breaks up the light into the pattern on the background paper (3.14).

Lighting the background is very important especially when the fashions to be photographed are sheer and flowing. The background must have enough brightness to silhouette her shape through the fabric. If it doesn't, the garment will appear to be opaque even though it's sheer.

Incident metering: Determines the amount of light striking an object. When an incident meter is aimed at the predominant light source, the reading indicates proper exposure for the diffused value.

Origin of light: The point from which light energy begins (such as electronic flash, flood light, sun, and so on).

Shadow edge transition: The area of transition between a diffused value (highlight) and a shadow. A transition that covers a small area results in a hard shadow edge. A harsh quality (from a small light source) of light is defined by a short shadow edge transition. One that covers a large area indicates a soft shadow edge. The quality of light from a large shadow edge transition is described as soft. This indicates a large light source.

Source of light: A two-dimensional surface that illuminates an object.

Reflective metering: Determines the amount of the light reflecting off of an object. This type of metering is used to establish the difference in contrast (brightness) between two objects or areas in a photograph (such as the subject and background).

After the scene is lit, the photography starts. Shoot until you are sure you have the image you want. Then experiment. Exploring your photographic creativity takes nothing but some time. This is the time to play, experiment, and explore. Put on music, turn on a fan, invite your model to participate and contribute to the session. The results will more often than not exceed your original ideas. When the session is working there is an energy that flows through everyone involved. When the photographer feels this energy it is a rush. The excitement shows in the final images.

In the next chapter I introduce raw capture and discuss some of its advantages. I use additional images from Laura's shoot to show how to create *bulletproof* archive discs. You can use the proofs from these discs to create photo galleries for clients, friends, and catalogs, so no matter how many CDs of raw files you have, finding exactly the right image is a snap. (Well, would you believe a few clicks?)

3.11

Chapter Four

Archiving: Creating Bulletproof Digital Negatives

Just for a moment step into *The Twilight Zone*. Imagine shooting a roll of color print film. Imagine taking it to the corner drugstore for processing and printing. Now imagine hallucinating as insane madness overcomes you. You open the envelope, pull out your negatives, and run them through a nearby shredder. You have not even glanced at the prints. *(Theme music swells and fades. . . .)*

This is not a dream. It is reality. Even worse, it is quite possibly *your* reality. Because this is exactly what happens when you shoot digitally and the camera is set to save in JPEG or TIF formats. These file types are a software team's best guess at what information in your photograph is important, just as the drugstore prints are the operator's best guess at what the colors were when you made the photograph.

Don't panic. There is a solution. Change the camera to save in raw.

Yes, saving raw files takes up more space on the memory card or microdrive. Now be honest. If a 35mm film camera had a setting for shooting quarter frames to get 144 shots on a 36-exposure roll, would you use it? Probably not. The quality loss compared to the cost savings just doesn't add up. The same is true for shooting raw.

Raw files are your digital negatives. They hold considerably more information than JPEG files or TIFs because they capture all the data the sensor sees when the photograph is made. And they do it in high bit depth. This is important. The greater the bit depth, the more information each pixel carries. In Chapter 1, the exercise on histogram combing demonstrates the power of high bit depth images (4.1). More information means that burned-out skies can be made blue again (it's like burning in a sky while printing from a negative), huge exposure corrections become possible, and upping the resolution of an image is way more effective.

4.1

Pre-Postproduction: Archiving Raw Files

The raw file is the digital equivalent of a color or black-and-white negative on film. This important distinction clearly defines the value of the raw file especially compared with 8-bit JPEG files and TIFs. Raw files are so important because they record *all* the data the sensor sees when light strikes it and in a significantly higher depth than the 8-bits traditionally used in Adobe Photoshop. The additional data that the raw format contains allows "impossible" photographs to be created in Photoshop. The Adobe Camera Raw plug-in (accessible from the File Browser) gives photographers a fast, efficient means of getting raw data into editable Photoshop files. Later on in this chapter Camera Raw is explained in depth.

ARCHIVE BEFORE OPENING

The temptation to work with the raw files right from the compact flash, microdrive, or hard drive is great. *Resist it with all of your being.* If there is a catastrophic failure of any of these volatile media, the shoot is lost.

Always have a means of downloading camera media cards to a hard drive and burning the data to CDs with you on a shoot. Compared with the cost of buying film, processing, scanning, and dust spotting it, a laptop with an external FireWire (PC: IEEE 1394) hard drive is truly inexpensive insurance. Protect your raw files (digital negatives) at all cost.

MEDIA VOLATILITY

Storage media with moving parts are inherently volatile. They are subject to catastrophic failure when any one of them fails. Hard drives are mechanical devices spinning at high speeds that hold massive amounts of data. Microdrives are mechanical devices spinning somewhat slower and holding less information. Compact flash cards and microdrives are susceptible to impact damage and static electrical disruption.

Then there is obsolescence. Try finding a SyQuest drive or even a Jaz drive to read that stack of cartridges in the closet. How many different formats of tape backup storage have come and gone over the years? Other problems with tape include stretching and layers sticking, rendering data irretrievable.

The only nonvolatile media that is reasonably universal in acceptance is the CD-ROM. It is stable over a period of years, won't break if dropped (just don't step on it), is inexpensive, and easy to duplicate. The possibility of readers disappearing before copies can be made to whatever will replace them (DVDs most likely) is remote. For the moment CDs rule for storage of raw files. Seven CDs' worth of data will fit on one DVD. This is good and bad. If a shoot is archived on a DVD and the DVD fails, the whole project is lost. If a CD fails only one-seventh of the shoot would be gone.

NAMING FILES AND FOLDERS

There are naming conventions to follow for files and folders that make cataloging and retrieving images easier. For every exposure use a four-digit job number followed by a dash followed by a three- or four-digit image number followed by the file extension. Adding a letter followed by another dash designates sections of an ongoing job number. A typical image number looks like this: *2062-E-047.DCR*. It means the job number is 2062-, the image is the

Note

The reusability of camera storage media – compact flash cards, microdrives, and so on – makes them incredibly cheap. On a shoot, having enough media to store the entire shoot is imperative. That makes the compact flash cards and/or microdrives backups in case the copies made to the hard drive were corrupted in transfer or the drive itself should fail.

Tip

Avoid the siren lure of the multi-gigabyte flash cards and microdrives. When a large card fails (notice I said *when*, not *if*) a whole day or more of shooting can be lost. Use 512MB cards. Their data fits nicely on a CD and a shoot will require multiple cards. When (not if) one fails, the whole shoot won't be lost with it.

Tip

When delivering a job on a CD, make a professional-looking label for it. Clients pay large sums of money for the data on the disc. Your image as a professional is boosted if the disc looks good.

Note

The hyphen after the job number is important. Including it in a search of an electronic catalog eliminates all the images that are numbered 2062 from being included in the result.

Note

35mm–style digital cameras that capture raw files have different file extensions. Some of the most common are, in alphabetical order by manufacturer, CRW (Canon), RAF (Fuji), DCR (Kodak), NEF (Nikon), and X3F (Sigma/Foveon).

forty-seventh shot of the fifth (E-) session, and it is a raw file from a Kodak camera.

Folders have the job number, a very brief description of the event, and/or the client name and the year. If you are cataloging back into the last century use four digits for the year. A folder might look like *2062E PsCS Laura Phillips 2003*. The job number is still *2062-E-*, the event or project is *PsCS* (Photoshop CS book), the subject is *Laura Phillips*, and *2003* is the year.

BULLETPROOF ARCHIVING FOR DIGITAL NEGATIVES (RAW FILES)

The set of steps that follow set up a destination folder for the Actions that are used in pre-postproduction. After they are done you probably won't have to repeat them again.

Step 1: **Create a new folder on your hard drive and name it *0 Automate Hot Folder*.**
The zero puts it at the top of hierarchy on the hard drive (4.2).

Step 2: **Make a new Photoshop document by pressing ⌘/Control+N.**
The New dialog box appears. In the Preset pull-down menu, select 2 x 3. Leave Resolution at 300. Set the Color Mode to RGB Color and select White as the Background Contents. The title doesn't matter. Click OK.

Step 3: **Find the USM Alias © Action in the Postproduction set in the Actions palette.**
This Action was built in Chapter 2.

4.2

[58]

Step 4: **Duplicate the USM Alias © Action by dragging it to the Create New Action icon at the bottom of the Actions palette.**

Step 5: **Double-click the copied Action's name and rename it** USM Alias © JPG.

Step 6: **Click the disclosure triangle next to its name and highlight the Fade step below Unsharp Mask.**

Step 7: **Click the Begin Recording button at the bottom of the Actions palette or select Start Recording from the fly-out menu in the upper right** (4.3).

Step 8: **Select Image→Image Size to open the Image Size dialog box.**
Make sure that the Resample Image and Constrain Proportions boxes are checked. Change the Resolution to 72 pixels/inch. Set the Resample Image pull-down menu to Bicubic Sharper. Click OK. A step named Image Size appears under Unsharp Mask and Fade in the Actions palette (4.4).

Step 9: **Click the Stop Recording button at the bottom of the Actions palette.**

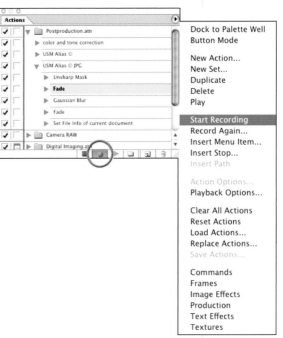

4.3

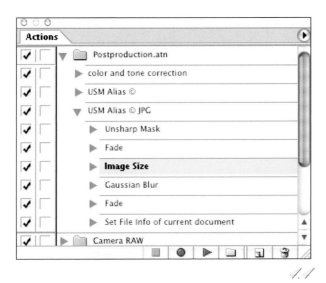

4.4

Note

In order to save files as JPEGs using an Action with the Automate command from the File menu or File Browser, you must include the Save As information including the destination when recording the Action.

Step 10: Highlight Set File Info of Current Document and click the Begin Recording button at the bottom of the Actions palette.

Step 11: Press ⌘/Control+Shift+S to enter the Save As dialog box and select JPEG from the Format menu (4.5).

Step 12: Navigate to the 0 Automate Hot Folder folder and click Save.

The JPEG Options dialog box opens. Set 12 in the Quality field. Click OK.

Step 13: From the menu bar choose File➞Close or press ⌘/Control+W to close the file.

The steps in the USM Alias © JPG Action should look like it does here (4.6).

Step 14: Click the Stop Recording icon at the bottom of the Actions palette.

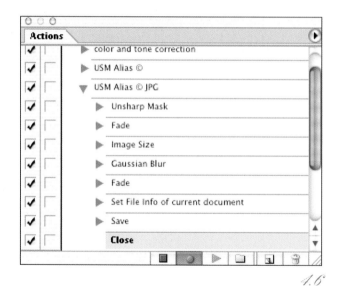

4.6

4.5

File Browser consists of four main viewing areas or panes. The Folders pane is the file and folder navigator. Below that is the Preview pane, which shows an enlarged view of the selected photograph in the Thumbnail pane. The Information pane has tabs for Metadata and Keywords. Individual panes in each column (there is one column on the left for the Navigation, Preview, and Information panes and one on the right for the Thumbnail pane) can be resized independently of one another by clicking and dragging on the sizing bars (4.7).

The Panes of File Browser

Step 15: **Highlight the Postproduction Action set and save the new Action by selecting Save Actions from the Actions palette fly-out menu.**
Replace the previously saved Postproduction.atn. The default location is Photoshop Actions in the Presets folder in the Photoshop CS folder.

Step 16: **Navigate to the 0 Automate Hot Folder folder and delete Untitled-1.jpg.**
The USM Alias © JPG Action and the 0 Automate Hot Folder come into play when the archived discs of raw files are proofed. Now it's time to prepare the raw files for archiving.

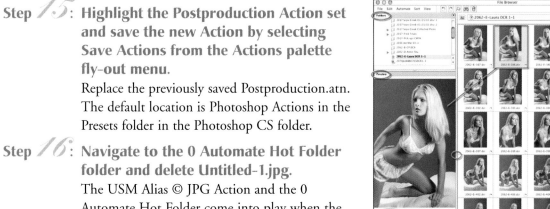

4.7

WORKING WITH FILE BROWSER

The next steps demonstrate some of the workflow features of File Browser. You'll rotate the image thumbnails for easy viewing, rename the files for easy cataloging, and save the cache files so the previews will appear quickly from the archive CD when it's viewed in File Browser.

Step 1: **Open the folder of raw files for this section by double-clicking it in the Folders pane of File Browser.**
You can also download the folder for Chapter 4 from www. amesphoto.com/learning. It contains the raw files to use in this section.

Step 2: **Scrolling through the Thumbnail pane, ⌘/Control+click to select images that you want rotated.**

Tip
You can set the image thumbnails to a custom size by choosing Edit➡Preferences from the File Browser menu. Type in the pixel dimension that you want in the Custom Thumbnail Size window. The thumbnails in the screen captures of File Browser are 325 pixels wide.

Note

Click a single image in the Thumbnail pane to select it. ⌘/Control+clicking on several non–adjacent images selects them. To select a contiguous group of images, click the first image and Shift+click the last image in the sequence. All the thumbnails between the first click and the Shift+click are selected. ⌘/Control+A selects all the images.

Step *3*: Click on the appropriate rotation icon (Rotate Counterclockwise or Rotate Clockwise, respectively) next to the File Browser menu bar.

The thumbnails rotate to the proper orientation (4.8).

Step *4*: Press ⌘/Control+A to select all the images in the Thumbnail pane.

Step *5*: Rename the raw files in File Browser.

Refer to the section, "Naming files and folders" to learn what numbers and descriptions to use.

Step *6*: Choose Automate➡Batch Rename from File Browser's menu bar.

In the Batch Rename dialog box, make sure that the Rename in Same Folder button is checked. In the File Naming section, follow the example shown here (4.9). Enter the starting number in the Starting Serial # field. If you are working with the supplied images, enter **380** in the Starting Serial # field. Click OK.

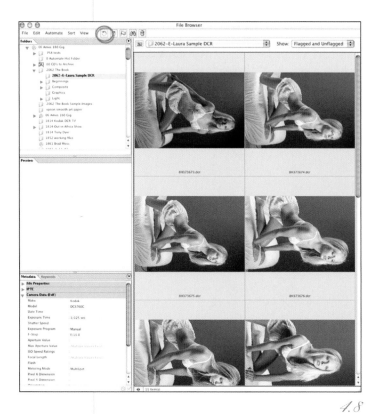

4.8

4.9

Tip

If you are using Photoshop 7, in the field 'X' Digit Serial Number, type a pound or number (#) sign, the starting number, followed by another pound or number (#) sign. This is the workaround for the missing starting number field in the Batch Rename dialog box.

Step 7: Choose File➜Export Cache from File Browser's menu bar (4.10) **and click OK on the Cache Exported Successfully confirmation dialog box.**

The next steps take place outside of Photoshop in the Finder on the Mac or in Windows on the PC.

Step 8: Burn a CD using the Clone Disc option in the software you are using.

Step 9: Burn another copy of the first CD using that CD as the source of the files, not the files on the hard drive.

To be really efficient, use a computer that has a CD player and a CD burner.

4.10

The Export Cache command creates three files that are hidden when viewed in File Browser (*cache* is French for hidden.) The cache files contain all the retrieved metadata and the generated thumbnail previews. The rotation data set in the File Browser is stored here as well. When a folder with the cache files is opened in File Browser, the previews appear almost instantaneously. Cache files can be included on a CD of images to speed things up when the disc is accessed in File Browser (4.11).

Cache Cachet

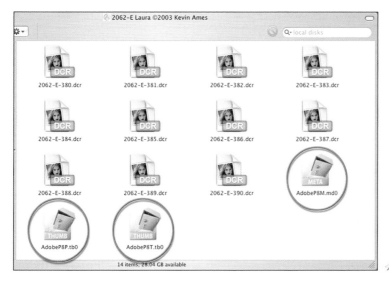

4.11

Pre-Postproduction: Proofing the Archives

Photo shoots are a lot of work. It doesn't matter if the photography is personal work made at home or if it is a major advertising project that involves professional models, stylists, makeup artists, hairdressers, wardrobe managers, assistants, clients, art directors, and account executives (never forget the AEs). No matter how many people are involved, the process of getting the lighting and composition to work in the context of the idea of what the end result will be is work. When it's personal, the stakes are sometimes higher because that is where the photographer is stretching her/himself, tackling new ground, experimenting, and daring beyond the comfort zone. The captured image is just plain important. After all, it's all that's left after everyone else has gone home.

Film shooters have evolved redundant procedures to make sure that no matter what happens, the film — or at least some of it — survives. They will shoot primarily color transparency film and back it up by shooting some color negative film, too. Each type of film then goes to different labs for processing to ensure that even a catastrophic failure at one lab won't ruin the whole take.

Digital capture isn't any different. Digital shooters have to either trust to luck (a very bad idea) or evolve a workflow that includes multiple backups and proofs that ensures the archives are good. This has to be an efficient *automated* process. Otherwise no one will do it and then we are all back to trusting to luck (still a very bad idea).

Film users really have it over the digital folks here. All they have to do is look at the processed film. "Yup, it's good. There's a picture there."

So how do digital photographers get to that "Yup, it's good" place? When shooting, we can check the results either on the camera's LCD screen or by moving files to a laptop and checking them. That's only half the story and it is like using Polaroids to check lighting and exposure. The Polaroids don't guarantee that the film is in fact *good*. Verifying disc burns or seeing a folder full of JPEGs doesn't either. The long-term answer has to do with actually looking at the JPEGs. First we'll use the USM Alias © JPG Action and the 0 Automate Hot Folder we set up earlier in this chapter to create JPEGs for viewing. And as a special feature for photographers whose camera only captures in JPEGs, there is a guide to archiving them safely as well. Let's go to the step-by-steps:

Step 1: **Insert the *copy* of the original archive CD into your computer and open File Browser (⌘/Control+Shift+O).**

Step 2: **Navigate to the CD and double-click the folder of images.**

The light box pane populates with thumbnails of the raw files (4.12). Do a quick review, checking the thumbnails for problems. This is a very good indication that the files on the CD are good. It also means the original CD is good, too, because the one open in File Browser is a copy of the original. The next step is the proof that the raw files have been archived successfully.

Step 3: **Press ⌘/Control+A to select all the images and then choose Automate➡Batch from the File Browser menu (4.13).**

Step 4: **In the Batch dialog box, select Postproduction.atn from the Set menu. Choose USM Alias © JPG in the Action drop-down menu.**

4.12

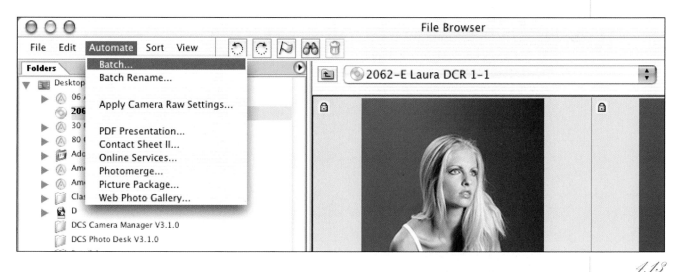

4.13

Tip

When the File Browser is active, pressing F5 (or choosing View➡Refresh from File Browser's menu) refreshes the view of volumes, folders, and files.

Step 5: In the Source drop-down menu, select File Browser.
Check the Suppress File Open Options so Camera Raw will run without opening its dialog box. Check the Suppress Color Profile Warnings box.

Step 6: Set Save and Close in the Destination drop-down menu and click OK (4.14).
The files selected in the File Browser are resized to 72 pixels per inch, unsharp masked, the color aliasing is reduced, your copyright information and symbol in the header bar is added, and the files are saved as high quality JPEGs in the 0 Automate Hot Folder.

Step 7: Navigate to the 0 Automate Hot Folder on the hard drive of your computer.
Make a new folder and name it 2062-PsCSBook Laura 2003 JPG (4.15).

Step 8: Press ⌘/Control+A to select all the files and the new folder in 0 Automate Hot Folder and then ⌘/Control+click the 2062-PsCSBook Laura 2003 JPG folder to deselect the folder.

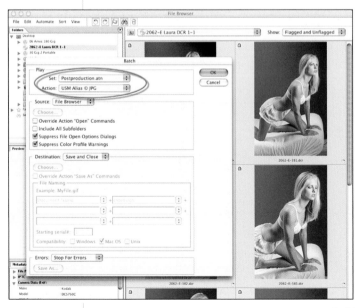

4.14

4.15

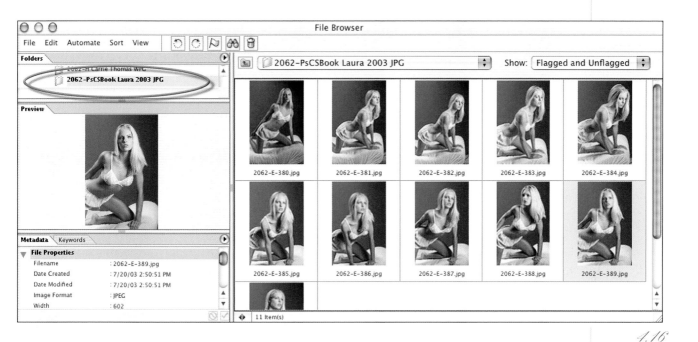

4.16

Step 9: **Drag the selected JPEGs into the folder and then drag the folder out of 0 Automate Hot Folder and onto the hard drive.**

Step 10: **Navigate to the 2062-PsCSBook Laura 2003 JPG folder in File Browser and double-click it.**
Thumbnails of the JPEGs appear automatically. This is confirmation that both CDs of raw files are archived and proofed (4.16).

Step 11: **⌘/Control+click any files that need to be rotated and then click on the appropriate Rotate button to rotate the selected images as needed.**

Step 12: **Choose File→Export Cache from File Browser's menu bar (4.17).**
A dialog box appears reporting the cache was exported successfully. Click OK.

Step 13: **Repeat Steps Two through Six for each set of raw file CDs.**
Burn all the folders to a single CD. This CD will be used for cataloging the images.

Tip
In Photoshop 7 hold down the Option/Alt key to rotate an image counterclockwise.

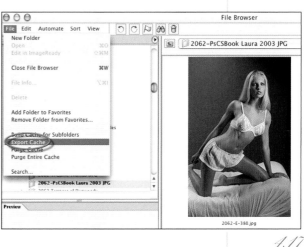

4.17

If you have four sets of raw file CD archive discs, for instance, add "1-4" to the end of the folder name (for example, *2062-PsCSBook Laura 2003 JPG1-4.*) This indicates that the CD is the first of four discs. Use a hyphen, not a front slash. The front slash is reserved for the OS X and other UNIX operating systems.

Exporting the cache places three files inside the folder that is open in File Browser. (Yes, I know I mentioned this earlier. And it is so cool — it's like your newest favorite song that you just can't help but play over and over again until you just can't stand it anymore. Please bear with me.) One saves the metadata that Photoshop has read from each raw file while making the JPEGs. Another file holds a copy of the thumbnails that File Browser generated when the folder of raw files was first opened. It also records any rotations that were made to thumbnail images. When an image is opened in Photoshop, the cache file is referenced and the appropriate rotation is applied. Thanks for listening . . .

Help! My Camera Only Captures (Gasp!) JPEG Files

JPEG files are compressed. This compression is a good thing for use on the Web where resolution or high quality in an image is not important. It is not quite a good thing when capturing images for the reasons outlined in the previous section. That said, let's face it there are times when shooting JPEG files *seems* to make sense. The two significant advantages of the JPEG capture workflow are small file sizes allowing more images on a card, and larger burst rates when shooting action. Remember the most important principle when working with original JPEG files is after opening a JPEG, *never* save it as a JPEG *with the same name*. Every time you save a JPEG without renaming it, the file recompresses and the image quality degrades. Think of JPEGs as deliverable images, not working files. If you must capture in JPEG instead of raw, here is how to safely archive them using Photoshop CS.

Step 1: **Copy the JPEG captures from your camera to a folder on the hard drive.**
Don't erase the data on the camera or capture media just yet.

Step 2: **Open File Brower in Photoshop by pressing ⌘/ Control+Shift+O or choosing File➥Browse from the menu bar.**

I'm so glad you asked. That bundle of JPEGs has a lot of uses beyond making sure your raw files are safely archived. Because they are in folders named by raw file set, you can drag them into Digital Asset Management software to create catalogs. And if your catalogs should ever be lost, the JPEGs are used to rebuild them (redundancy, redundancy, redundancy). Canto Cumulus, Extensis Portfolio, and iView Media Pro are all good choices. (See the appendix in the back of this book for contact information.) Another use is to build galleries of the work that you can post on the Web or burn to CDs for client review. Self-running PDF presentations can be generated, too. Guess what? The next chapter goes through all the how to's step by step. Before we get to that there is another burning (well, maybe smoldering is more like it) issue to address.

So, Kevin, What Do I Do with All These JPEGS?

Step 3: **⌘/Control+click on image thumbnails that need to be rotated counterclockwise.**
Click the Rotate Counterclockwise button on File Browser's toolbar. Press ⌘/Control+D to deselect them. Now ⌘/Control+click the ones that need to be rotated clockwise. Click the Rotate Clockwise button in File Browser toolbar. Deselect the newly rotated images (4.18).

Step 4: **Press ⌘/Control+A to select all the thumbnails.**

Note

Naming folders with a job or event number, a brief description, and the year is a good idea. For more information see the section, "Naming files and folders" earlier in this chapter.

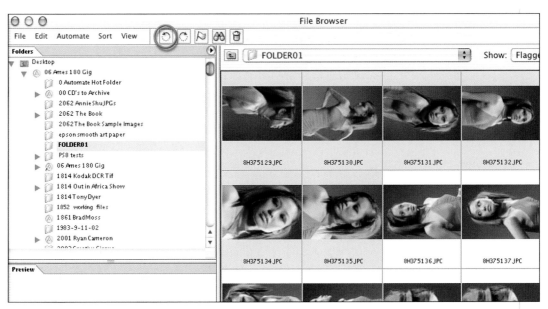

4.18

Step *5*: **Choose Automate➡Batch Rename from the File Browser menu bar and click the Rename in Same Folder button.**

Step *6*: **Enter the job number followed by a dash in the first File Naming field.**

Step *7*: **Select 3 Digit Serial Number from the drop-down menu in the second field.**
Be sure Extension is selected for the next field.

Step *8*: **Enter the starting number in the Starting Serial # field.**

Step *9*: **Click OK.**
The thumbnail files are renamed.

Step *10*: **Choose File➡Export Cache from the menu bar in File Browser** (4.19) **and click OK in the confirmation window.**

Step *11*: **Burn the folder of JPEGs and the two cache files to a CD.**

Step *12*: **Burn a copy of the CD (not the folder on the hard drive) to serve as a backup or archive copy.**
Follow the steps in "Pre-Postproduction: Proofing the Archives" to ensure that the copies of the original JPEG files are good.

4.19

All the work has been done using the thumbnails of the JPEG files. They have never been opened. Any changes that would have required opening the JPEG and resaving it is done by referencing the thumbnails. The data of the changes is archived in the exported cache files. When you open the burned CD in File Browser, it reads the cache data and displays the rotations (4.20).

The CDs of JPEGs that have been created in this section are the *digital negatives*. The original files have been copied from the camera or storage media. The files on the CDs have *never been opened.* They are pristine and hold all the data the camera that captured them was able to record. Store the extra CD in a safe place at another location. You'll always have a backup of your precious digital photographs.

"Come on, Kevin, you don't do this to everything you shoot, do you?"

Yes, as a matter of fact I do all of these steps to every image after every shoot. Yes, it takes time and lots of CDs. (Thank goodness they are cheap!) And it is the best investment of time and resources I can think of. Not only does this process guarantee that the images are available for further work in Photoshop, it also gives an overview of the work. This viewing begins the editing process.

4.20

Coming up in Chapter 5, we use Photoshop to generate a Web photo gallery of the proofed JPEGs for review with a Web browser. The Web photo gallery can be on a hard drive or on a Web site on the Internet. Later on in the book you refine your image-editing skills even further when I show you how to narrow down sixteen images to three and combine them into a final composite.

Chapter Five

Proofing and Reviewing Digital Photography

I hate to think of the countless hours that have been spent by photographers with an eye glued to a loupe bending over a light box reviewing their film. Clients, too, have squinted at contact sheets wishing that their magnifying glasses could really show the detail held in the negatives of the miniature photographs.

Reviewing images has always been the result of the way they are proofed. Transparency film originals received scrutiny with a 4X to 8X loupe. Editorial black-and-white negatives were ganged on contact sheets with 36 one-inch by one-and-a-half-inch frames on an 8 x 10 sheet. Wedding shots were shown on 4 x 5 color prints or projected on a screen when they were proofed to slides.

Today, digital capture has revolutionized the reviewing process. We are demanding instant feedback. Polaroids offered a tantalizing glimpse of the possibilities a shoot offered yet were not the final product. The translation from the test to the finished film worked well sometimes and sometimes it didn't.

Digital images can be seen at the moment of capture on the LCD screens of the cameras making them or on laptop screens to which the cameras are tethered, through File Browser in Adobe Photoshop CS in their original raw form. The JPEG files you created in the last chapter prove that the archive discs are good. These JPEGs are also used to create catalogs of digital negatives and finished photographs using software packages.

Now we begin to look critically at photographs with an eye toward choosing the best work to show clients. In this chapter we make an Action to prepare files for display and explore Camera Raw's ability to create great-looking files automatically. This chapter shows you how to create proofing tools that you can use to view images from a CD or use to post images on the Internet. In both cases a browser such as Apple Safari, Microsoft Internet Explorer, or Netscape Navigator functions as a contact sheet and a magnified proof as well. Let's jump right in.

Sharp Presentation

Showing work in the very best possible light is always a good idea. Dressing up the work for review by the client is important. Before digital photography, transparencies from a shoot were often mounted in custom-cut mattes for presentation. Contacts sheets sported logos printed on them in the darkroom. Wedding proofs were shown in book form. Fortunately presenting digital image files is straightforward, requires no sharp instruments, contact frames, chemicals, or plastic pages. Actually, all it takes is Adobe Photoshop CS and half a buck or so for a CD, label, and envelope.

And, of course, first there is a little bit of file preparation (surprise, surprise) before showing the digital proofs to anyone! Remember that digital images come to us in a not-quite-sharp state. They lack borders. (Remember how nice those custom mattes were?) And how about adding some beveled edges with embossing? I'm glad you asked.

PREPPING YOUR PRESENTATION

Step 1: **Download Marie.jpg from www.ames-photo.com/learning and open the file in Photoshop CS.**

Step 2: **Highlight the Postproduction.atn set in the Actions palette and click the Create New Action icon from the bottom of the palette.**

Step 3: **Name the new Action WPG Prep USM.JPG (*WPG* is, of course, a TLA for Web Photo Gallery) and click Record.**

Step 4: **Choose Image→Image Size from the menu bar.**
Make sure that Scale Styles, Constrain Proportions, and Resample Image are checked in the Image Size dialog box (5.1). The sampling method drop-down menu should read Bicubic. Type **72** into the Resolution field. Click OK.

Step 5: **Make a duplicate of the background layer by pressing ⌘/Control+J.**

Step 6: **Highlight the Background layer and press D on the keyboard to set the default colors.**
Press ⌘/Control+Delete/Backspace to fill the Background layer with white.

Step 7: **Choose Image→Canvas Size from the menu bar and check the Relative box in the Canvas Size dialog box.**
This distributes additional area according to the amount entered in the Width and Height fields (or subtracts it if a minus sign precedes the value). You assign distribution by clicking the arrows in the Anchor graphic. Enter **.25** inches in both Width and Height fields. Leave the Anchor set in the center. Choose White in the Canvas extension color drop-down menu. Click OK.

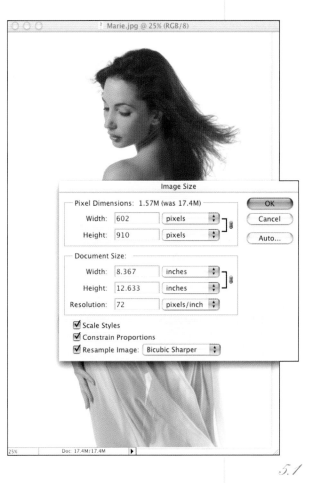

5.1

Note

Some digital cameras have their resolution set at 72 pixels per inch (the TLA is PPI not DPI). If your camera works this way, insert a step in the Action before down-sampling the images to 72ppi to convert the resolution to 300ppi. Choose Image→Image Size, deselect the Resample Image box, and set the Resolution field to 300 pixels/inch.

Step *8*: **Press ⌘/Control+A to select the entire Background layer.**

Step *9*: **Choose Edit➡Stroke from the menu bar and enter 5 px in the Width field of the Stroke dialog box** (5.2). Click the Inside button in the Location section. Click OK. A black border appears around the image. Press ⌘/Control+D to deselect the selection.

Step *10*: **Double-click the thumbnail in Layer 1.** The Layer Style dialog box opens.

Step *11*: **Click the words *Drop Shadow* on the left-hand side of the dialog box to open the Drop Shadow dialog box.** Set the Blend Mode to Multiply and Opacity to 37%. Deselect Use Global Light. Enter **128°** into the Angle field. Set Distance to 6 pixels, Spread to 27%, and Size to 8 pixels.

Step *12*: **Double-click the words *Bevel and Emboss*.** The Bevel and Emboss dialog box replaces Drop Shadow (5.3). Set Style to Inner Bevel, Technique to Smooth, Depth at 150%, Direction to Up, Size at 6 pixels, and Soften at 4 pixels. Again deselect Use Global Light. Enter **128°** in the Angle field and **30°** in the Altitude field. Set Highlight Mode to Screen at 75% and Shadow Mode to Multiply at 75%. The Highlight Color should be White and the Shadow Color should be Black. Click OK.

Step *13*: **From the fly-out menu in the Layers palette, select Flatten Image.**

5.2

5.3

Step 14: **Choose Filter➧Sharpen➧Unsharp Mask from the menu bar.**
In the Unsharp Mask dialog box set the Amount to 100%, a Radius of 1 pixel, and 0 levels for Threshold (5.4). Click OK.

Step 15: **Choose Edit➧Fade Unsharp Mask from the menu bar.**
In the Fade dialog box, set the Mode to Luminosity and click OK (5.5).

ADDING YOUR COPYRIGHT

Step 16: **Choose File➧File Info from the menu bar.**
The File Info dialog box opens (5.6). Click on Advanced, click the Append button, navigate to 2004.xmp, and click Load. Click OK.

Step 17: **Choose File➧Save As and navigate to the 0 Automate Hot Folder (5.7). Click Save.**
Set the Quality slider to 6 (Medium) and click OK.

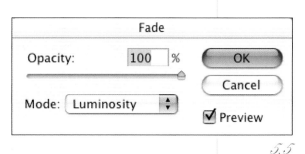

5.4

5.5

5.7

5.6

Step *18*: **Press ⌘/Control+W or choose File·Close to close Marie.jpg.**

Step *19*: **Click the Stop icon at the bottom of the Actions palette and select Save Actions from the fly-out menu of the Actions palette.**

Step *20*: **Navigate to the 0 Automate Hot Folder and delete Marie.jpg.**

This action dresses up the files in similar fashion to the way photographs were presented when they were on film. The finished presentation for Marie.jpg is shown here (5.8).

The extra effort is a subtle way of setting your Web Photo Gallery apart from those who use shortcuts in the process. The next section shows how to set up Camera Raw to make the very best proofs automatically and then run the WPG Prep USM JPG Action on selected images in File Browser.

Getting to Know Camera Raw

Adobe introduced a Camera Raw/JPEG 2000 bundle as a plug-in for Photoshop 7 downloadable from www.adobe.com for $99.00. Photoshop CS has a much-improved Camera Raw built right in. While some of the higher-end digital cameras are not supported in Camera Raw, the software that comes with them offers great workflow solutions that fit well into Photoshop. Raw files from Canon, Fuji, Kodak, Nikon, and Olympus have been tuned to work much better in Camera Raw than in the manufacturer's software.

Camera Raw has been fully integrated into Photoshop CS and is accessible through File Browser. In the last chapter, Camera Raw was used as a brute-force image processor to create JPEG files for cataloging and to confirm that the archive discs were good. This section is about working with finesse on a series of images. It becomes the basis for the high-quality workflow for files to be retouched and prepped for output.

5.8

There are minor differences from camera to camera when a file is displayed in Camera Raw. The demonstrations in this chapter were created with DCR files from a Kodak DCS 760. The flavor of raw file that your camera produces will be slightly different in Camera Raw. The workflow is the same. Settings will change based on the personality of each type of raw image.

A folder with six DCR files (2062-F Marie) is on www.ame-sphoto.com/learning for you to download. This demo will use more files from the same shoot.

5.9

Step 1: **Choose Edit→Preferences from the File Browser menu bar** (5.9).

The Preferences dialog box sets up File Browser's parameters. The Adobe engineers understand that photographers have different working requirements. My files tend to be quite large, so I want File Browser to display thumbnails of my images even though all of them together might reach half a gig in size. (Don't worry: The exercises in this book will not reach the default 100MB setting.) I also like big thumbnails, so I set the Custom Thumbnail Size to 325 pixels wide. (This setting creates the big thumbnails you see in the screen captures.) Select the Allow Background Processing check box, which lets File Browser build thumbnails behind the scenes (5.10). Click OK.

Step 2: **Navigate in File Browser's Folder pane to the folder 2062-F Marie and double-click it.**

Thumbnail previews open in the light box pane.

Step 3: **Choose View→Custom Thumbnail Size from the File Browser menu.**

Step 4: **Double-click 2062-F-0260.DCR to open the photograph of Marie holding a Gretag Macbeth ColorChecker Gray Balance Card in Camera Raw.**

Step 5: **Click the Rotate Image 90° Counterclockwise button and then select 25% in the Zoom Level drop-down menu** (5.11).

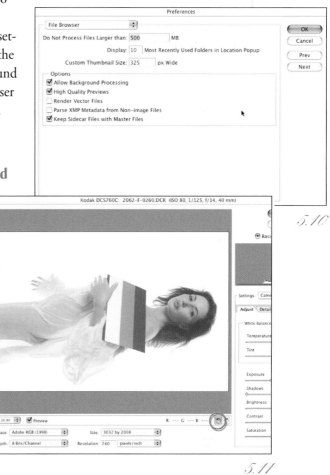

5.10

5.11

Step 6: Continue setting up Camera Raw.

Select Adobe RGB (1998) in the Space drop-down menu and 8 Bits/Channel in the Depth menu. Click the White Balance tool located in the upper-left toolbar in the Camera Raw interface (5.12).

Step 7: Click anywhere on the GretagMacbeth Gray Balance Card in the image.

You use the White Balance tool to neutralize white, gray, or black simply by clicking. The important thing to remember is that any change made to a raw file is applied to the file that is built from the data. The raw file itself is not changed.

Step 8: Fine-tune the exposure while observing the histogram.

Individual color channel as well as luminosity information is displayed graphically. Unfortunately, there is no way to place color samplers for dynamic readouts in the Info palette when working in Camera Raw. Any of the three tools — Zoom, Hand, and White Balance — show the value of the area they are on in the single RGB readout window to the left of the Rotate buttons. The photograph of Marie is high key with a predominant number of pixels in the highlight areas of the histogram. Driving the exposure up until the histogram has data in the right area won't help in this instance because there is already lots of highlight exposure.

Step 9: Place the Hand tool on the white swath of the GretagMacbeth Gray Balance Card.

The readings are R: 236, G: 233, B: 233, indicating a slight underexposure.

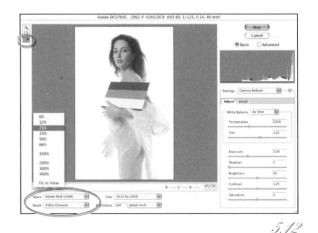

5.12

Step 10: **Click the Exposure slider and move it to the right.**
Take it up in small steps, checking the values each time. A setting of +.35 gives a reading of R: 247, G: 244, B: 244. The background is almost completely white. This setting is fine for the highlights.

Step 11: **Move the Hand tool over the black patch.**
The readings show R: 80, G: 81, B: 79. This is a double-edged problem.

Step 12: **Hold down the Option/Alt key and push the Shadow slider to the right.**

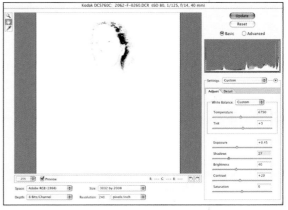

The image goes completely white. Keep moving it until some black breaks through the Posterized colors (5.13). The black swath reads in the low sixties. Now look at Marie's hair. All the detail close to her head is gone.

Step 13: **Back the shadow slider toward the left and move the Hand tool over her hair until the shadow readings there are in the low thirties.**
The colors won't balance because her hair is brown. That's okay. It's the detail that is important. The setting will be close to 22.

5.13

Step 14: **Now back the Brightness slider off to the left and watch the histogram.**
The shadow end expands toward the left in concert with the Brightness slider. Set it at 40 and check the readings in Marie's hair. The contrast has improved and the numbers are still in the very high twenties or low thirties. Move the Contrast to flavor and not too much now. Watch the numbers to retain detail. A setting of 20 is close to perfect.

Doing this for every frame would be more painful than slow tooth extraction without painkiller and half as much fun. Life would be great if only there were a way to use these settings in an Action. If only. Well (fortunately) there is.

Color and
Exposure
References

Color and exposure references are very useful to have when working in postproduction. Shooting a reference on the first frame of each new scene is a good photographic habit. This example shows the difference between the image on the left that was shot with flash versus the image on the right that was balanced with the White Balance tool (5.14). The RGB numbers at the bottom of each frame tell the story. Notice that Camera Raw displays the camera type, the image name, ISO, shutter speed, aperture, and focal length in the document header.

5.14

Step *15*: **Click the disclosure triangle to the right of the Settings drop-down menu and choose Save Settings. Leave the name set to the new file 2062-F-0260.xmp.**

Click OK to have Camera Raw build out a TIF. (Even though it carries the .DCR extension in this case it's still a TIF.) Or, click Cancel to quit Camera Raw without making an editable file.

Compare the three histograms shown here (5.15). The top one is the distribution of pixels for the image as it was captured using the camera's settings. There is an area from the left side indicating that there is no data in the blacks or lower shadow values (arrow). The middle histogram shows expanded shadow data resulting from the tweaks to the default settings in Camera Raw. This histogram shows that data exists across the entire dynamic range of the image. The blue channel extends color into the lowest value. This histogram represents the pixels of the file that will be produced when OK is clicked. The last histogram represents the output file of Marie shown on the right. The photograph has not had any postproduction exposure or contrast tweaks. It is shown as output from Camera Raw.

Histograms: Before, During, and After

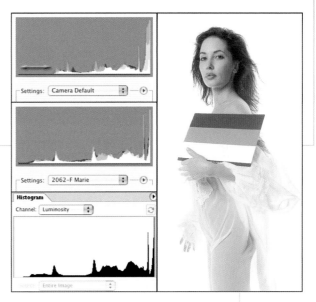

5.15

Step 16: **Return to File Browser and press ⌘/Control+A to select all the thumbnails.**

Step 17: **From File Browser's Automate menu choose Apply Camera Raw Settings** (5.16).

Step 18: **In the Apply Camera Raw Settings dialog box select 2060-F-2060.xmp from the drop-down menu and click Update** (5.17).

The settings are transferred to all the selected thumbnails in File Browser. And what's really cool is the thumbnails update to reflect the new information.

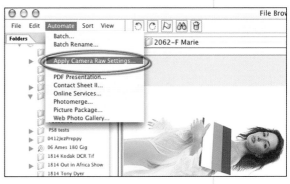

5.16

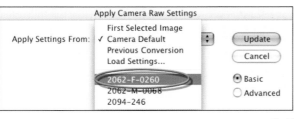

5.17

Naming Conventions Continue

Anything that has to do with a job carries the job number. This is true for levels, curves, and special Action sets. Camera Raw files that may have to be found later are no exception! Including the job number on Camera Raw files is useful when a client wants changes. The raw settings are the starting point for postproduction.

Step : **Click any thumbnails that need rotating.**

In this case they all do and it's 90° CCW (Counterclockwise). Click the Rotate button. If the annoying rotation dialog box appears quickly check Don't Show Again and OK to dismiss it forever (5.18). (Actually, you can reset the warnings in Preferences.) Press ⌘/Control+D to deselect all the thumbnails.

Now it is time (finally) to edit the picks into the set that will get presented to the client. Yes, I know you thought that I had forgotten that presentation was the point of this chapter. . . .

Step 20: **⌘/Control+click on the thumbnails that are going to get the "I-want-people-to-see-you" treatment.**

Almost there. . . .

Step 21: **Choose Automate➡Batch to open the Batch dialog box.**

Select Postproduction as the Set and WPG Prep USM JPG as the Action. Set the Source to File Browser. Deselect (if selected) both the Override Action "Open" Commands and Include All Subfolders.

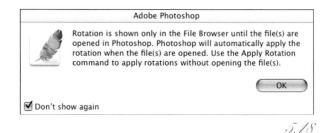

5.18

Step 22: **Select the Suppress Color Profile Warnings option.**
This option ensures that if the working color space is not Adobe RGB (1998), the process will not generate the Missing Profile dialog box requiring an input from the user for every file as it opens. In the Destination drop-down menu choose Save and Close.

Step 23: **Click OK.**
The Batch process opens every image sequentially using Camera Raw, adds the enhancements, and saves them as JPGs to the 0 Automate Hot Folder. Take a break. Go pour a cup of coffee and bring it right back. The prep work will be finished and waiting to become a gallery of work for presentation.

Welcome back. All that's left is to navigate to 0 Automate Hot Folder and create a new folder.

Step 24: **Name the folder with job number and description, in this case, 2062–F Marie WPG.**
Drag the JPG files into the new folder. Drag that folder out of 0 Automate Hot Folder.

Done. On to the next exciting section.

Creating Web Photo Galleries

One of the most powerful features of Photoshop CS is the ability to create Internet-ready Web sites of images. These mini-sites can be posted to the Web, burned to CD, or left on the hard drive. All that is required to view them is a browser. You'll use the files of Marie that were prepped in the previous section for your Web Photo Gallery. This exercise will use the Simple template. At the end of the section I'll go over how to modify the HTML code so that the style looks like the one with my Web site's logo and background.

Step 1: **Create a new folder on your hard drive to hold the Web Photo Gallery. Name it 2062_wpg_marie.**

Tip

Now this is important. Really important. Because it is written in Adobe-speak, a language known only to a select few who spend their days and nights in incense-infused surrounds chanting transient witticisms to one another and writing things like *Suppress File Open Options Dialogs,* which actually means *Allow Camera Raw to Work with Actions.* Be sure to check this box (5.19)!

Really means: "Let Camera RAW work with actions!"

5.19

Web Templates

Photoshop CS offers eleven templates in the Web Photo Gallery Styles drop-down menu and many more on the CD. The templates are HTML based and feature cascading style sheets (CSS). They are customizable using Adobe's Go Live, Macromedia's Dreamweaver, Bare Bones Software's BBEdit, and even in a text editor (though that choice requires some serious expertise in HTML). The path to the templates is Adobe Photoshop CS➡Presets➡Web Photo Gallery.

Note

The folder, 2062_wpg_marie, is named according to conventions for posting on the Internet. Lowercase letters separated by underscores or dashes (no spaces) ensures it will work no matter what type of operating system an Internet hosting company is running on its servers.

Step 2: **From File Browser navigate to the folder, 2062-F Marie WPG, created in Step Twenty-four in the last section and click on it.**

The thumbnails populate in the light box pane in their proper orientation (5.20). These files were edited in the previous section before they were made into JPGs.

Step 3: **Press ⌘/Control +A to select all the thumbnails.**

Take one last look through the chosen ones to see whether any should be left out. If so, ⌘/Control+click on them and they will be deselected.

Step 4: **Choose Automate➡Web Photo Gallery from File Browser's menu.**

The Web Photo Gallery dialog box appears.

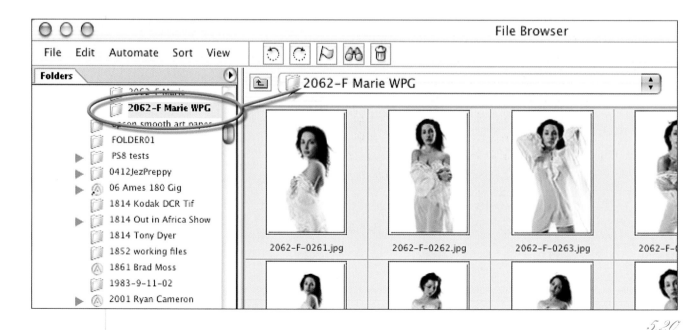

5.20

This dialog box has several sections, which you'll fill in over the next several steps.

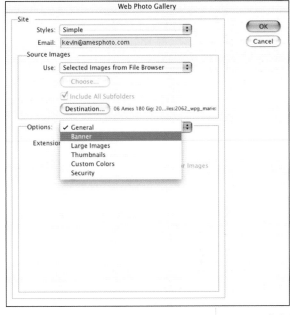

Step 5: **In the Styles drop-down menu choose Simple and fill in the Email window.**
Now set up the Source Images section.

Step 6: **Choose Selected Images From File Browser in the Use drop-down menu, click the Destination button, and navigate to the folder where you would like to store your Web Photo Gallery.**

Step 7: **Select Banner from the Options drop-down menu (5.21) and fill in the Site Name with 2062-F Marie Proofs–Not for Publication.**
Because I shot the photographs, go ahead and use my name and phone number as shown in this figure. The date is filled in with the day the site was generated (the field is modifiable). My font choice is **Arial** in a Helvetica world. Set **3** as the font size.

5.21

Step 8: **Select Large Images in the Options drop-down menu and make sure the Resize Images box is selected.**
Now make sure the photographs are big enough to see.

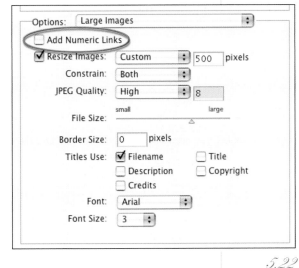

Step 9: **Choose Custom from the Resize Images drop-down menu and enter 500 in the pixels box.**
Set Constrain to Both and JPEG Quality to High — **8** (or better). The Border Size is **0**. Check the Filename box in the Titles Use section. Continuity demands that Font and Font Size remain **Arial** and **3**, respectively (5.22). If your gallery will have more than a page, be sure to deselect the Add Numeric Links check box.

5.22

I am an admitted resolution junkie. I like big files. And I want others to have them, too. For client reviews, I ask clients about their Internet connection in order to the give them large files balanced with reasonable download times. (The size and usage is then contractually agreed upon in advance.)

The images are downsized to 72 ppi. Whenever possible I save them page sized in High JPG quality. High-speed connections to the Internet (cable modem, DSL, and even T1 connectivity) are becoming more commonplace. And they will continue to. Size and speed — you really can have cake and eat it, too! Cool.

Step *10*: **Select Thumbnails from the Options drop-down menu.**

I prefer bigger thumbnails so once again look to the Custom Size and fill in **150** pixels. Fill in **5** for Columns and **3** for Rows. Again the Border Size is **0**. Whew. Easy step. Onward. . . .

Step *11*: **Choose Custom Colors in Options. Click the Background color swatch (white in this case) to open up the custom colors dialog box.**

Select the Only Web Colors check box; the number of colors shrinks greatly. New browsers are capable of rendering more colors than the Web-safe colors this dialog box represents. The reason for using them is there is more than just a noticeable difference in the neutral (gray) tones shown. There are four grays, black, and white — more than enough to fill the dialog box requirements.

Step *12*: **Click the first gray swatch down from white or enter R: 204, G: 204, B: 204.**

You can also enter this color in the #field as **CCCCCC** (5.23). (It's the HTML code for this color.) Click OK.

Step *13*: **Leave the Banner color where it is. Click the Text swatch and click the first gray above black or enter R: 51, G: 51, B: 51 or #: 333333. Click OK.**

Step *14*: **I like to keep the Link and the Active Link colors the same. Click on the Link swatch and click the second gray below white or enter R: 153, G: 153, B: 153 or #: 999999. Click OK.**

Repeat this step for Active Link.

Step 15: **Click the Visited Link swatch and choose black. R: 0, G: 0, B: 0 or #: 000000.**

When you are finished the color scheme will be non-distracting and completely neutral. The black Visited Link selection makes the photographs that have been enlarged stand out when a user reviews the contact page. This is important when your client goes back to make a list of favorites (5.24).

Step 16: **Click OK.**

Photoshop opens every file selected in File Browser, makes a large and thumbnail image, places them in HTML pages, and opens the default browser automatically so the new Web Photo Gallery can be reviewed before posting on the Internet or burning to a CD.

Step 17: **Click an image to see it larger.**

Look at how finished it is with a beveled edge, drop shadow, and black border (5.25). It's more than well worth all the extra effort. (As if running Actions is tough — don't tell anybody!)

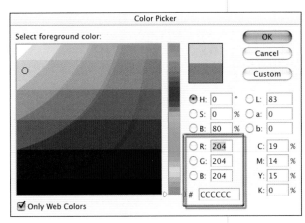

5.23

5.24

5.25

Open a Web Photo Gallery in a browser by navigating to the folder it's in and double-clicking index.htm. If you know what page you want to view, double-click on the page index_#.htm, where the number sign is the page you want to visit.

Note

If an agreement on usage and price has not been reached with the people who will view the work, click on the Security portion of the Options drop-down menu. Fill in the dialog box to taste and Photoshop will overprint the choices on the large image, providing security against unauthorized use. The next section on customizing the gallery shows how to put a copyright notice on every thumbnail in an image page automatically.

Note

The Simple template that is installed in Photoshop CS has had features added and removed. The original Simple template is on the Photoshop CS disc in the Optional Content folder and is installed in Photoshop 7. It is the version used in the following steps. Drag a copy of the original Simple template into the Web Photo Gallery. This is the template you modify.

This example uses the custom template for amesphoto.com's Web photo gallery. (Call the templates and graphics for your site names that make sense to you.)

5.26

Leisurely peruse your work. Click another thumbnail. Enjoy the enlarged image (5.26). Click on the Next icon and view another big photograph. Life is good, very good. You rock!

Creating the Custom Gallery

Branding and identity are important marketing tools. One of the elements of a marketing plan is a cohesive Web presence. A consistent look throughout the site is crucial. Photoshop CS builds great Web galleries that don't look anything like the site you've already poured your blood, sweat, and tears into (or paid your hard-earned money to have someone else design). What to do?

Once again those Adobe marvels in San Jose know the way to help. They made every Web gallery style an editable template in the Web Photo Gallery folder. This section shows how to customize the Simple templates.

Step 1: Look inside the Photoshop CS folder and find the Presets folder. Inside is a folder named Web Photo Gallery. Find the folder named Simple (5.27).

Step 2: Rename the Simple folder to Simple Numerics.

Step 3: Rename the folder amesphoto.com and add the graphic files (usually .gif) for logo, background, and navigation buttons if you want to use your own like my site does (highlighted in blue) (5.28).

IndexPage.htm and SubPage.htm are the files you'll modify.

Step 4: Open IndexPage.htm in a text editor.

The screenshots in this section are from Microsoft Word. You can drag the file onto the Word icon to open it. Choose View➡HTML Source.

Note

Dragging a copy of the original Simple folder leaves the newly renamed Simple Numeric in the menu in case a site has to be built for someone else. And your custom template appears in the Automate➡Web Photo Gallery menu, too!

| Simple |
| 4 items, 18.94 GB available |

A Better Finder Rename for OS X	Adobe ImageReady CS	Keyboard Shortcuts	Centered Frame 1 – Basic
Acrobat Reader 5.0	Adobe Photoshop CS	Layouts	Centered Frame 1 – Feedback
Address Book	Adobe Photoshop CS ReadMe.rtf	Optimized Colors	Centered Frame 1 – Info Only
Adobe InDesign 2.0	Adobe Photoshop Install Log.txt	Optimized Output Settings	Centered Frame 2 – Feedback
Adobe Photoshop 7	Help	Optimized Settings	Horizontal – Feedback
Adobe Photoshop CS	Helpers	Patterns	Horizontal Neutral
AppleScript	Legal	Photoshop Actions	Horizontal Patterned
Applications (Mac OS 9)	Plug-Ins	Scripts	Horizontal Slideshow
Art Directors Toolkit 3	Presets	Styles	Simple
Calculator	Samples	Textures	Table 1
Chess	Scripting Guide	Tools	Table 2
Clock		Web Photo Gallery	
DCS Applications		ZoomView	

5.27

| amesphoto.com |
| 5 of 9 items selected, 18.94 GB available |

amesphoto.com	ani_ames_logoweb.gif
Centered Frame 1 – Basic	background2.gif
Centered Frame 1 – Feedback	Caption.htm
Centered Frame 1 – Info Only	home.gif
Centered Frame 2 – Feedback	IndexPage.htm
Horizontal – Feedback	next.gif
Horizontal Neutral	previous.gif
Horizontal Patterned	SubPage.htm
Horizontal Slideshow	Thumbnail.htm
Simple	
Table 1	
Table 2	

5.28

Tip

Mac users will want to use Microsoft's Word in OS X or Simple Text in Classic. Sometimes TextEdit will not allow HTML editing.

Step 5: **In IndexPage.htm find the code that is displayed in this figure** (5.29). **Change it to read** `<BODY bgcolor= FFFFFF background="background2.gif" text= %696969% link=%LINK% vlink=%VLINK% alink= %ALINK%>`

The site, amesphoto.com, features a white background with a vertical gray stripe pattern. These modifications permanently change the background color to white (FFFFFF), the text color to dark gray, and add the graphic file background2.gif as the pattern. This overrides the color choice dialog box in Photoshop.

Step 6: **Scroll down the page and locate the following text:**

```
</TD>
</TR>
```

Between them add this code:

```
<TD ALIGN="LEFT"><a href="../../index.html">
<img height="76" width="225" src="ani_ames_
logoweb.gif" border="0"></a></TD>
```

This HTML positions the graphic, ani_ames_logoweb.gif, to the upper-right side of the page, sets its dimensions, and tells a browser to go to the home page (`<a href="../../index. html">`) when the logo is clicked. The "`../../`" tells the browser to look two levels up in the hierarchy of the site for the home page file, index.html. Before modifying the templates for your site make sure you know how it's set up. It may be different from this example.

5.29

Step 7: **Find the text that says:**

`<BR>%PHOTOGRAPHER%`

Add the copyright symbol and the year right
after `<BR>` and before the first % sign. This automatically inserts a legal copyright notice when the
photographer's name is entered in the Web Photo
Gallery dialog box. The text now looks like this:

`<BR>(c)2003 %PHOTOGRAPHER%`

That's it for IndexPage.htm. The modified areas
are highlighted in yellow so you can see the modifications in place and check yours against them
(5.30). Save the changes to IndexPage.htm.
There's one more page to go.

Step 8: **Open SubPage.htm in Word, choose
View➞HTML Source, and find the
following code:**

`<BODY bgcolor=%BGCOLOR% text=%TEXT% link=%LINK%`
`vlink=%VLINK% alink=%ALINK%>`

5.30

Step 9: **Change** `bgcolor=%BGCOLOR%` **to read** `bgcolor=FFFFFF`.
Change `text=%TEXT%` **to** `text=696969`.

That makes the SubPage background white, the text dark gray,
and overrides Photoshop's background and text color dialog
boxes. (If you want to be able to modify these colors in
Photoshop, leave this part alone.)

Step 10: **Add** `background="../background2.gif"` **after**
`bgcolor=FFFFFF`.

The code now reads:

`<BODY bgcolor=FFFFFF background="../back-`
`ground2.gif" text=#696969 link=%LINK%`
`vlink=%VLINK% alink=%ALINK%>`

Notice that "`../`" has been added before background2.gif.
The hierarchy of the Web photo gallery puts the SubPages in a
folder named Pages. The "`../`" tells the browser to look one
level above the Pages folder for the background image.

Step 11: **Scroll down and find** `<BR>%PHOTOGRAPHER%` **and add
the copyright info so that it reads** `<BR>©2003`
`%PHOTOGRAPHER%`.

Step *12*: **Find the following tags**:

```
</TD>
</TR>
```

Between them insert this code:

```
<TD ALIGN="LEFT"><a href="../../../index.html">
<img height="76" width="225" src="../ani_ames_
logoweb.gif" border="0"></a></TD>
```

This code has *two* very important differences from the code in Step Five. There is and extra "../" in `<a href= "../../../index.html">` and in the logo graphic: `scr="../ani_ames_logoweb.gif"`. The home page is now three levels above the Pages folder. The logo graphic is one level up. The modifications you make to your SubPage.htm will probably be like the ones for IndexPage.html. Remember the extra "../" (5.31).

You can still change the active, visited, and link colors on both pages in Photoshop. If you want to you can make the colors permanent. You now know how.

5.31

Step *13*: **Copy your custom graphics files from the custom style folder (in this case amesphoto.com) into a new folder and name it** 2062_wpg_marie_customized.

Step *14*: **Select the images you want for the site in File Browser and then choose Automate➡Web Photo Gallery.** Choose your custom style, fill in the Banner data, thumbnail and large image sizes, fonts and font sizes, colors, and security, if any. Click OK. While Photoshop builds your site, look at these figures (5.32). Compare the standard Simple to the custom style. There really is no comparison and no compromise in the presentation.

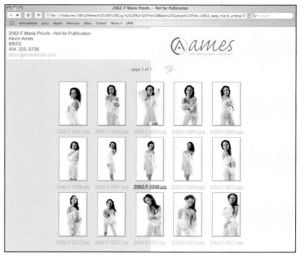

5.32

Hey, look — it's finished!

You have just created your own signature Web photo gallery with bevel and embossed edged photographs floating above white surrounded by a black border. Your site is now awesome!

The Web photo gallery is ready to be uploaded to the Internet. Soon clients or friends anywhere in the world can see the work and let you know which ones rock their boat. Or for that matter, you can browse it on your laptop in a hotspot-equipped coffee house while enjoying an espresso and editing the take to the final hero. Relax, you've earned it.

The next chapter rounds out the section on workflow by exploring non-destructive Photoshop. My friend and fellow digital photographer, Jim DiVitale, calls this style of working the "Way of the Fast Retreat." It allows extreme flexibility by using layers in 16-bit. This next chapter puts the whole section to productive and dynamic work.

Chapter Six

Non-Destructive Photoshop: "The Way of the Fast Retreat"

*The "Way of the Fast Retreat" protects me from art directors who want
things changed. They always want things changed.*

Jim DiVitale

Adobe Photoshop CS offers its users many different styles
for working on photographs. An image can be color-
corrected, have its exposure tweaked, be retouched, and
sent to the client without your knowing a thing about layers.
Photoshop's Auto/Magnetic/Magic style features will make most
photographs close to good enough. The Image→Adjustments
method pragmatically, and often with heavy-handed finesse, works
the image through color, exposure, and retouching. (The finesse part
involves using the Edit→Fade command. The heavy-handed part is

TLA

For brevity's sake, allow me to create a new one: NDP for *non-destructive Photoshop*. Thank you very much.

the degradation of the original file that occurs that leaves no way to go back to the original image once the file has been saved and closed.)

The inevitable need to "go back" brings up the Photoshop style that causes the least damage to the image, and creates the ability to easily rework the file long after it has been archived. What commercial digital photographer Jim DiVitale calls "The Way of the Fast Retreat," I refer to as *non-destructive Photoshop*.

This style of editing is not new. As a matter of fact it goes all the way back to the first days of Photoshop. Before layers (Photoshop 3.0) *non-destructive* meant saving a copy of the file for every change. This also meant burning through hugely expensive (at the time) hard drive and CD space. Back then (ten or so years ago), blank CDs cost $15.00 each. They burned successfully three out of five times on $4,000 burners writing at 1x. A 1GB hard drive cost $1,500. The result was Photoshop users often gambled (unsuccessfully) against the possibility that no one would want to make changes later. It was balancing the cost of saving many versions against how much time it would take to do the work over. Today that gamble is silly.

Still, we were thrilled to be able to work on our photographs and these prices were cheap considering the control we gained. (Photographer is a synonym for *control freak*.) Those were the "good old days." I, for one, am very glad to have them in the past.

Today, computers are powerful. They have ultra-fast processors, huge amounts of RAM and hard drive storage, and built-in high-speed optical recorders. They are cheap — less than the price of a 1x CD burner of ten years ago. Layers are available and Photoshop CS sports a 4GB limit for a single image. Life is good. It is comforting to know that three years from now when a client wants the background color changed, doing so won't be a hassle.

This chapter presents editing practices that always leave a way to get back to the present from the future. An added bonus is a simple tutorial on learning the most powerful tool in all of Photoshop — the Pen tool.

Non-destructive Photoshop involves using techniques that can be undone and/or modified after the file has been saved, closed, and reopened. The two areas for consideration in this style of working are Tools and Layers.

Avoiding Photoshop's "Forbidden" Tools

Fifty-five tools are in Photoshop CS's toolbar. Twenty-two are always visible on the palette. Of this formidable number of instruments only four are destructive. One tool is useful and three have such destructive potential they must be banned outright. (These tools exist only to annihilate pixels.)

The Crop tool destroys pixels. Cropping an image throws pixels away. That is destructive. It is also useful and safe when used on TIFs destined for a client. The chances of using the Crop tool in the middle of editing a photograph are non-existent. Cropping is the last thing done. The Crop tool gets the yellow caution square.

The tool that is banned for life from the world of NDP is the Eraser tool and its two buddies: the Background Eraser and the Magic Eraser tools. It's not that they are intrinsically evil; it's just that they kill pixels. That's right. Their whole purpose in life is to destroy pixels. When the Eraser tool's work is finished there is no hope of recovering a single pixel after the file is closed. ("The Eraser" sounds like an *X-Men* villain, doesn't it?) A better way exists. You can do the Eraser's work using layer masks. This is not to say that there are no circumstances in the non-destructive style that the Eraser tool is not appropriate.

I can think of a few. The problem lies in the huge potential of doing fatal damage with this tool. If you are willing to adopt the rule that the Eraser is a never-to-be-used *weapon of mass destruction* (WMD) and is banned from civilized Photoshop, you won't even select the tool. This means you won't ever use it inappropriately by accident, let alone on purpose. Therefore, the Eraser tool and its cronies receive the big red "Do Not Use" symbol with a drop shadow for foreboding emphasis (6.1).

The remaining fifty-one are fully cleared for use in NDP as long as you use them on layer masks and duplicate layers.

This section is not about rules other than no WMD's allowed. It is a way of thinking when working in Photoshop to always leave a way back. After all the work is finished the goal is to say, "No pixels were harmed during the creation of this photograph."

6.1

Getting to Know the Layers Palette

The Layers palette holds the canvas, paper, or graffiti wall upon which layers of pixels are brushed, sprayed, blended, or pasted. Each layer is a block building the final image. Layers can carry pixels, paint, type, adjustments, or vectors. The combinations are limitless. So are the creative possibilities. The potential for confusion seems to be limitless, too.

The Layers palette is powerful. It is the place in Photoshop where everything happens. It is safe to say that all the other palettes and menus support the Layers palette. This illustration has callouts naming each of the sections and functions that will be used in projects starting in the next chapter (6.2).

The temptation is to launch into a description of every feature and turn the book into a user's guide instead of one on photographing women. Instead, the Layers palette will be explained as each step-by-step project is completed. This process is learning by doing. After finishing the projects in this book you will have layers down cold.

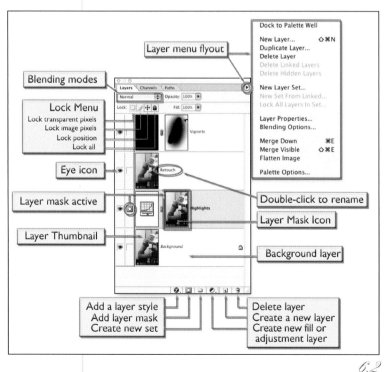

6.2

The Background layer is a flattened version of the opened file. It is always locked and cannot be moved, blended (it is always Normal), or made transparent. Grayed-out areas indicate options not available. NDP practice is to duplicate this layer (⌘/Control+J) when editing is required. This leaves the Background layer intact. Think of it as the Backup layer (6.3).

**The
Background
Layer**

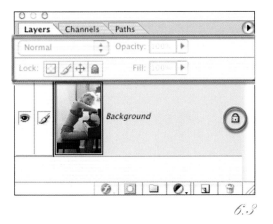

6.3

6.4

Creating a Vignette

This exercise introduces non-destructive Photoshop techniques. It involves brightening a photograph of Carrie and creating a vignette with it. Download 2062-M-0368.tif from www.amesphoto.com/learning. It is a 16-bit file. One of the best new features in Photoshop CS is the ability to work with layers in 16-bit. This is non-destructive Photoshop at its best.

Step 1: **Open 2062-M-0368.tif by double-clicking it in File Browser.**
 The layers palette now has its first layer automatically named Background.

Step 2: **Hold down the ⌘/Control+Option/Alt keys and press ~ (tilde, the key next to the number 1.)**
 This combination makes a selection out of the tones above middle gray (127) (6.4).

16-bit Info

The Info palette displays 16-bit RGB tonal values in 8-bit numbers by default. This option saves you from doing a lot of math conversions and having to recognize big numbers. To display the 16-bit values, choose Palette Options from the Info palette fly-out menu and select the Show 16 bit Values check box.

Step *3*: **Double-click the Quick Mask icon in the toolbar** (6.5). The Quick Mask Options dialog box opens. Check Selected Areas in the Color Indicates section. Set the Color Opacity to 100% (6.6). Click OK.

Step *4*: **Choose Image→Adjustments→Levels (or press ⌘/Control+L). Drag the highlight slider until the highlight input window reads 205** (6.7).
This adjustment is to the Quick Mask, not the image. The adjustment has increased the contrast of the Quick Mask, reducing the amount of the selection (6.8).

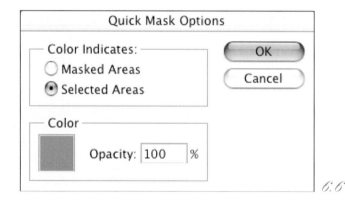

6.6

6.5

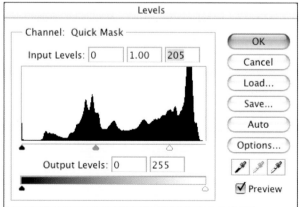

6.7

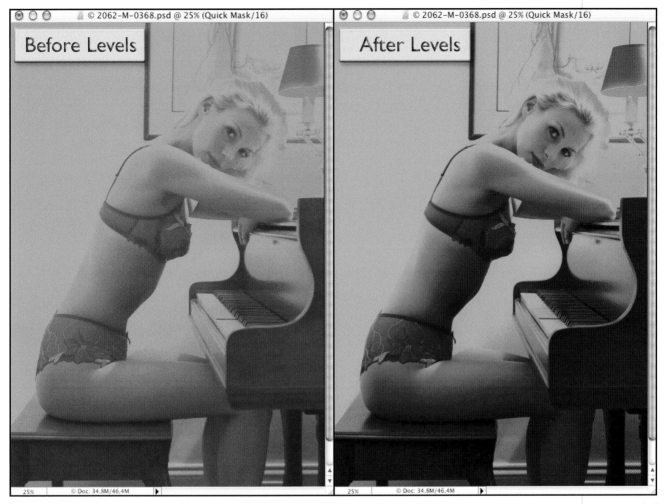

6.8

Before Photoshop, masks for placing color separations were cut by hand using X-Acto knives out of a red-colored material named *Rubylith*. Rubylith masks created clear areas on the film, which was blind to red. Color separations would later be stripped into clear places on the film. These negatives were used to burn the plates that ran on the printing press.

Setting up Quick Mask to show the selected areas mimics the convention of masking selected areas in the red of Rubylith. That's also the reason the default Quick Mask color is red.

Rubyliths Revisited

Solid Color...
Gradient...
Pattern...

Levels...
Curves...
Color Balance...
Brightness/Contrast...

Hue/Saturation...
Selective Color...
Channel Mixer...
Gradient Map...
Photo Filter...

Invert
Threshold...
Posterize...

6.9

Note

When you create a new layer it always appears just above the active (highlighted) one in the stack.

Step 5: **Press Q to exit Quick Mask.**
The marching ants of the modified selection appear.

Step 6: **Click the New Adjustment Layer icon at the bottom of the Layers palette. Choose Curves** (6.9).
The Curves dialog box appears. Option/Alt+click in the grid to set the fine grid.

Step 7: **Count two boxes over and down from the upper-right corner. Drag the curve up one box. Count a box and a half up and over from the bottom-left corner. Drag the curve down half a box** (6.10).
The new Curves layer appears in the layer stack above the Background layer (6.11). Click OK.

Step 8: **Double-click the word *Curves* to open the rename dialog box. Type Highlights in the highlighted window. Click outside the rename window or press Enter to accept the new name.**
The curves adjustment layer, Highlights, is active.

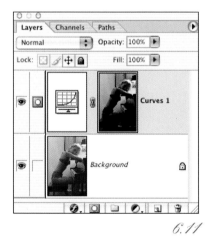

6.11

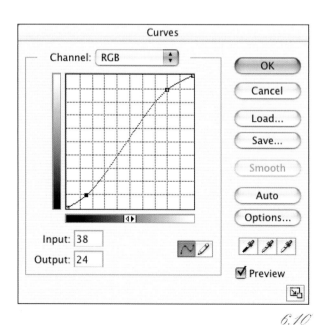

6.10

Step *9*: **Create a new empty layer by clicking the New Layer icon at the bottom of the Layers palette. Rename it** Retouch.

Step *10*: **Hold down the Option/Alt key and choose Merge Visible from the Layers palette fly-out menu.**
The Background layer and the effects of the curve adjustment layer, Highlights, are copied onto Retouch (6.12). This is the layer that would hold the retouching for the photograph. Upcoming chapters cover many techniques that would normally be done next. This section is about understanding NDP and the layers palette.

Step *11*: **Make a new layer and rename it Vignette.**

Step *12*: **Select the Elliptical Marquee tool and draw an oval around Carrie** (6.13).

Note

Retouching work is done on a copy of the layers below it. If the work gets to the point where it is overdone, the layer can be thrown away and a new one made from the ones below.

6.12

6.13

Step *13*: Choose Select➡Transform Selection from the main menu. Hover the cursor outside any corner of the bounding box. The rotate cursor appears. Drag the corner clockwise until her body fits inside the marching ants (6.14). Pull the selection away from her head by dragging the top middle handle outwards. Repeat at the bottom (6.15). Click the Commit Transform check mark in the options bar or press Enter.

Step *14*: Hold down the Option/Alt key and click the Add Layer Mask icon at the bottom of the Layers palette (6.16).

The layer mask icon appears next to an empty thumbnail icon on the layer named Vignette.

6.14

6.15

Step 15: **Press D to set the default colors: black and white.**

Step 16: **Click the empty layer thumbnail icon of Vignette to make it active. The thumbnail icon itself is high-lighted in black. A paint brush icon replaces the layer mask icon in the box next to the eye icon (6.17). Choose Edit➡Fill.**

In the Fill dialog box, choose Foreground Color and 100%. Click OK. The result is a sharp-edged black oval with Carrie looking through it (6.18). This is a vignette. Let's refine it.

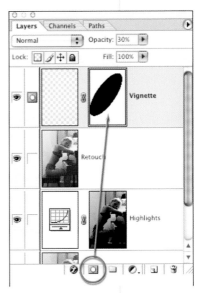

6.16

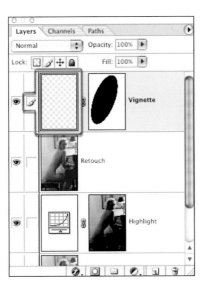

6.17

6.18

Layer masks work in grayscale. Black on the mask shows the pixels on the layers beneath it. White shows the pixels on the mask's layer. Shades of gray create transparency on the mask. Darker grays produce less transparency; lighter grays make more. One way to remember which color does what is "black conceals, white reveals."

Layer Masks in Black and White

Step *17*: **Click on the arrow next to 100% displayed in the Opacity area.**

A slider appears. Drag it to read 50%. The vignette reveals detail underneath it (6.19).

Step *18*: **Choose Filter➡Noise➡Add Noise from the main menu. In the Add Noise dialog box, set 3% as the amount, Uniform, and Monochromatic. Click OK.**

Step *19*: **Click on the Vignette layer mask thumbnail to make it active.**

A layer mask icon appears next to the eye icon replacing the brush.

Step *20*: **Choose Filter➡Blur➡Gaussian Blur from the main menu.**

In the Gaussian Blur dialog box, set the Radius at 250 pixels. Click OK.

Tip

Add noise? Yes, add noise. This layer will later have a massive blur applied to its layer mask. Without added noise, the vignette might band or posterize during output.

6.19

Changing the amount of blur on the layer mask makes the vignette go from a spot light to a subtle darkening of the edges (6.20). There is even more variability. Move the layer's opacity back and forth to control the amount of the final effect.

Vignettes are great. They can have a beautiful soft edge that blends almost imperceptibly into the background. Large amounts of blur also blend into the subject. The mask can easily be modified to override areas of the effect. This is non-destructive Photoshop at its best!

Variable Vignettes

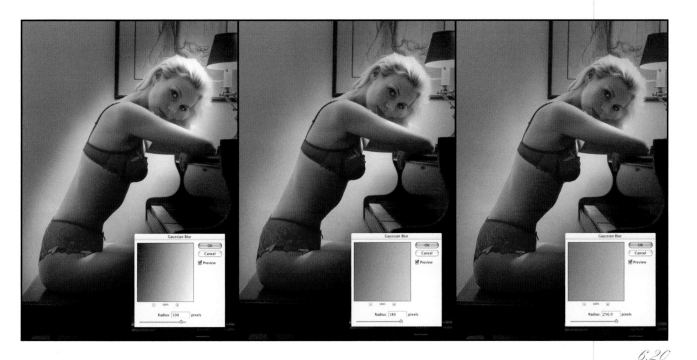

6.20

Step 21: **Select a soft-edged 200-pixel Brush at 100% opacity with black as the foreground color. Paint over Carrie's face, letting the soft brush bring back the highlights in her hair.**
Use the brush to follow the line down her back and around her hips. A quiet highlight returns.

Photoshop is a tool to be wielded with subtlety. The lamp on the piano has fallen into the vignette's darkness.

Step 22: **Zoom into 200%. Reduce the brush to 20 pixels. Paint black over the inside of the lampshade. Paint down the stem (6.21).**

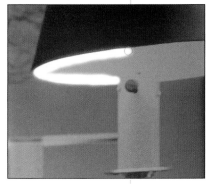

6.21

Painting Straight

Painting a perfectly straight line is easy in Photoshop. Click the brush at the starting point. Hold down the Shift key and click the brush where the stroke should end. A straight line of paint appears (6.22).

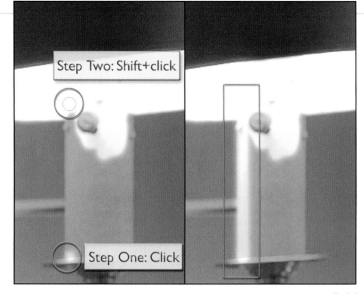

Step Two: Shift+click

Step One: Click

6.22

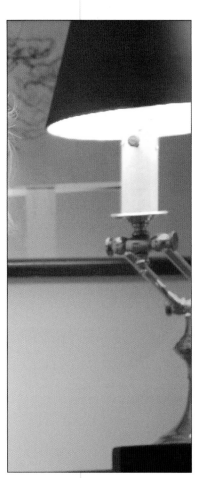

6.23

Step 23: **Use the click, Shift+click technique with an 8-pixel brush and bring back the highlight on the base of the stem. Change the brush opacity to 50%. Continue painting back just the highlights on the lamp** (6.23).

Dull highlights give away the vignette. Painting them back in on the layer mask makes the vignette appear natural.

Step 24: **All the work on this file is finished. Create a new layer at the top of the layer stack. Name it** Final. **Merge the visible layers to Final. (See Step Ten.)**

The final layer stack contains the layers Background, Highlights, Retouch, Vignette, and Final (6.24).

Option/Alt+click on the layer mask thumbnail. The image is replaced with the mask itself (6.25). The areas in black are protected from the effects of the vignette. It is useful to review the mask by itself to see areas that might need to be cleaned up. This is an editable view. Option/Alt+click to return to the normal view.

Study the layer stack. You can undo all the work that you've done in this project within the final image all the way back to the original that lives in the Background layer. Every step can be modified at anytime in the future. The essence of non-destructive Photoshop is the question, "After this step is finished, can it be returned to the version before it?" When the answer is "yes," you are a practitioner of the "Way of the Fast Retreat."

Step 25: **Save the file as a Photoshop document (.psd).**
Two files are now in the folder: 2062-M-0368.tif and 2062-M-0368.psd (6.26).

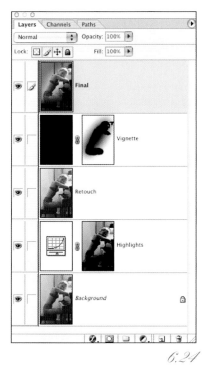

6.24

6.25

6.26

When setting up a workflow, deciding which type of file goes to the client, which is a working file, and which file is for use on Web sites or e-mail is important. Here's how I assign file types to specific uses:

.PSD – These are working files and are the only files in my workflow that contain layers and 16-bit information. Output devices cannot use 16-bit (yet) so it is important to keep them in-house.

.TIF – These files serve two purposes. First, they are origination files. This means they have been built out of either Camera Raw or another manufacturer's raw converter. They have not been edited. Second, after editing, the saved .PSD is flattened and saved as a .TIF overwriting the original 16-bit .TIF. It is then converted to 8-bit for delivery to the client. After postproduction, all files with .TIF extensions mean that they are 8-bit flattened files. This is still non-destructive. The original raw file has been archived. .TIF files *never* contain layers. Layers are work products. They are proprietary to my studio. We do not deliver layers to clients. Inexperienced Photoshop users can cause much havoc and chaos playing with your layers.

.JPG – These are 72-pixel-per-inch files saved at high quality for clients to use on their Web sites. .JPG files are used in-house to create Web photo galleries.

The next section is a tutorial for the most powerful and avoided tool in the toolbar: the Pen. It is true in the world that the pen is mightier than the sword. It is true in Photoshop, too.

Tutorial: Using the Pen Tool

The Pen tool is considered by beginning and some advanced users of Photoshop to be intimidating and difficult. Back in the day of Photoshop 2.0 when I was dragged kicking and screaming into the digital world, my guru and part-time studio mate, Eddie Tapp, told me that the Pen tool was "the most powerful tool in Photoshop." Like you, I *really* didn't want to hear it. He was (and is) right. The power of the Pen tool is the ability to make very exacting selections with complete control. Now this appealed to the control freak in me, so I learned. Slowly. I taught the Pen tool by giving students images of telephone handsets with coiled cords to outline. A method I now consider brutal, unkind, and Neanderthal. Then another friend, Joe Glyda, head of photography for Kraft Foods and the man who took that venerable organization from film to digital, said, "Kevin, it's as easy as ABC." Here's how Joe teaches the Pen tool.

My in-depth QuickTime movies on the techniques of NDP are available on CD-ROM from Software Cinema. They expand on this section of the book with additional step-by-step projects, a section-by-section explanation of the Layers palette, and exercises for working with layer masks. The title is Non-Destructive Photoshop. How to order? Go to www.amesphoto.com/learning and click "Chapter 6" or the "Learn More" link.

More on NDP

6.27

Step *1*: **Press ⌘/Control+N to bring up the New dialog box.**
Choose the 5x7 preset. Make it 7" wide and 5" high. Name it **Pen Tool**. Click OK to accept the rest of the default settings.

Step *2*: **Click the Type tool.**
The Options bar setup is Helvetica, 225pt, Sharp, Left Align Text, and Black as the color (6.27).

Step *3*: **Click inside the new file and type** ABC **in capital letters** (6.28). **Center the text with the Move tool if necessary. Click the Commit check box in the Options bar. Choose Flatten Image from the Layers palette fly-out menu.**

Step *4*: **Select the Pen tool or press P on the keyboard to select it. Zoom in to 100%. Press F to invoke the Full Screen Mode. Click the Paths button in the Options bar and choose Rubber Band from the blue Pen Options drop-down arrow** (6.29).

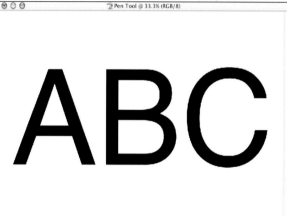

6.28

6.29

ABC Easy

The three letters teach each of the outlining functions of the Pen tool: straight lines on the A, straight and curved lines on the B, and sweeping curves on the C.

Tip

The Pen tool creates a *vector* path that can be resized without loss. Working at a view of 200% or more when creating outlines with the Pen tool is a good practice. Paths drawn at higher viewing percentages are that much more precise.

Tip

Hold down the spacebar to temporarily use the Hand tool. Click and drag to scroll around the image.

Tip

The enclosed or hollow part of a letter is called the *counter*.

Step *5*: Start at the lower-left corner of the A and click to set the first anchor point. Move up the left side to the top of the A. Click to set another anchor point. Mouse to the next corner point and click.

Continue around the A until the path is closed by clicking on the initial anchor point with the Close Path icon that appears automatically when a path is ready for completion (6.30).

Step *6*: Outline the counter of the A. Click on the apex of the inside of the A to set an anchor point.

Continue around the counter and close the path.

Step *7*: Click on the Paths tab. Double-click the thumbnail.

The Save Path dialog box opens and the default name Path 1 is offered. Click OK.

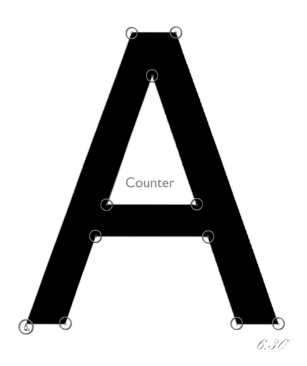

Counter

6.30

Saving Paths

Every time a new path is started Photoshop names it *Work Path*. Saving the path as a name preserves it. If a path is named *Work Path* and a new path is begun the original work path is replaced with the new one. If this happens to you and you have not gone too far (20 undos is the default) you can recover by going back in the History palette and saving the work path. You lose the new work path when you do this. Saving paths saves a lot of time redrawing them not to mention frustration and the occasional less-than-polite expletive.

Step 8: Click on the lower-left corner of the B to set an anchor point. Go up the left side and set another point at the top-left corner. Follow the top of the B to the point where the curve starts and click and drag straight out.

This sets an anchor point and pulls out a direction handle. Actually you get two direction handles pointing in opposite directions. In this case, they follow the line between the last two anchor points exactly. The direction handles are the key to drawing paths around curves. They are powerful and require some practice to master. Be patient. This is a skill most worth learning.

Step 9: Let up on the mouse button. At the midpoint between the curves of the B, click and drag.

The rubberband of the path is starting to bend around the bottom part of the upper curve of the B. When the bend matches the B, stop dragging. Release the mouse button (6.31).

Step 10: Hold down the Option/Alt key and move the cursor over the first direction handle.

The cursor becomes the Convert Point tool. Keep holding down the Option/Alt key and click and drag the handle pulling the shape of the curve around the upper portion of the B. Continue working the direction handles until the path bends around the B perfectly matching the curve (6.32).

6.31

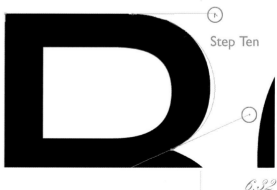

6.32

[115]

Step *11*: Once again, hold down the Option/Alt key and move the cursor over the direction handle that is in the lower counter of the B. Click and drag it out to the right until it is parallel to the baseline (6.33).

Step *12*: Release the Option/Alt key. Move the mouse down to the point where the lower curve of the B becomes a straight line. Click an anchor point and drag out the direction handles.

The direction handle that is pulled along the bottom line of the B rests on the baseline.

Step *13*: Hold down the Option/Alt key. When the Convert Point cursor appears over a direction handle, drag it to bend the path around the B. Alternate until the path is as close to the top and bottom parts of the lower curve.

The path will bulge out at the front of the lower curve of the B.

Step *14*: Hover the cursor over the bulge in the path. It changes to the Add Anchor Point tool. Click to set an anchor point.

The direction handles automatically appear without being dragged. Press the left arrow key to move the new anchor point into the curve. The path moves with it (6.34).

Tip

The *baseline* is the imaginary line on which the capitals and most of the lowercase letters in a line rest.

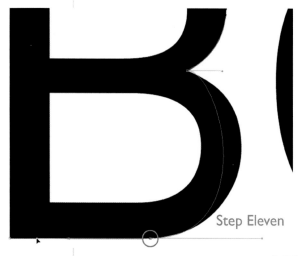

Step Eleven

Step Fourteen

6.33

6.34

Step *15*: Use the Option/Alt key to drag the new direction handles to smooth the path around the B (6.35). Hint: This works much better at 200% view. Close the path.

Step *16*: Outline the counters of the B using the same procedures.

Step *17*: Now for the C, start by placing an anchor point and dragging down to create direction handles at the top outermost corner. After the handles are out, hold down the Option/Alt key without releasing the mouse button. Drag the lower direction handle until it bisects the straight edge of the C. Release the Option/Alt key (6.36).

Step *18*: Click to place an anchor point at the inside top corner and drag left to draw the direction handles out from it.

The direction line that appears along the straight edge of the C should be parallel to it and the handle bisects itself on that edge. Hold down the Option/Alt key and drag the direction handle under the mouse cursor along the curve of the C (6.37).

Tip

An alternate way to move the anchor point is to hold down the ⌘/Control key and drag the anchor point into position.

Tip

Drag the directional handle from the anchor pointing it toward the route that the path is being drawn.

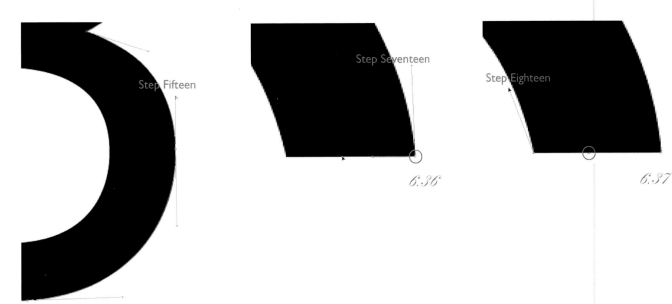

6.35

Step Fifteen

Step Seventeen

6.36

Step Eighteen

6.37

Step *19*: Place an anchor on the inner curve of the C opposite of the last anchor point.

Drag out direction handles and rough-in the upper curve. Hold down the Option/Alt key and drag the handle under the cursor in the direction of the next point. Release the mouse. Using the Option/Alt key, drag the inner handles to bend the path to the curve. Add an anchor point and smooth the path.

Step *20*: Add anchors and drag out direction handles the rest of the way around the C.

When the path is closed the handles will look similar to this figure (6.38). Note that the path for the entire letter was created using only ten anchor points.

Step *21*: Click on the Path tab.

The thumbnail for Path 1 shows the ABC outline. ⌘/Control+click Path 1 to make it into a selection.

Step *22*: Click the Layers tab. Cut the selection out of the background and into a new layer by pressing the shortcut ⌘/Control+Shift+J. Click the background layer eye icon.

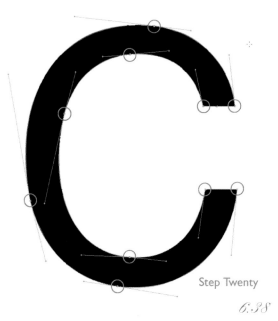

Step Twenty

6.38

Step _23_: **The ABC has been cut from the background by the selection made from the path. Click the eye icon on for the Background layer and off for Layer 1.** The outline of ABC left behind looks like an emboss. It is important to leave a little of the edge behind. Doing so ensures that the cutout will be sharp edged. An accurate path of the letters looks like this (6.40).

All right! This wraps up Part One. Many of the skills for preparing files for review and retouching are now well in hand. The Pen tool along with a lot of new and improved features of Photoshop CS are spotlighted in Part Two's projects. It introduces specific retouching techniques that build on non-destructive Photoshop editing. Jump right in. The next chapter shows how to turn a normal woman into Barbie. Why anyone would want to is beyond me. Well, it is a fun, campy way to get into the power of Photoshop CS. Wouldn't it be nice if there were a "Good Taste" adjustment layer, too?

Tip

You can also make a selection by dragging Path 1 to the Load Path as a Selection icon at the bottom of the Paths palette (6.39).

6.39

6.40

part 2

Projects: Behind the Camera and In Front of the Computer

Barbie: From the Ridiculous to the Sublime

I'm a Barbie girl in the Barbie world. Life in plastic, it's fantastic!
Lyric from "Barbie Girl" by Aqua

Barbie. You know her, the Barbie doll. She's the feminine ideal aspired to by generations of little girls who dream that their grown-up lives will become her fantasy world. Fortunately little girls outgrow Barbie and refine those dreams to become the real women we love. Fortunately, too, the techniques in this chapter are invaluable basics that when applied in subsequent chapters with finesse, sensitivity, and refinement turn the ridiculous into the sublime. It is important to start the project section of the book with an exploration of the global effects that make skin plastic and perfect. There is a sense that women in fashion aren't real. Nothing could be further from the truth. At the same time, the camera records a moment, freezing it forever. It translates a four-dimensional breathing human being that lives in height, width, depth, and time on to the two dimensions of monitor or print.

Men's magazines seem to consider Barbie to be the male ideal of physical feminine beauty. Flip through their pages. The photographs portray women whose faces feature full, bee-stung lips; wide, clear eyes of intense unworldly color; and skin that is smooth and flawless. Their bodies are perfect, too. Their curves flow in graceful lines with neither unseemly bumps nor unsightly creases. Midriffs are toned, sculpted with the precision of dreamworld perfection.

Barbie is perfect, you see. Her skin is perfect. So are her wardrobe, accessories, car, house, and life with Ken for that matter. Her figure is genetically unobtainable. The list goes on.

This chapter is about fantasy, not reality. It is about creating an "ideal," the digital Zen of "Barbie-ness." The stage is set. The players are pictured here (7.1). On the left is Barbie. On the right is Mindy, a woman desperately seeking to reveal to the world her inner Barbie. So it is that with a tongue-in-cheek, quite ridiculous sense of drama, with not a single iota of seriousness at all, we shall wave that magic wand whose secret name is Adobe Photoshop CS and cast the spells that turn our heroine Mindy into Barbie . . . .

7.1

Strategy

How will this transformation from normal girl to fantasy Barbie take place? In spite of the belief of most casual readers that this is done simply, the process is in fact quite complex. It encompasses four distinct postproduction phases: retouching, color correction, skin smoothing, and finally, body sculpting.

One of the things I do when planning a session is to create a *retouching strategy map*. Drawn on a separate layer in Photoshop, this map contains all the areas to be reworked. It serves as a guide during the retouching process and a warning in case something has been overlooked. To check your work against the strategy map, simply click the eye icon on the retouch layer on and off. If an area in the strategy map doesn't blink, it's been missed.

The retouching strategy map for Mindy's ascension (or decline, you choose) to Barbie-ness shows that there is much work to be done (7.2). We'll start with the overall retouch.

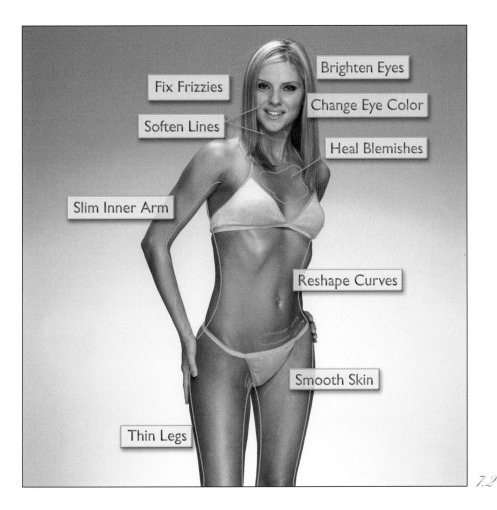

7.2

Retouching

The first set of steps covers removing the frizzy hair, fixing blemishes, and softening the lines on Mindy's face, neck, and armpit, as identified in the strategy map.

Step *1*: **Download the images for this chapter from www.amesphoto.com/learning and save them in your working folder.**
Navigate to the folder in File Browser and click it. Select the files 2062-O-0032.psd and 2062-O-0130.tif by ⌘/Control+ clicking them. Double-click one of them to open them both in Photoshop CS. Make the photograph of Mindy (2062-O-0032.psd) active by clicking it.

Step *2*: **Press F to invoke the full screen mode and zoom in to actual pixels view (100%) by pressing ⌘/Control+Option/Alt+0 (zero).**
Hold down the spacebar to temporarily activate the Hand tool. Drag the image until Mindy's face fills the screen.

Step *3*: **Duplicate the Mindy layer by pressing ⌘/Control+J or dragging the layer to the New Layer icon at the bottom of the Layers palette.**
Name the layer **Retouch**.

Step *4*: **Press S or choose the Clone Stamp tool and Option/Alt+click next to the frizzy hair to the left of Mindy's head.**
Clone out all the frizzies.

Step *5*: **Make a new layer and name it** Healing.

Step *6*: **Switch tools to the Healing brush by pressing J on the keyboard.**
In the Options bar click Use All Layers.

Step 7: **Sample an area of clear skin on Mindy's forehead above the left eye** (7.3).

Heal the slight skin textures on her forehead. Now move to her cheeks and heal the blemishes and textures. Without resampling, heal under both of her eyes.

Step 8: **Sample just to the left of the laugh line on the left cheek. Heal down to the point where the line curves by her lip. Resample on her check and continue healing toward her chin. Heal the lines and textures on her chin.**

The goal is to have smooth skin for the make-it-plastic part of the show. Compare the healed left side to the unretouched right side of Mindy's face. The healing process takes time and a lot of small strokes to get a smooth result. Finish healing the right side of the face.

Note

Healing to layers is a new feature of Photoshop CS. Photoshop 7 users will do their healing on the Retouch layer.

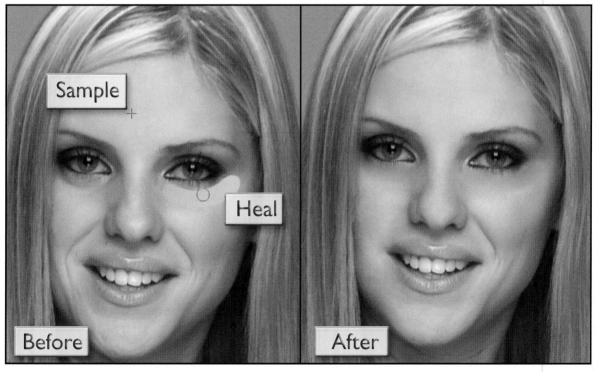

7.3

Note

The Healing brush will also take care of the fly-away hair on her forehead. Start the stroke at the end of the hair and brush toward the scalp.

Step 9: **Sample between the horizontal lines on Mindy's neck. Heal the lines.**

Overhealing is all right. In this case the goal is artificially smooth skin. In reality, the overhealed layer opacity would be lowered, resulting in softer, not plastic, skin. Heal the tendons in Mindy's neck. Usually, only the shadows would be softened (7.4).

Step 10: Highlight the **Retouch** layer then press **Shift+J to switch to the Patch tool. Draw a selection around the wrinkles at the armpit** (7.5). **Drag the selection to her upper arm.**

The original selection previews the area that the dragged selection is covering (7.6). When the selection looks clean, release the mouse button or lift the pen. The wrinkles are gone and yes, it looks weird (7.7). Remember, Barbie would never have wrinkles at her armpit.

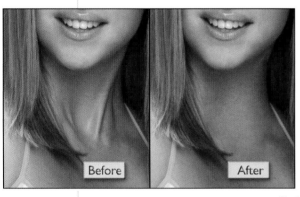

Before   After

7.4

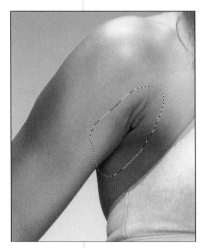

7.5

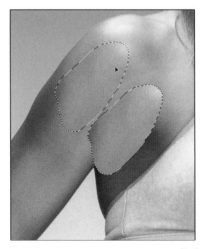

7.6

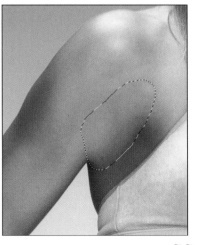

7.7

Smaller, hard-edged brushes work best when you're using the Healing tool. This tool looks outside the actual sampled area. Notice that the color changes when you initially brush over an area. When the stroke is applied by Photoshop, the oversampled area is blended outside the healed area making the healing smooth and for the most part undetectable.

Brushes for Healing

Step *11*: **Scroll over to Mindy's chest.**
We'll use the Patch tool to heal the blemishes here. Draw a selection and drag it to her stomach just to the left of the navel ring (7.8). Deselect.

Step *12*: **Scroll down to the lines just above the waistband of her bottoms. Patch these, too.**

Step *13*: **Heal the blemish on the centerline of her breastbone while you are at it.**
You can use the Patch tool on it as well. Patch the line on the right knee.

One last bit of patching to do. Mindy's ribs have to be softened.

Step *14*: **Draw a selection around the ribs on the left (7.9). Drag it down to the smooth skin on her stomach. Patch any artifacts.**
The major retouching is finished.

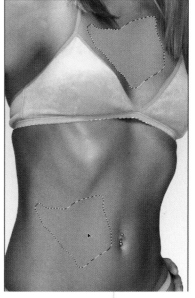

7.8

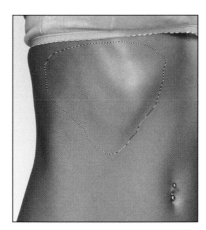

7.9

[**129**]

The Blending Mode drop-down menu is not labeled *Blending Mode.* Unless you idle the cursor over it and wait for the tool tip to appear telling you it set the Blending Mode for the layer, you have no way of knowing it is, in fact, the Blending Mode drop-down menu. (Was that redundant?) It displays Normal and lives right under the Layers tab.

Brightening and Coloring Eyes

There are two goals in this section: the first is to brighten Mindy's eyes and the second is to color them. Take a close look at Barbie's eyes (7.10). They are an intriguing shade of teal — Pantone 325C for the graphic designers in the audience. Mindy's aren't teal yet. They will be.

Step *1*: **Create a new layer above Retouch and name it** Retouch 2.

Step *2*: **Hold down the Option/Alt key and choose Merge Visible from the Layer palette fly-out menu.**
The visible layers are copied to Retouch 2.

Step *3*: **Make a new Curves adjustment layer. Click OK. Name it Bright eyes.**
Set the default colors (D). Press X to make the foreground color Black, hold down the Option/Alt key, and then press the Delete/Backspace key to fill the layer mask of Bright Eyes with black. Change the Blending Mode to Screen. Your Layers palette should now look like this (7.11).

7.10

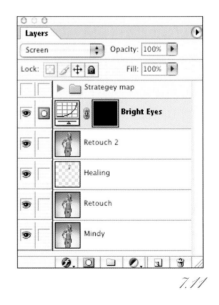

7.11

Step 4: Zoom in to 300%. Select a soft edge brush with a 7-pixel diameter. The brush opacity is 100%. Press X to set White as the foreground color. Brush over the catch lights in both eyes.

Step 5: Press 5 on the keyboard to set the brush opacity to 50%. Paint over the irises of her eyes. Avoid the pupils.

Step 6: Press 25 to set the brush opacity to 25%. Brush in the whites to lighten them some.

This is rarely done in real life. The eyes are the windows of the soul — not the whites. Then again, we are bringing out her inner Barbie. . . . Compare the left eye (after brightening) to the one on the right without brightening (7.12).

Step 7: Click the Retouch 2 layer to highlight it. Select the Rectangular Marquee tool. Draw a selection around both of Mindy's eyes (7.13).

Step 8: Press ⌘/Control+J to jump the selection to its own layer. Rename it Eye Color.

Step 9: Select 2060-O-0130.tif from the Window menu and then choose the Eyedropper tool.

Set the Sample Size to 3 by 3 Average in the Options bar. Zoom Barbie up to 200% and click in the color of the iris of her eye.

> *Note*
>
> In Photoshop 7 you can find 2060-O-0130.tif by choosing Window➡ Documents.

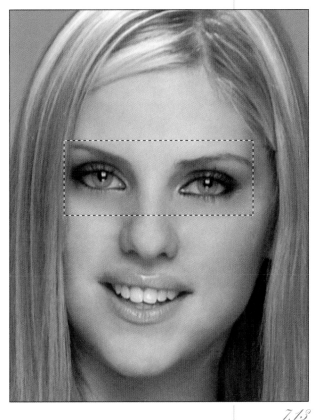

7.13

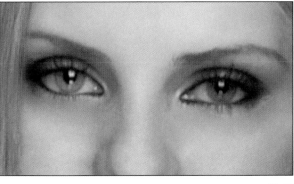

7.12

Step *10*: **Return to 2062-0-0032.psd and choose the Color Replacement brush from the Healing tools flyout in the toolbar.**

Select a 3-pixel soft edge brush. In the Options bar, set Mode to Color, Sampling to Continuous, Limits to Contiguous, and Tolerance at 30%.

Step *11*: **Paint in the irises with the Color Replacement brush.**

And yes, it looks artificial. So does Barbie.

Click the eye icons on the Bright Eyes and Eye Color layers on and off to see the changes. Isn't it great to always be able to go back? Non-destructive Photoshop rocks!

Smoothing Skin, Plastic Style

One of the hallmarks of the women in the magazines is their flawless skin. In the first section, you retouched Mindy's skin to remove blemishes and lines. Now you'll turn a copy of it into the plastic perfection that we all believe is supermodel real (sure we do).

Step *1*: **Use the Pen tool to outline Mindy's legs, midriff, arms, hands, chest, and face.**

Don't include the bikini or her hair. The areas to be pathed are shown in green (7.14). Next comes the setup for the skin smoothing.

Pen Tool Panic

If you are already friends with the Pen tool, skip this sidebar. Okay. Here it is — the time you have been dreading. It is time to use the dreaded, misunderstood, and much maligned Pen tool. A tutorial in Chapter 6 teaches you how to use it. If you still aren't quite ready to tackle the job, click the Paths tab and find the ones I have drawn for you. Here's hoping my fellow Pen tool fanatics will forgive me. . . . Don't put off learning this "most important tool in Photoshop." Remember, your photographs won't have the luxury of pre-drawn paths!

7.14

Tip

To create a new layer and merge visible layers to that new layer on the Mac, hold down ⌘+Option+Shift and press N then E. In Windows, the keys are Control+Alt+Shift and then N and E. Rename the layer, and you're done faster than you can read Step Two.

Step 2: **Highlight the Bright Eyes layer. Create a new layer, name it** Retouch 3, **and merge the visible layers to it.**

Step 3: **Click the Paths palette. ⌘/Control+Shift+click on midriff & legs, right arm, and face & chest to select them. Choose Select➡Modify➡Contract and enter 1 pixel.**

Step 4: **Return to the Layers palette and copy the selection to its own layer (⌘/Control+J.) Name it** Skin.
Complete the steps in the sidebar "Seeing Feathers" before going on to Step 5.

One of the not-so-intuitive functions in Photoshop is the Select➡Feather dialog box. How much feathering is 3 pixels really? On top of being non-visual, the effect of the command depends on the native resolution in the file. Whew. There is a better way. It requires some setup first. Here we go:

1. **Step 1:** Double-click the Quick Mask icon in the toolbar. The Quick Mask Options dialog box opens. Change the Color Indicates to Selected Areas and set the Opacity to 100%. Click OK (7.15).

2. **Step 2:** The shortcut key for Quick Mask is Q. Press Q to turn off Quick Mask. Press Q again to reenter Quick Mask, this time with the new settings. The selected areas appear as solid red (7.16).

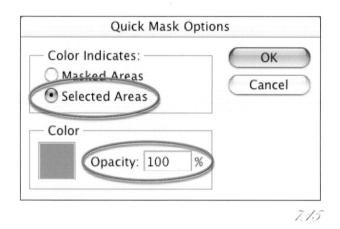

7.15

Step 5: **Click the Lock Transparent Pixels icon in the Lock section of the Layers palette.**

This means that only the existing pixels on the layer can be changed and not outside of their own edge. A padlock icon appears on the Skin layer.

Step 6: **Choose Filter➡Blur➡Gaussian Blur. Set the Radius to 2.0 Pixels.**

Notice in the preview that only the skin gets the blur. The transparent areas are unaffected because they have been locked (7.17). The blurred skin cannot bleed over its own edges. This step softens the edges. Click OK.

Step 7: **⌘/Control+click on the Skin layer to make a selection from the layer information. Choose Select➡ Modify and contract this selection 10 pixels.**

3. **Step 3:** Here's the payoff. Zoom into 100%. Choose Filter➡Blur➡Gaussian Blur. Click on a red edge. The example shows her elbow. Move the Radius slider to 10 pixels. The glow around the solid edge is the feather and exactly matches a 10-pixel feather.

4. **Step 4:** Highlight 10 in the Radius window and enter **0.3**. This is just enough feather on the selection to keep the edge from being sharper than the image. A too-sharp edge is a dead giveaway that the image has been manipulated. Click OK.

5. **Step 5:** Press Q to return to normal mode. The now slightly feathered marching ants reappear.

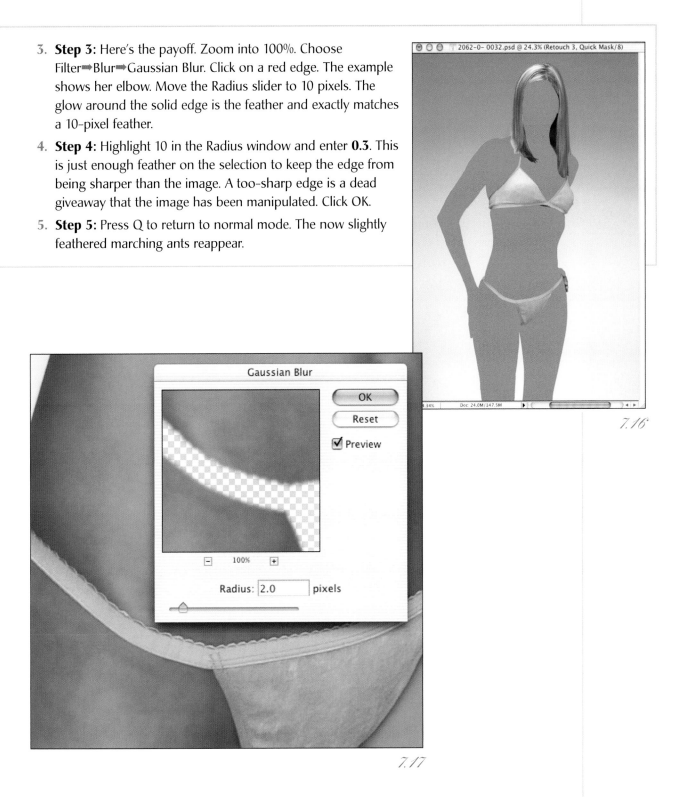

7.16

7.17

Step *8*: **Press Q to enter Quick Mask mode.**

The red area shows the selected area. If it were blurred now there would be a line on the edge of the selection. Not good.

Step *9*: **Bring up the Gaussian Blur filter by choosing Filter➡Blur➡Gaussian Blur. Enter 8 in the pixel Radius box.**

Look at the preview. The quick mask softens. The edge is spread wide and into the previous 2-pixel blur (7.18). Click OK and press Q once more to exit Quick Mask mode.

Step *10*: **Open the Gaussian Blur Filter once again. Stay with the 8-pixel setting and click OK. Press ⌘/Control+D to deselect.**

Perfect. Mindy's skin is smooth and soft as well — as soft as Barbie's. Of course, so are parts that need to be sharp: her eyes, lips, teeth, nostrils, belly button, fingernails, and ears, to mention a few.

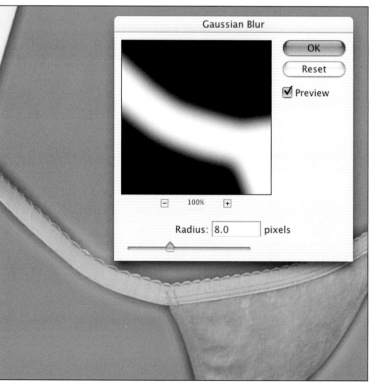

7.18

Step 11: **Click the Add Layer Mask icon.**

Step 12: **Start in the center of Mindy's blurry eyes and paint black on the layer mask with a 30-pixel soft edge brush at 100% opacity.**
Use the soft edge of the brush to bring out her eyelashes, lower lid, and corners of her eyes. Paint on her teeth and work the edge of the brush along her lips until they are once again sharp (7.19).

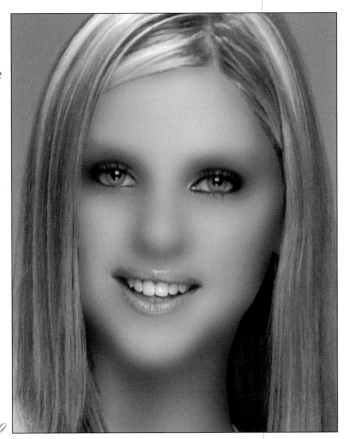

7.19

Soft focus filters were common when photographs were made on film. There was no cost-effective way to isolate wrinkles, lines, and other skin "imperfections" and smooth them individually. It had to be done globally. Out-of-focus images are larger than sharp images. When these filters blurred the image focus, they caused a halo effect making highlights bloom and colors bleed into each other. One of the telltale signs of using Gaussian Blur over an entire photograph to smooth skin is this edge-bleed effect caused by blurring (de-focusing and therefore enlarging) the whole image and painting sharpness back as desired.

Selecting only the areas to be blurred and constraining them to non-transparent pixels on a layer eliminates edge bleed and halos. Just the edge area is blurred, and then only slightly. The success of this technique is contracting the selection, blurring the Quick Mask until the selection barely overlaps the first blur, and *then* applying Gaussian Blur to the pixels after leaving Quick Mask. Look at the scallops on the waistband of Mindy's bikini. They are sharp while the skin is smooth. And there is no color bleed of the pink fabric into the skin. The technique fools the viewer by eliminating the visual cues of soft focus.

Multiple Stage Blurring for Soft Focus

[137]

Step *13*: **Press 5 to set the Opacity of the brush to 50%. Start at the far-left edge of the left eyebrow and paint over it to the right and all the way down the left side of her nose, over her nostrils, and back up the right side of the nose.**

Continue painting over her entire right eyebrow. This step is done without lifting the pen off of the tablet. If you are using a mouse, do the stroke without releasing the button. Press the left bracket ([) key twice to get a 10-pixel brush. Stroke over just the eyebrows (7.20).

Step *14*: **Use the 50% brush to bring her hairline back in where the transition is too sharp. Paint along the edge line of the jaw and chin, too.**

Step *15*: **Scroll down to the shadow line at the center of the lower bra strap.**

This requires a 100% Opacity and the 30-pixel brush. Paint out the line.

7.20

Brushing with Opacity

When the brush is set to an Opacity less than 100%, it will build up paint only to the amount it is set to. This is useful, especially when using a pressure-sensitive tablet and pen. Starting to brush with a light pressure allows the paint to build density gradually up to the opacity set point. In Step Fourteen, the brush stopped adding paint at a density of 50%. Lifting the pen (or releasing the mouse button) allows another 50% build up to begin.

Step 16: **Press X to exchange the colors. Set the Opacity of the brush back to 50% and brush the softness back in.**

The line was left in the path on purpose to make certain that this naturally occurring shadow continued to look natural. Don't worry about the noise in the unblurred shadow. You'll take care of that when you add noise to the Skin layer to prevent banding.

Step 17: **Go over all the skin and paint back areas that want a bit of sharpening.**

Be sure to paint her belly button back in. The navel ring needs to be brought all the way back to full sharpness. Brush the hand on the right back in a little. The important part is the contact shadow where the hand meets her leg. Paint in the contact shadows and fingernail on the hand on the left side.

Step 18: **Highlight the thumbnail of the Skin layer by clicking it.**

The Layer Mask icon to the right of the eye icon changes to a brush.

Step 19: **Choose Filter➡Noise➡Add Noise.**

In the Add Noise dialog box, set the Amount at 3%, the Distribution to Uniform, and check the Monochromatic box (7.21).

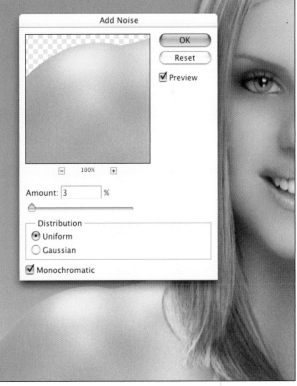

7.21

7.22

Step *20*: **Make a new layer and merge Retouch 3 and Skin to it. Name it Smooth. Save your work.**

We have come a long way. Mindy is looking softer and more doll-like. Barbie hasn't changed (duh). Compare this figure (7.22) with where we started. Now to put some serious curves on the girl to complete her transformation.

Body Sculpting

Mindy is slender and beautiful. In person she does remind one of Barbie. In a side-by-side comparison, injection molding beats nature every time when it comes to curves. Remember, the proportions sported by Barbie are fictitious. This section is designed to introduce methods of body sculpting using the Pen tool and Liquify filter. This is all done in good fun and quite frankly, to point out that what appears in some magazines might well be taken with a grain of salt.

Step 1: **Make a new layer and name it** Curves Guide.

Step 2: **Select the Pencil tool and set the size to 5 pixels. In the Swatches palette click the third color from the upper-left corner, RGB Green, to set it as the foreground color.**

Step 3: **In the Paths palette, click Curves. From the fly-out menu choose Stroke Path.**
The Stroke Path dialog box appears. Click OK. Click off of the paths to deselect Curves.

Step 4: **Click the Layers tab.**
Curves Guide shows Mindy's new shape (7.23).

Step 5: **In the Layer stack, click and drag Curves Guide under the layer named Skin. Click the Skin layer to highlight it.**

Step 6: **Choose Filters→Liquify. Click the Show Backdrop check box in the dialog box on the right of the preview window. Click the Use drop-down menu and highlight Curves Guide.**
It becomes visible in the preview. Curves Guide won't be affected by Liquify's tools so it will show us exactly how much Barbie to apply.

Step 7: **Zoom in to a 50% view. Use the drop-down menu in the lower-left corner of the dialog box, or click the + next to it, or press ⌘/Control++ (plus). Scroll until her arm guide is in the upper-left quadrant of the preview.**

7.23

Photoshop currently can address up to 2GB of memory. Some filters such as Liquify are memory intensive. If your computer does not have oodles of RAM or if the files are huge, Photoshop will page the extra data to the hard disk. Make sure you have plenty of space on your scratch disc (by default the boot drive). Photoshop likes a combination of RAM and disk space at least four times the size of the file being worked on. You can assign additional drives as scratch disks in Preferences (choose ⌘/Control+K then ⌘/Control+7).

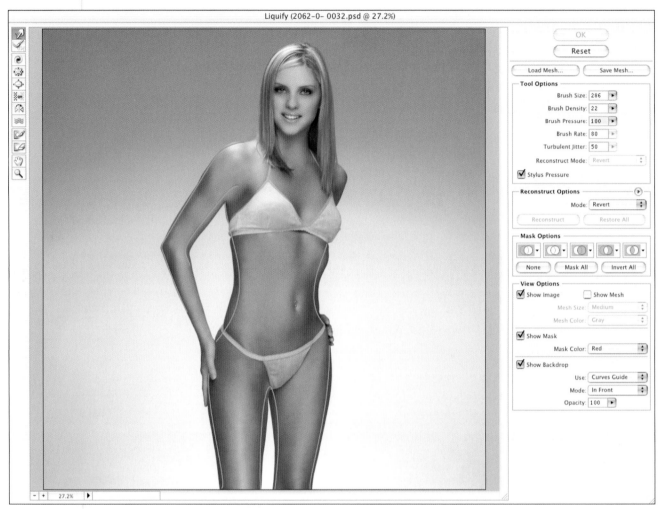

7.24

7.25

Step *8*: **Select the Forward Warp tool.**

In the Tool Options section set Brush Size to 286, Brush Density to 22, Brush Pressure at 100, Brush Rate to 80, and Turbulent Jitter at 50. If you are using a mouse, reduce the Brush Pressure to 35 and leave the Stylus Pressure box unchecked. This tool works more intuitively with a graphics tablet and stylus than with a mouse (7.24).

Step *9*: **Click the cross hatch in the center of the Warp tool cursor just below the top of the arm and drag the skin to the guide.**

Work your way around the shoulder and down the arm to the wrist (7.25).

The Photoshop standard undo (⌘/Control+Z) and redo (repeat ⌘/Control+Z) shortcuts work in the Liquify tool. Step Back in history is the same, too: ⌘/Control+Option/Alt+Z. Step Forward in history is ⌘/Control+Shift+Z. Handy! The forward and backward in history shortcuts work in the filter and do not affect the History palette.

Step *10*: **Set the Brush Size to 150 pixels. Select the Freeze tool (press F) and paint red over Mindy's left side.** This step locks out the painted areas from being liquified (7.26).

Step *11*: **Reset the Brush Size to 286 pixels and select the Warp tool. Using very small and close together strokes, pull the skin of her inner forearm and upper arm into the guide.** The work doesn't have to exactly match the guide (7.27).

Step *12*: **Use the Thaw tool (D) to unfreeze Mindy's side. Then freeze her upper arm.** You might want to use a smaller brush.

Note

Below Freeze in the tool-bar is the Thaw tool. Its icon looks like an eraser. It removes any of the frozen areas you paint over. The shortcut for the Thaw tool is D.

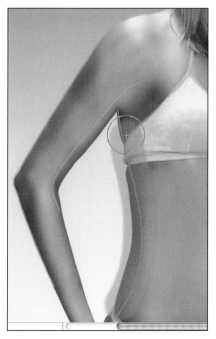

7.26

7.27

Step *13*: **Warp tool time again. Start at the upper part of Mindy's side and pull the skin toward the guide. When you get below her top, go outside and push the hand and hip in to the guide.**

This keeps the contour shadow from becoming too wide (7.28). Continue pushing until her outer leg matches the guide (7.29).

Step *14*: **Go to the right side and push the skin and the hand into the guide.**

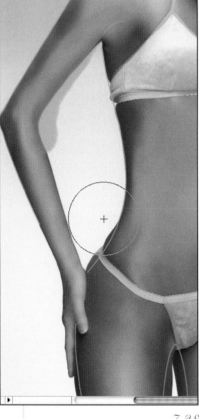

7.28

7.29

Keyboard Brush Sizing

Hold down the left bracket key ([ ) and watch the brush icon or pixel setting in the menu. The longer the key is held, the smaller the brush gets. The right bracket ( ]) key makes the brush larger.

In the Liquify tool reconstruction has nothing to do with carpetbaggers after the *War of Northern Aggression* (a.k.a., the Civil War). It is a tool that allows the original image to be painted selectively. The lower the brush size and pressure, the more strokes it takes to go back. This is very useful when you exceed the number of undos (20 by default).

Reconstruction

Step 15: **Click the Show Backdrop check box off and check the work.**
Reconstruct and rework as needed. Then click OK. Save the file.

Mindy's shape is almost Barbie's. Barbie has teeny tiny hips. Mindy (for the sake of this image) wants them, too.

Step 16: **Duplicate Smooth (⌘/Control+J) and name it** Barbie Shape 1.

Step 17: **Go back into Liquify (Filters→Liquify). Choose the Warp tool. Set the Brush Size to 600 and reduce the Brush Pressure to 51. If you are using a mouse, stay at 35.**
Gently push and pull her hips and hands toward each other rounding down the leg. When you think it's right click OK. Look at the result. If you don't like it, press ⌘/Control+Z, go back into Liquify, and do it again.

Step 18: **There is a different technique to reduce her inner thighs. Click the Paths tab and ⌘/Control+click Inner Legs to make it into a selection. Zoom into 300% view. Go into Quick Mask mode. Open the Gaussian Blur filter dialog box.**
Compare the sharpness of the Quick Mask to the outer edge of her leg. Adjust the Radius until the mask matches the leg edge, about 0.3 pixel. Click OK. Exit Quick Mask.

Step 19: **Select the Clone Stamp tool (S) and set a 50-pixel soft edge brush.**

Tip
Remember the Show Backdrop check box. Click it and choose the Smooth layer. Set the Opacity to 100%. Click it on and off and see how the new hip size looks compared to the original.

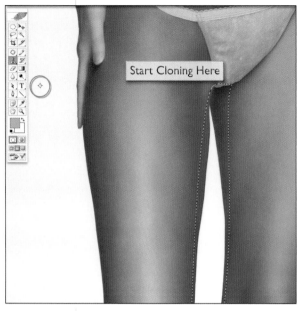

7.30

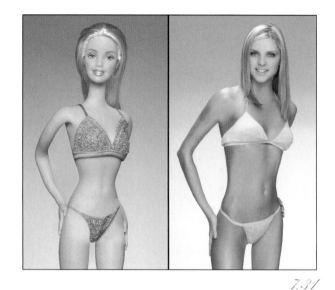

7.31

Step 20: **Option/Alt+click on the background to the left of the left hand** (7.30). **Clone the background from the top of the selection down both of her legs. Clone in the center area so it will match the background.** Do this cloning without lifting pen or mouse button. Press ⌘/Control+D to deselect the image once you're done.

Let's bring up Barbie and see how Mindy stacks up. Not bad. Not bad at all if you are into dolls. There is one difference that isn't in the text. Look at Mindy's lips. I used the Color Replacement brush to put some of the pink from her bikini onto her lips — digital lip gloss if you will (7.31).

Go back to the layer stack and click and click all the eye icons off except for Mindy and Barbie Shape 1. Click Barbie Shape 1's eye icon on and off to see just how much of Mindy's inner Barbie has shown through.

Just Because We Can . . .

There is one last little thing. Make sure that 2062-O-0130.tif is open. Put our Mindy makeover in a window next to it. View Actual Pixels. Click on Barbie Shape 1 to make sure it's active.

There is one last little thing that really bugs me about Barbie. She really doesn't have a belly button. . . .

Step 1: Select the Lasso tool. Draw a selection around Mindy's navel (7.32).

Step 2: Feather the selection 10 pixels (⌘/Control+ Option/Alt+D.)

Step 3: Choose Window➞Arrange➞Match Zoom and Location.

Step 4: Hold down the ⌘/Control key and drag the selection onto Barbie's tummy. Let go. Hmm, Mindy's tan is better than Barbie's (7.33).

Step 5: Add a layer mask to Layer 1. Use a soft 60-pixel brush and paint out the tan skin leaving only the belly button and navel ring.

Step 6: Add a new Curves adjustment layer. Click OK. Press ⌘/Control+G to group the Curves layer with Layer 1.

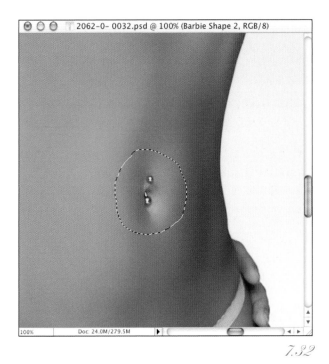

7.32

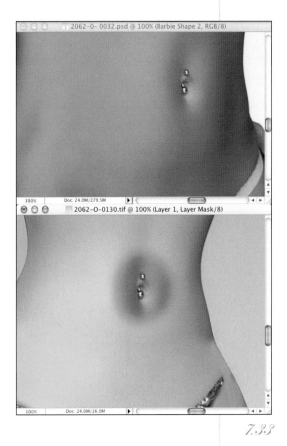

7.33

Step 7: **Reopen the Curves dialog box by double-clicking the Curves icon in that layer. Count two boxes up and over from the lower-left corner of the Curves dialog box and click to set a point** (7.34).

Step 8: **⌘/Control+click on the navel skin just to the right of the navel ring.**

Another point is set at exactly the value of the skin. Click on the new point and drag it straight up slowly until the skin tones match (7.35). Click OK.

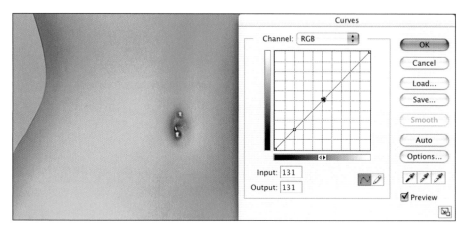

7.34

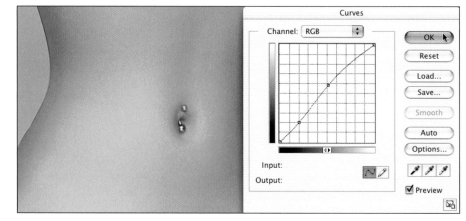

7.35

That's much better (7.36). Now Mindy looks like Barbie!

The next chapter deals with doing the enhancements that make a beautiful face able to stand the scrutiny of long and close observation. We revisit the healing brush in depth, explore making eyes the same size, and work with a realistic method of brightening them, all without hurting a single original pixel! How much does that rock?

7.36

Chapter Eight

Pinups: Modern Girls in a Digital World

Pinups have a storied history in the art of the twentieth century. Today they hold a special place in the hearts of romantics around the world. The artists who painted them are many. Rolf Armstrong is considered the father of the American pinup. George Petty and Alberto Vargas created pinups for *Esquire* magazine. Vargas went on to paint for fan and admirer Hugh Hefner who published his pinups in *Playboy* during the 1960s and '70s.

Women also practiced the art. Zoë Mozert, protégé of Armstrong, was often her own model. Her images evoked charm, romance, and sex appeal. Joyce Ballantyne and Pearl Frush were also standout female artists of the genre. Pinups appeared on calendars, advertisements, movie posters, and magazine and romance novel covers.

So much for the history lesson. A burning question arises! What's wrong with this picture? Notice that it is only about painters. There is not a photographer in the bunch. "What's up with that?" you ask. Then you cry, "Not fair!" No, it isn't fair at all and it is easily explained. This art form has always been the exclusive purview of artists who turned their imaginations to painting fancifully sleek women featuring ever-so-slightly elongated legs, torsos, and accented curves. Their creations were simply beautiful and beyond the abilities of literal rendering cameras. Until now.

Pinups are back! And this time they are not paintings. Now they are photographs with all the qualities that made pinups so very popular. Girls with impossibly long legs and graceful flowing bodies in wonderful lingerie (or not) float on backgrounds in weightless-looking poses. They are modern romantic visions frozen forever by the shutter of a camera. What's so different now? Adobe Photoshop.

The previous chapter introduced several of the techniques that are applied to the pinup girls in this chapter. This time we apply those techniques with delicate and craft-like sensibility.

Pinups are art. Thanks to Photoshop we leave reality behind. We are now artists creating works of art.

Taking Pinup Photographs

Photographically, pinups are exaggerated, over-posed, too expressive, and way too much fun to shoot. The set is simple — a roll of white background paper is enough. Having white or similar light tone behind your model's hair is important. The camera angle, too, is often not what it appears. Shoot your model upside down and flip the image later. Believe me, if she looks great upside down, she will look fabulous right side up. There's something about shooting a subject from above with the top of her head closest to the lens and her feet in the distance that is exceedingly nice.

Rembrandt lighting is defined as the triangle of light on the cheek opposite the light source formed by the shadow cast by the forehead and nose. The light source is either 45° up and behind the subject, which casts the shadow on the camera-forward cheek, or 45° up and aimed at the cheek closest to the camera. Then the trademark triangle of light appears on the cheek farthest from the lens (8.1).

Butterfly lighting is defined by the butterfly-shaped shadow cast by the nose on the upper lip. The light source is placed slightly to either side of the camera and up about 45°. The shadow cast by the subject's nose should end somewhere halfway between the nose and upper lip. This butterfly example shows catchlights in the pupil produced by the model lifting her chin. The raised chin minimizes the telltale shadow (in the red circle).

8.1

The lighting is simple, too. Pinup artists used Rembrandt lighting on their moody efforts. Butterfly (Paramount) lighting has always been a favorite in high-profile pinups. The lighting is usually low contrast (not much brightness difference between shadow and highlight) and is somewhat harsh in quality (distinct shadow edge transitions.)

Sweater Girl

Cosmopolitan magazine cover girl Adair Howell from Elite Atlanta is wearing a Pringle of Scotland Georgina cashmere sweater dress and python shoes by Manolo Blahnik. Her pose and expression are pinup classics. This project will include dropping out the background to white; lengthening, smoothing, and slimming her legs; tucking her tummy; softening wrinkles; and appropriate healing work. Download 2062-K-0001.psd from www.amesphoto.com/learning. The 16-bit file has already been through the pre-postproduction process. The strategy map outlines the desired changes (8.2).

8.2

Note

The 16-bit workflow can cause computers that handle 8-bit files well to slow down substantially. If you experience the slow-downs, feel free to convert the file to 8-bit.

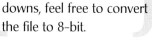

8.3

8.4

Step 1: Use the Pen tool to draw a path around Adair and outline inside the wispy hair as shown (8.3). **Save the work path as Path 1.**

There is a path available in the Paths palette. As you can see, paths are very useful. I encourage you to embrace this most powerful tool.

Step 2: ⌘/Control+click Path 1 to make it into a selection.

Step 3: Feather the selection 0.3 pixels (choose Select➞Feather).

Step 4: Return to the Layers palette. Make the selection into a new layer (⌘/Control+J) and name it Adair. Click the eye icon on the Background layer off. Zoom into Actual Pixels and scroll to her head.

Her hair has been chopped into the shape of the path. This might be all right for a stylized pinup (8.4). Personally, I prefer a more natural flow to the hair that only the camera and a few photorealistic painters can execute. Click the Background layer's eye icon on.

Step 5: Activate the Background layer and then select the Elliptical Marquee tool.

Draw a selection around the outside of Adair's head.

Step 6: Click Path 1 to make it visible.

Hint: Click the Paths tab.

Step 7: Select the Lasso tool. Hold down the Subtract from Selection key – Option/Alt – and make a selection inside the line of the path.

Step 8: Enter Quick Mask mode (press Q) and open the Gaussian Blur dialog box (Filter➞Blur➞Gaussian Blur).

Set the Radius to 15-pixels. Click OK. The soft edge of the Quick Mask does not cross the line shown by the path (8.5). Exit Quick Mask. Click in the Paths palette to deactivate Path 1.

Step 9: Return to Layers. Press ⌘/Control+J to make the selection into its own layer and name it Adair's Hair.

Step 10: **Drag Adair's Hair above Adair. Activate the Background layer.**

Step 11: **Make a new layer named** White **and fill it with white (Edit→Fill).**

Adair now has a full head of hair and a dirty-white halo, which would be fine if this were the Renaissance, she were a saint and we were old masters. (It isn't, neither is she, and we aren't, thank goodness.)

Step 12: **Double-click the Adair's Hair's thumbnail icon to open the Layer Style dialog box, arguably the largest screen real estate hog in all of Photoshop.**

There is a lot of power per square foot in this box. We are concerned with Blending Options and the Blend If section in particular.

Step 13: **Click the highlight slider on the line labeled This Layer, drag it to the left, and watch Adair's halo.**

As the slider moves toward a value of 186, the halo fades to white. At 186 the halo is gone and her hair has breaks in it where it was light against the background (8.6).

8.5

8.6

Blending Magic

Any sufficiently advanced technology is indistinguishable from magic. This comment from Arthur C. Clarke, the author of *2001: A Space Odyssey*, pretty much sums up my reaction the first time I saw Katrin Eismann demonstrate this somewhat hidden feature of Photoshop. This layer blending feature is powerful, cool, and fun to play with. It is important to remember that this is a blending feature, meaning that the layers blend with one another to create what is seen on the photograph. If you move or modify one of the layers, the effect changes. To preserve the blending effect you must copy it onto its own layer.

Step *14*: **Notice the line splitting the slider in half. Hold down the Option/Alt key and drag the right side to the right.**

Watch the hair. As the slider approaches 229, the hair is brought back. Move the slider farther to the right and the halo starts to return. Put it back to 229 and click OK (8.7).

8.7

Step _15_: Click the eye icons off for the Background and White layers. Make a new layer above Adair's Hair. Name it Stretch. **Hold down Option/Alt and select Merge Visible from the fly-out menu to merge the visible layers to the Stretch layer** (8.8).

Step _16_: Choose Image➡Canvas Size.
Click the Relative check box. Enter **.5** inches into the Height window and click OK. The expanded canvas is transparent. Activate the White layer and fill with white again. Turn off the eye icons for both the Adair and Adair's Hair layers.

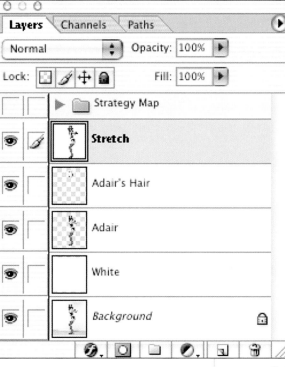

8.8

This is the first stretch of our artistic license. One of the characteristics of pinups is their model's extra long bodies and legs. Adair is tall already, almost six feet in her bare feet. She is about to become taller still.

Step _17_: Activate the Stretch layer. Press ⌘/Control+T to enter Free Transform mode. Highlight H: 100% and type in 106%. Click the Commit check mark.
Avoid the temptation to overstretch!

Step _18_: Click the Paths tab and duplicate Path 1 by dragging it to the New Path icon at the bottom of the palette. Rename it Stretch 106%.

It sure is! Look under the Stretch layer. The layers White, Adair, and Adair's Hair are still available. The Way of the Fast Retreat: Merge them onto a new layer. In this project we've named it Stretch. To go back, you can make a new layer from the ones under it.

Kevin, Is This Non-Destructive Editing?

Keeping on the Path

When you apply a transform to a layer of pixels that was created with a path-based selection, the path is unchanged. It is important in non-destructive Photoshop editing to keep copies of transformed paths. Remember: *Every time* pixels are transformed, apply the same transformation to a *copy* of the matching path. One never knows when the ability to make a precision selection will come in handy. (Like when an art director changes something. Nah. That *never* happens.)

Step *19*: **Select the Path Selection tool and then click on the path outline around Adair.**

Filled anchor points comprising the path appear. Notice that the path no longer matches the pixel information. This is because you enlarged the data vertically 106%. Press ⌘/Control+Shift+T to apply the last transform settings to the path. This command is called Transform Again (8.9). Click on the path at the hole formed by her arm on her hip. Apply Transform Again to it as well.

Step *20*: **Return to the Layers palette. Duplicate Stretch and name the duplicated layer** Retouch. **Then heal the blemishes on Adair's legs.**

8.9

Tutorial: Modifying Paths

One of my personal peeves is when an author assumes (and we all know about *assume*) that his readers already know how to do something. Especially when that something is as confusing and convoluted as paths can be. Granted, paths aren't easy to wrap your mind and hand-eye coordination around. If you are already hot on the path path, skip this section. On the other hand. . . maybe a refresher might be useful. This tutorial walks step-by-step through modifying the path of Adair's back leg. The same techniques pertain to the path for the front path.

Step 1: **Click the Paths tab.**
Duplicate Stretch 106%. Rename it **Back Leg**. Duplicate Back Leg and rename it **Forward Leg**.

Step 2: **Activate the Back Leg layer and then select the Path Selection tool (A). Its icon is a black arrow.**

Step 3: **Press Shift+A to change to the Direct Selection tool (white arrow) and draw a box starting above Adair's head and continue down to just above her legs.**
All the anchor points in the box are solid, indicating they are selected (8.10).

8.10

Step 4: **Press the Delete key.**
The anchor points around Adair's legs are left. They will be used to isolate the back leg. Note that the remaining anchor points are now solid.

Step 5: **Switch to the Pen tool (P) and hold down the ⌘/Control key.**
The cursor changes to the white arrow. Click away from the path. The solid anchor points disappear. Still holding down the ⌘/Control key, click the path with the white arrow again and they reappear, this time hollow. Click the anchor at the top of the dress and drag it down to the top of her knee (8.11).

Step 6: **Release the ⌘/Control key and hold down the Option/Alt key. Hover the cursor over the direction handles of the newly placed anchor point until it turns into the Convert Point cursor.**

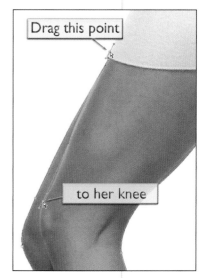

Drag this point

to her knee

8.11

8.12

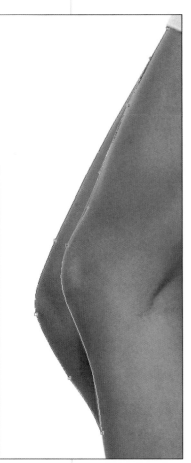

8.13

Step 7: **Click and drag the handles until the path flows along the top of her front thigh.**

Hint: The handles are reversed. The one pointing up her leg actually needs to be pulled toward her knee. The other handle will shape the existing path.

Step 8: **Hover the cursor over the top of the path midway up her thigh.**

The cursor changes again to the Add Anchor Point tool. Click and add a point. Hold down the ⌘/Control key and drag the anchor to the top of her quadricep, about two-thirds of the way up her thigh. Hold down the Option/Alt key and drag the new direction handles to shape the path to the muscle.

Step 9: **This path has to be broken before it can be completed. Choose the Direct Selection tool (white arrow) and click the first anchor point on the front of her shin below where the back leg intersects the front leg, then Shift+click on the anchor below that (8.12). Press Delete.**

The path is now a segment.

Step 10: **Select the Pen tool. Click the anchor point at the top of her shin.**

This connects the new path to the segment.

Step 11: **Hold down the Option/Alt key and drag the down-ward-pointing direction handle up toward the knee. Close the path and adjust the direction handles until the top of the back leg is outlined.**

Hint: ⌘/Control+click on an anchor point to reveal its direction handles (8.13).

Step *12*: **Hold down the ⌘/Control key and click the anchor point at the back of Adair's front leg at the hem of her dress to select it.** Add the Shift key and click the next three anchors moving down her leg, selecting them. Press Delete to remove them (8.14).

Step *13*: **Hover the cursor over the path at the top of the back high heel shoe.** When the cursor turns into the Add Anchor Point tool, click to set an anchor.

Step *14*: **Hold down the ⌘/Control key and click the next anchor down the back of the shoe. Add the Shift key and draw a box around the anchors remaining on the shoes. Release the ⌘/Control and Shift keys and press Delete.**

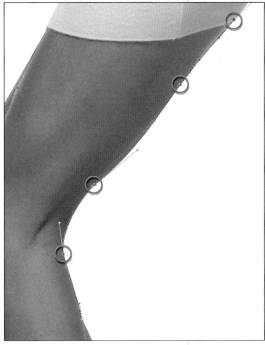

8.14

Step *15*: **Click the anchor at the top of the shoe to connect to the path segment. Set a point at the overlap of the edge of the back shoe with the heel of the front one. Drag out a direction handle and point it up the calf. Adjust the direction handles until the path follows the lines of the shoes. Draw the path along the line of the calf of her front leg. Close the path.**

Step *16*: **Use these techniques to modify the Forward Leg path** (8.15).

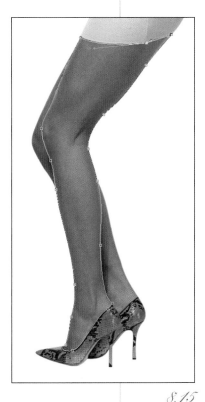

8.15

8.16

Smoothing Subtlety

This section covers the preparation of the skin on Adair's legs. Then the skin is reapplied to achieve a painterly smoothness. Use the paths you created in the previous exercise or the ones provided to complete the next steps. Before moving on to Step One, use the healing brush to soften any blemishes on her legs and feet. (It is the same process you used in Chapter 7.)

Step *1*: ⌘/Control+click on the Forward Leg path.

Step *2*: **Go to the Layers palette. Press ⌘/Control+ Option/Alt+D and feather the selection .3 pixels. Make the selection into its own layer by pressing ⌘/Control+J. Name the new layer Front Leg Skin.**

Step *3*: **Click the Preserve Transparency icon.**
A lock icon appears in the layer.

Step *4*: **Use Gaussian Blur (Filter➡Blur➡Gaussian Blur) to blur the layer 2 pixels.**

Step *5*: **⌘/Control+click the Front Leg Skin layer to make the pixel edge into a selection. Choose Select➡ Modify➡Contract to contract the selection 8 pixels.**

Step *6*: **Enter Quick Mask mode (press Q) and Gaussian Blur 20 pixels. Click OK and exit Quick Mask mode** (8.16).

Step *7*: **Gaussian Blur the selection 4 pixels.**
See the difference in the skin texture between the front and back legs (8.17)?

8.17

Step 8: **Go to the Paths palette and ⌘/Control+click on the Back Leg path to load it as a selection. Return to the Layers palette and feather the path .3 pixels.**

Step 9: **Click the Retouch layer in the Layers palette to activate it.**

Make the selection into its own layer by pressing ⌘/Control+J. Name it **Back Leg Skin**. Click the Lock Transparent Pixels icon.

Step 10: **⌘/Control+click the Back Leg Skin layer to make the pixel edge into a selection. Choose Modify➡Contract to contract the selection 4 pixels.**

Step 11: **Enter Quick Mask mode (Q) and use Gaussian Blur to blur the edge 40 pixels. Click OK.**

The double-sized blur on the selection will help maintain the shadow cast from the front leg onto the back one. Exit Quick Mask mode (8.18).

Step 12: Use **Gaussian Blur to blur the selection 4 pixels.**

The skin on the back leg softens and the shadow is preserved. Deselect the selection by pressing ⌘/Control+D.

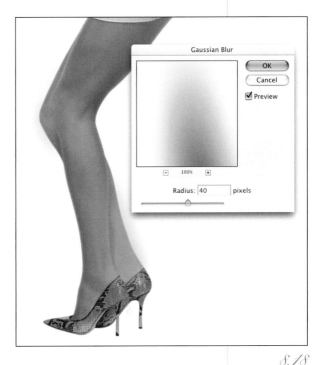

8.18

Note

Using greater Gaussian Blur pixel counts on the Quick Mask makes the skin smoothing technique more realistic. The lower blur of the skin helps retain important shadow detail. It minimizes the "plastic" look that pervades the fashion industry.

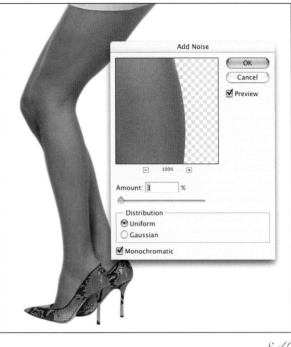

8.19

Step *13*: **Click the Front Leg Skin layer to highlight it and then choose Filter→Noise→Add Noise.**
In the Add Noise dialog box, set the Amount to 3%, the Distribution to Uniform, and put a check mark in the Monochromatic box (8.19). Press Enter.

Repeat Step Thirteen for the Back Leg Skin layer.

Retouching

This section concerns softening the lines on Adair's face, fixing the flaws on the dress, and smoothing her hand. Her eyes are also brightened.

Step *1*: **Click the White layer's eye icon off. Create a new layer above Front Leg Skin and merge the visible layers to it. Name it** Retouch 2. **Make White visible.**

Step *2*: **Zoom in to 100% Actual Pixels View. In the Strategy Map set, click the eye icon off of Strategy Blocks and Strategy Map. Click the eye icon on for Strategy Map 106%** (8.20).
After reviewing the work to be done, close the Strategy Map set and click its eye icon off. Start by brightening the eyes.

Step 3: **Create a new Curves adjustment layer. Click OK to accept the defaults in the dialog box. Close the layer and name it** Bright Eyes. **Move the layer below the Strategy Map set and just above Retouch 2.**

Step 4: **Fill the layer mask with black. Change the blending mode to Screen.**

Step 5: **Select a 15-pixel brush with a soft edge. Make the Foreground color white. Paint in the area of her eye from lid to lid.**

If you hit any of the skin outside of the lids, press X to exchange the colors and paint the skin back to its original tone.

Step 6: **Press V to select the Move tool and then enter 5 to set the Opacity of Bright Eyes to 50%.**

Step 7: **Make a new layer above Retouch 2 called** Healing.

Step 8: **Select the Healing brush and click Use All Layers in the Options bar.**

Use a 10-pixel hard-edged brush to sample high on the left cheek. Heal the laugh line from her nose to her lip in one stroke by painting up and down the line in order to make the finished stroke wide enough to cover the line. (8.21).

8.20

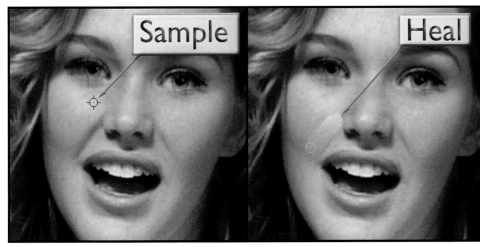

8.21

8.22

Step 9: **Soften the result by choosing Edit➡Fade Healing Brush or pressing ⌘/Control+Shift+F.**
In the Fade dialog box, set the Opacity to 62% and click OK. This causes a little bit of the laugh line to show through (8.22). Repeat Steps Eight and Nine on the remaining one.

Step 10: **Heal the blemish above the right eyebrow, the lines on her neck, and anything else you might notice.**
I like her freckles, so I left them alone

Step 11: **Click the eye icon for the White layer off. Make a new layer. Name it** Body Sculpting. **Drag it above Bright Eyes. Merge the visible layers to it. Make White visible.**
This sets up the layer needed in the next section of transforming the photograph of Adair into pinup art.

Body Sculpting

The next part of creating Adair's pinup is to do a little bit of body shaping. This time the technique will be done in Photoshop CS in 16-bit. It is easy, clean, and *painterly*.

Step 1: **Draw a path defining a slimmer shape for her tummy.** Close the path in front of her.

Step 2: **Draw another path that slightly slims her bottom and makes a smooth line of her leg by removing her hamstring** (8.23).
Remember this is a pinup not an athletic poster.

Step 3: **Draw one more path that will cut out her back elbow that shows through the hole created by her forward arm with its hand on her hip (or click on the Paths tab to find Sculpting Path).**
Remember to save your paths as you create them. They will disappear as soon as you start a new path. This can be frustrating!

Step 4: **⌘/Control+click on your path or on Sculpting Paths to make a selection.**
Return to the Layers palette and make sure Body Sculpting is activated. Inverse your selection by choosing Select➡Inverse or by pressing ⌘/Control+Shift+I.

8.23

Step 5: **Enter Quick Mask mode (press Q).**

What you see is weird at first. The selection is the area *inside* the path (8.24). The challenge is to use Gaussian Blur to duplicate the edge softness of her back.

Step 6: **Zoom in to 400% to a portion of her sweater that's visible next to a mask edge. Choose Filter➡Blur➡ Gaussian Blur to bring up the Gaussian Blur dialog box.**

Compare the edge of the Quick Mask with that of her sweater. To match up the edges, try using a .5-pixel Radius.

Step 7: **In the Gaussian Blur dialog box, set Radius to .5 pixels and then click Cancel. Zoom back to 50%. Exit Quick Mask mode.**

Step 8: **Inverse the selection by pressing ⌘/Control+Shift+I. Feather the selection .5 pixels.**

Step 9: **Make a new layer mask on Body Sculpting.**

Step 10: **Repeat the procedure on the other side. Deselect.**

This time choose the Brush tool. Set an 80-pixel brush. Paint with black on the layer mask to reveal the white background and cover her tummy where it is outlined by the selection. The selection will keep the brush *inside the lines* and soften it, too (8.25).

8.24

8.25

Note

The purpose of Step Six is to determine the amount of blur to match the edges. When a selection is inversed, it loses any applied feathering. That is why Gaussian Blur is canceled in Step Seven and the inversed selection is feathered .5-pixels in Step Eight.

8.26

Note

When you apply a layer mask to a layer, it is removed from the layer. This seems contrary to the philosophy of non-destructive Photoshop at first glance. Looking deeper, the paths that created the sculpting on the layer mask are still in the Paths palette. To go back, you make a new body sculpting layer and recreate the mask from the paths. The "Way of the Fast Retreat" is alive and well.

Step *11*: Control+click (right-click) inside the layer mask on Body Sculpting and choose Apply Layer Mask.

There you have it. Body sculpting is super-easy against plain, evenly lit backgrounds. The Pen tool allows the shape of the sculpture to be altered at the artist's whim. If you (the artist, that is) don't like it, undo the work, revise the path, and go at it until you do. How hot can this be (8.26)?

Toning Down Wrinkles (Of the Fabric Persuasion, That Is)

One of my clients, Fred Mastroianni, designs apparel for men and women. He is also the art director on the shoots. Then he sits with me for hours creating the retouching strategy maps of every detail that he wants changed, softened, or slimmed. As the designer of the clothing, he knows the fabrics and how they must appear in print. The time I spent with him has given me a huge appreciation for how to make apparel look fresh.

Wrinkles in fabric are really shadows. They are supposed to be there. The fabric would look painted on without them. The real problem is that these shadows are dark and the eye naturally is pulled to darker areas in a high-key photograph (a photo with more white than other tones). The trick, therefore, is to lower the contrast of the shadow. Reduce contrast by adding light to the shadows (discussed in Chapter 3). Here is one technique I developed to make such wrinkles less obvious.

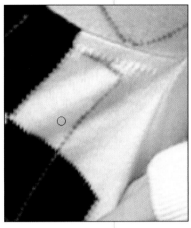

8.27

Step 1: **Turn off the eye icon on the White layer. Make a new layer above Body Sculpting. Merge the visible layers to it. Rename it** Wrinkles. **Turn the White eye icon back on.**

Step 2: **Make a new** Curves **adjustment layer. Click OK. Name it** Lighten Wrinkles. **Fill its layer mask with black. Set the layer-blending mode to Screen. Zoom in to 200%.**

Step 3: **Select a 7-pixel brush with a soft edge. (This technique works better with a pressure-sensitive tablet and pen.)**

Step 4: **Set the brush Opacity to 20% by pressing 2 on the keyboard. Make the foreground color White. Paint over a shadow in front of her arm. Hit undo to see it lighten up. Hit redo.**
If you want the shadow lighter still, paint over it again without lifting the brush. This method takes advantage of the feature that allows paint to build up the limit of the brush opacity and not exceed it until you lift the brush (8.27).

Step 5: **Work throughout the sweater and reduce the shadows. Look at the work by zooming back to 100%. Click Lighten Wrinkles' eye icon on and off. Leave the eye icon off for the next step.**

To Undo, press ⌘/Control+Z on the keyboard. Repeat the same keystroke to *redo* — literally *undo* undo. Add the Option/Alt key to the sequence to step back through history (multiple undos.) ⌘/Control+Shift+Z steps forward through history (multiple redos).

Undoing Undo

Sample   Heal   Fade

8.28

8.29

Step 6: **Scroll down the ribbing where the skirt of the dress begins. Click the Wrinkles layer to highlight it and then select the Healing Brush.**

Set 10 pixels for the size for a hard-edged brush. Option/Alt+click the edge of the skirt just below the shadow. Center the brush on the shadow and stroke away from the edge (8.28).

Step 7: **Select the Healing Brush and set its size to 6 pixels.**

Sample next to each of the pulls under her arm and heal them (8.29).

Adding the Shadows

The pinup of Adair is almost finished. Without shadows she looks like she is floating in (white) space. After we add the contact shadow and drop shadows our work here is done.

Step 1: **Turn off the White layer's eye icon.**

The only other layers with eye icons on should be Wrinkles and Lighten Wrinkles.

Step 2: **Merge the visible layers to a new layer by clicking the Add New Layer icon then holding down Option/Alt as you select Merge Visible Layers from the Layers palette fly-out menu.**

Name the new layer **Retouch Final**. Turn off the eye icons for Wrinkles and Lighten Wrinkles.

Note

Aligning the sample point with the healing point is the trick to healing textures. Sample on the edge of the texture and the background in this example. Align the healing brush so the edge begins in the same place relative to the sample point. Brush the entire area with one continuous stroke.

Step *3*: **Duplicate Retouch Final and drag the duplicated layer *under* the original Retouch Final layer. Rename the duplicate** Shadow.

Step *4*: **Click the Lock Transparent Pixels icon.**

Step *5*: **Click Retouch Final's eye icon off. Fill Shadow with black.**

Adair's shape is filled with black (8.30). The transparency is unaffected. Make Retouch Final visible.

Step *6*: **Press ⌘/Control+T to enter Free Transform mode. The Shadow layer is active.**

Step *7*: **Press the Control key (or right-click) inside the bounding box and choose Distort from the menu** (8.31).

8.30

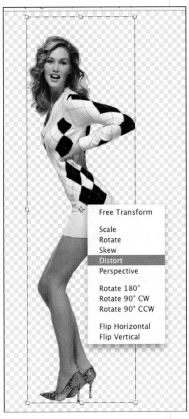

8.31

Step *8*: **Drag the center point straight down to the middle reference point at the bottom of the bounding box. Click the top-middle reference point. Drag the shadow down and to the right. Release the mouse button. Click the bottom-right reference point. Drag it toward the center until the right high heel shadow slips under the real shoe** (8.32).

Step *9*: **Select the Commit Transform check box. Make White visible.**

Step *10*: **Duplicate Shadow. Rename it** Contact Shadow. **Hold down the Option/Alt key and click the New Layer Mask icon.**

The layer mask icon appears. It is filled with black.

Step *11*: **Highlight Shadow. Set its Opacity to 50%. Click the Lock Transparent Pixels button off.**

The lock icon on the layer disappears.

8.32

Step *12*: **Press D to set the default colors.**
Black is the foreground color.

Step *13*: **Double-click the foreground color to open the Color Picker.**
Enter **20** in the B: text box of the HSB group. Click OK. This sets a dark gray as the foreground color.

Step *14*: **Exchange the foreground color for the background color. Double-click on White to enter the Color Picker. Enter** 80 **in the B: text box. Click OK.**
The foreground color is now a light gray.

Step *15*: **Select the Gradient tool.**
Check the Linear Gradient button. Then click the Foreground to Background Gradient button. Both of these are in the Options bar.

Step *16*: **Add a layer mask to Shadow. Click at the point where the shadow starts under the toe of Adair's front shoe. Drag across the shadow to the top of her head** (8.33).
The shadow fades from being dark close to her feet to lighter the farther is gets away (8.34).

8.33

8.34

Step *17*: **Press the Control key (or right-click) and click the layer mask icon on Shadow. Choose Apply Layer Mask.**

Step *18*: **Duplicate the now layer mask-less Shadow. Drag the copy above Shadow. Add a black layer mask to it.**

It is already named Shadow Copy. (See Step Ten for a refresher on the black layer mask.)

Step *19*: **Highlight the Shadow layer and open the Gaussian Blur dialog box.**

In the Gaussian Blur dialog box, set the Radius to 25 pixels. Click OK.

Step *20*: **Highlight the Shadow Copy layer. Set its Opacity to 20%. Highlight the layer mask.**

With a soft 700-pixel white brush, bring in the sharpness of this layer under her feet. Let the big, soft edge fade the sharp edge into the blur of Shadow.

8.35

Step *21*: **Go to Actual Pixels view and scroll down to the feet.**

The shadow is almost finished. Use a black, harder-edge brush on the layer mask to clean up the offset shadow (8.35).

There's a final touch to do on the shadow.

Step *22*: **Make a new layer above Shadow Copy. Name it** Contact Shadow. **Set the Opacity to 50%.**

Step *23*: **Get a 20-pixel soft brush. Paint with black under Adair's shoes at the balls of her feet.**

Let the soft edge make a slightly darker shadow where the shoes meet the floor.

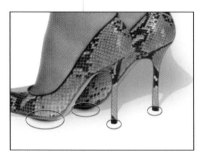

8.36

Step *24*: **Use a smaller brush and make a shadow under each heel.**

These are very subtle. If you can barely notice them, they are right (8.36).

Contact shadows is the glue that keeps things from floating away, makes drop shadows believable, and separates the photographers from art directors and graphic designers in Photoshop. It is that teeny-tiny shadow that is at the base of everything. It locks the object in the photograph to the background. It is a very deep dark shadow. It is the secret handshake that *only* photographers know. When it's missing, photographers look at the output then smirk, "It's fake! A graphic designer (or art director) must've made that shadow." Now I know that only photographers are going to read this so I'm not worried. Okay, maybe a little bit. Tell you what: If you are an art director or a designer, don't tell anybody. Everything will be just fine.

Contact Shadows

Creating a High-Key Vignette

White subjects on a white background are called *high key*. The only lower tones are those of the subject herself. In this project, we will drop out the background and remove both the clamps holding up the collar of the model's jacket and the white card that is bouncing light in on the left.

Our model is Amy Lucas from Houghton Talent Agency. She is wearing a Gucci ski jacket with a fur collar (8.37). She has already been color and tone corrected, as well as retouched.

Step 1: **Download 2062-L-0031.tif from www.amesphoto.com/learning. Open 2062-L-0031.tif by double-clicking it in File Browser. Make a copy of the Background layer by pressing ⌘/Control+J. Rename the layer White.**

8.37

Step 2: Select the Pen tool and set up the Option bar by clicking the Paths icon and the Subtract from Path Area icon (8.38). Draw a path around the background, skirting around Amy. Save your path.

The path is outlined in green (8.39).

Step 3: Click the Paths tab to reveal the Path palette. If you have drawn your own path, ⌘/Control+click it to load it as a selection.

You can use Path 1 if you haven't drawn one.

Step 4: Choose Selection➟Feather Selection or press ⌘/Control+Option/Alt+D to open the Feather Selection dialog box. Enter 1 pixel in the Feather Radius field. Click OK.

Step 5: Press ⌘/Control+J to make the selection into a layer. Rename it Amy.

Step 6: Highlight the White layer. Set the default colors by pressing D, and then pressing X to make the foreground color white. Press Option/Alt+Delete/Backspace to fill the layer with white.

The background is now white (8.40). The tips of the clamps used to hold up Amy's collar were left behind. We are not going to rebuild the collar, just clean up the colors.

8.38

8.39

8.40

Step 7: Create a new layer above the Amy layer and name it Collar. Choose the Clone Stamp tool. Set the brush to soft edge and 125 pixels in size. Sample the fur below the clamps. Clone fur over the clamp remnants all the way to Amy's hair.

Reduce the brush size as you get closer to her hair. Avoid overspraying the hair (8.41).

Step 8: Select the Healing brush from the toolbox. Sample in the fur below the clamps and brush into the white.

Remember to click the Use all layers checkbox in the Options bar.

Step 9: Select the Elliptical Marquee tool from the toolbox.

Step 10: Draw a selection around Amy that includes her hair and most of her lower hand (8.42).

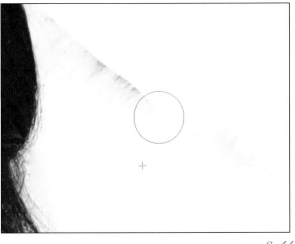

8.41

8.42

Step *11*: **Click the Create a New Layer icon located at the bottom of the Layers palette. Rename the layer Vignette.**

Step *12*: **Hold down the Option/Alt key. Click the Add Layer Mask icon also at the bottom of the Layers palette to make a layer mask on the Vignette layer.**
The Layer Mask icon displays a black circle the same shape as the selection.

Step *13*: **Click the Vignette layer thumbnail to activate it.**
A brush icon appears next to the eye icon. Set the foreground color to white. Hold down the Option/Alt key and press Delete (Backspace) to fill the layer with white (8.43).

Step *14*: **Click the layer mask to activate it.**
A Layer Mask icon replaces the brush next to the eye icon indicating that the layer mask is ready for editing.

8.43

Step *15*: **Choose Filter➡Blur➡Gaussian Blur from the menu bar. Enter** 114.3 **pixels in the Radius field and then click OK.**
If the blurred mask lightens some of her hair or face, select a black brush and paint it back in.

That's all there is to it (8.44). The major difference between a white and black vignette is that usually the white layer is left at 100% Opacity to bleed the image to paper white when it is printed.

There you have it. The secrets behind making glamorous pinups. If you want more practice, download the Going Further folder for this chapter from www.amesphoto.com/learning. There is also CD-based training available on the site for learning the Pen tool and some of the techniques described in this chapter.

In the next chapter the focus is close up and intimate as we explore the post-production work in retouching a beauty photograph.

8.44

Chapter Nine

From Many, One:
A Digital Portrait

Artists have been piecing together images long before digital manipulation of imagery was even a dream. Stained glass windows, religious paintings, frescos, and mosaics are all examples of manipulated art. When stripped of semiotics, art is about manipulating materials to represent a concept. Sculptors shape stone and metal into their vision. Painters use pigments and dyes. Architects draft their dreams on paper for builders to build.

Photography is also an artist's medium, albeit rather new when compared to other forms. And photographers have experimented with and manipulated their work since it was possible to fix an image onto metal more than one hundred and sixty years ago. They cut up photographs, pasted the parts together, and rephotographed the results. They made multiple exposures on a single piece of film. Film was boiled during development to form patterns of reticulation.

This constant push has helped evolve imagers who can see photographs as parts of a whole to be assembled after shooting. Ansel Adams taught himself to look at a scene and see the finished print in his mind before he released the shutter. He called this *pre-visualization*. Conversely, Jerry Uelsmann developed *post-visualization* — seeing an image after the exposure and then producing the finished image in the darkroom.

In-camera montages became predecessors to the more efficient digital techniques of today — teaching photographers how to see the components of a finished image. The photographers who learned to work within the compromises of in-camera composites on film and those created in the darkroom were uniquely ready to embrace the possibilities of digital postproduction. Digitally captured images moved the possibilities forward to a place dreamed of with film and accomplished only with extraordinary difficulty.

Often I shoot with the camera mounted on a tripod or studio stand. Yes, it limits my mobility and definitely keeps me from

Photographic History Lives in Photoshop

Photography started with ephemeral images that faded in the light. The first permanent images were fixed on pieces of copper covered with silver. Then silver (and other light-sensitive metals) was made into emulsions and coated on paper, glass, and finally, on sheet or roll film. This media was exposed to light then developed. The chemicals tarnished the metal that had seen light. This became the negative. Silver-coated paper was used again this time for prints made from glass plates and film.

Interesting, isn't it? A traditional silver gelatin photograph is really nothing more than tarnished metal on a paper base. The rate the density of the processed "tarnished" silver builds up in relation to the amount of light is called *densitometry*. Each film has a *characteristic curve* based on its own particular reactions to light and development. The adjustment Curves in Photoshop works on digital images exactly the way the characteristic curve does on film.

even vaguely resembling the fashion photographers on television and in the movies and this is a good thing. An even better thing is that the lack of camera movement guarantees sharp images. Best of all is that nothing except the model moves. Everything is in register. It becomes possible to choose the best elements from a series of the same image and put them together in Adobe Photoshop.

I often experience a visual flow while making photographs of a model. The feedback of seeing each exposure on a monitor as it is made shows me possibilities of combinations that can be evolved into one image in postproduction. I direct the model so that my postproduction options increase. It is this *concurrent visualization* that pushes my photography to be more than my original idea.

Constructing Christina

The project in this chapter is divided into three parts. The first part involves a critical review of the images of Christina, the model for this shoot. One frame that forms the base of the photograph is chosen. Then individual elements that will enhance the composite are selected. In the second part, the elements are assembled into an image for retouching. This section shares ideas about composition, positioning images using Photoshop's Free Transform and the Difference blending mode, and using layer masks to put it all together.

The third and final part covers the steps of retouching and finishing. It begins with creating a digital strategy map covering all the work to be done. Then we go step-by-step through smoothing skin, healing blemishes, expanding backgrounds, and even do a bit of color changing.

To work along with the project in this chapter, download the folder for Chapter 9 from www.amesphoto.com/learning. These files have already been color balanced and sharpened, anti-aliased, and of course, copyrighted. As with all the tutorial files, they are licensed to you only for purposes of learning these techniques. You may not use them in any manner for public display including but not limited to posting on the Internet and inkjet prints.

Analyzing the Take

Take a close look at this figure (9.1). This is the entire take of this pose in the order it was shot. In this section we analyze the photographs for overall composition. Then we choose the best individual parts. Look carefully at the model's hands and feet. Pay close attention to the angle of her face. Which face works the best?

In selecting the components of the photograph I often grid them out and then make a large print. I draw a green box around frames with possibilities. Then I circle the parts in those frames that I might want to use. I go through the grid quickly, relying on intuition more than reason. I can always change my mind later. The important thing is to connect with the creative side of the brain during this process, making logic secondary. That said, it is impossible to describe the intuitive process. So I must rely on the rational. Please practice the gut-feeling style of selection on your own.

A study of the pose in the first nine frames reveals a disconnected composition. Christina's right leg doesn't seem to be a part of the shot. There is nothing that *connects* it to the image. A more extreme example is in frame 10 (2062-B-0314). Her right arm is behind her back. This leaves her right leg

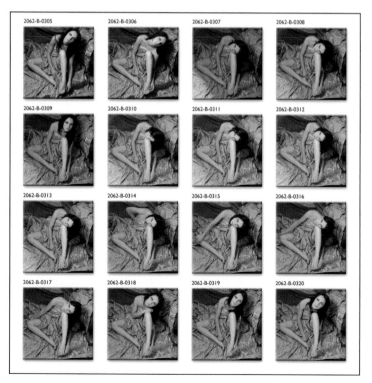

9.1

completely disassociated from the rest of image. In the next three frames (2062-B-0315, 0316, and 0317) her right hand is resting on her right knee, under her knee, or behind it, respectively. This arm position connects her leg with the rest of the photograph. Frame 0315 has a relaxed feel to the arm.

Unfortunately, her hand is flat to the camera, making it less graceful. Frame 0316 is better with just the side of her hand showing. Frame 0317 is my choice because the shape of her hand follows the line around her knee (9.2). This one gets a green box. It might become the base image, too.

9.2

Look at her left foot and hand. In the first three frames there is little if any connection between them. In the remaining frames there is a connection of some kind. Become aware of them. Do any of these 13 show a flow or particular sense of grace and femininity? Of these, which one is well . . . *pretty*? Frames 0310, 0311, 0312, 0316, and 0317 are almost identical. Her hand is long and slightly under her foot. Her foot is wide and boxy-looking because it, too, is flat to the camera. These five frames are out of the running.

Frames 0308, 0309, 0313, 0318, 0319, and 0320 are very similar as well. The first six show her hand curled, touching her little toe. In the last three frames her thumb is touching the top little toe joint. These are better though not perfect. That leaves Frame 0314 as the best left hand and foot combo. Her hand gracefully caresses her foot and covers a portion of her toes. A green box for the frame and a circle around Christina's left leg and hand go on this one (9.3).

9.3

Let's choose a face and some hair. One of the problems with this type of pose is that the top of the model's head naturally goes toward the camera. Telling the model to look at the camera will only raise her eyes. Check out 0310. The solution is to have the model raise her chin to bring the plane of the face more closely parallel to the chip in the camera, as in frame 0312. I love the hair in 0313 so it gets a green box and a circle (9.4).

Now review all the frames for the shape of the face. I love the poses where Christina rests her cheek on her knee. That eliminates Frames 0305, 0306, 0309, 0318, 0319, and 0320. The frames with her chin toward her chest are out: 0307, 0308, 0310, 0311, and 0314. Frame 0312 shows too much forehead. In 0313 she is looking away. I think eye contact is important for the feeling in the final image. Her eyes are almost closed in 0316. Frame 0315's chin is lowered. The nod for the face is Frame 0317.

More often than not the base image has several things in it that work. This is certainly the case for 0317. The right arm and knee, the body, and face all work well. In the steps that follow, we'll use Frame 0314 for the left hand, arm, foot, and leg, add hair from 0313, then move on to retouching the composite.

9.4

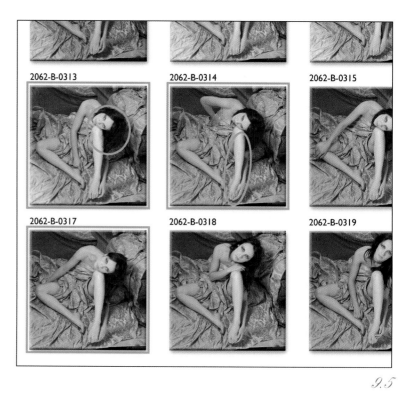

9.5

This process has reduced the take from sixteen frames to one hero and two supporting images (9.5). It seems like this is a lot of work. Editing is as important to the successful photograph as is shooting it and doing the post-production. Each is one leg of the tripod that supports a great image. Next we'll assemble the parts.

Creating the Composite

Step *1*: **Open the File Browser and select the files 2062-B-0317, 2062-B-0313, and 2062-B-0314. Double-click one of them to open all three in Photoshop.**

Step *2*: **Select the Move tool from the toolbar or by pressing V on the keyboard.**
Make sure you can see 2062-B-0317. Click 2062-B-0313, hold down the Shift key, and drag the image over file 2062-B-0317.

Step *3*: **Double-click Layer 1 in the Layers palette and rename the layer** 0313 hair.
Close 0313 by clicking on it and then pressing ⌘/Control+W. Press D for "Don't Save" when prompted.

Step 4: Click 2062-B-0314 to make that file active and then hold down the Shift key and drag 2062-B-0314 on top of 2062-B-0317.

Double-click Layer 1 in the Layers palette and rename it **0314 foot**. Close 2062-B-0314 without saving it.

Step 5: Back in 2062-B-0317, double-click the Background layer.

The New Layer dialog box appears. Change the name of Layer 0 to **0317 Base**. Click OK. Only one file remains open: 2062-B-0317.tif.

Step 6: Press ⌘/Control+Shift+S and save –B-0317.tif as 2062-B-0317.psd.

The layer stack should now look like this (9.6).

Step 7: Click the 0314 foot layer to activate it and then select the Lasso tool from the toolbar (or press L on the keyboard). Click and drag a selection around Christina's hand and foot (9.7).

Step 8: Press ⌘/Control+J to copy the selection to its own layer. Double-click the words *Layer1* and rename the layer hand & foot. Click the eye icon in layers 0314 foot and hand and foot to hide them.

9.6

Tip

Naming layers is a useful habit to adopt when working in Photoshop. It might not seem important while work is ongoing, but naming layers is hugely valuable when you reopen the file for modifications at a later date. It saves time and experimentation when trying to remember how you accomplished an effect.

9.7

A Burning Issue: TIFF or PSD?

A .*tif* extension represents a photograph that is either ready for editing (in 16 bit) or for delivery to a client (8 bits). The .*psd* extension indicates that it is a working file containing layers of a work product. *PSD files are never supplied to clients.* Adoption of this protocol ensures that a quick glance at the extension of an image file tells the photographer what is in it. *Danger:* It is possible to save layers as TIFs. Don't do it. Layered TIFs — as of this writing — open only in Photoshop and might cause problems for other software (non-Adobe page layout programs for instance).

Step *9*: **Click the 0313 hair layer to activate it and draw a selection with the Lasso tool around Christina's head.**

It's okay to include her face, shoulder, and knee (9.8).

Step *10*: **Press ⌘/Control+J to copy the selection to its own layer and rename the layer** hair.

Step *11*: **Click the eye icon next to 0313 hair to hide the layer. Click the hair layer and drag it to the top of the layer stack.**

Only two layers are visible now: hair and 0317 Base. The next step aligns the hair layer with the base layer.

Step *12*: **Select Difference from the Blending Modes drop-down menu** (9.9).

Zoom in to 100% to view the actual pixels by pressing ⌘/Control+Option/Alt+0. Choose the Move tool (V). Click and drag until the catchlights of her right eye go black.

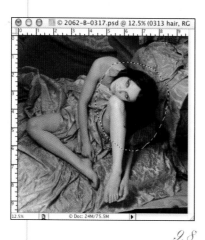

9.8

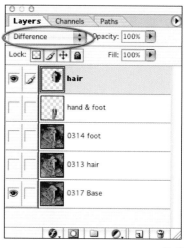

9.9

The Difference blending mode finds areas of similarity between the active layer and the one visible below it. When areas are identical they appear as black. The more black there is, the more perfectly registered an image is.

To see how this blend mode works, open 2062-B-0314.tif from the construction folder. Press ⌘/Control+J to duplicate the layer. Make sure that none of the Lock icons are active. The Lock icons are right under the Blending Mode drop-down menu. Change Layer 1's blending mode to Difference. The photograph is completely black. Press V to activate the Move tool and press the down arrow on the keyboard five times. The two layers are now out of register with each other (9.10). Now press the up arrow five times and watch the whole image become black again as the two layers reregister. This technique is useful for registering images when compositing them. It is most often used when registering scans from two or more pieces of film shot at the same time.

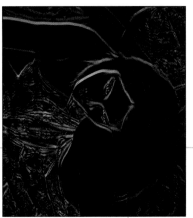

9.10

Step *13*: **Zoom out by pressing ⌘/Control+– (minus sign) until you see the whole image and press ⌘/Control+T to go into Free Transform (Edit➡Free Transform).**
A bounding box appears. Locate the center point and drag it over the aligned right eyes (9.11).

Step *14*: **Zoom back in to 100% by choosing ⌘/Control+Option/Alt+0.**
At this magnification the bounding box is not visible.

9.11

Step 15: Highlight the Rotate field in the Options bar. Hold down the Shift key and press the down arrow 10 times.

The number in the Rotate: field reads –10.0 degrees (9.12). The left eye catchlights should be almost completely black indicating that they are also in register.

Step 16: Release the Shift key and use the up or down arrow to fine-tune the rotation.

Hair and the 0317 Base layer are now a very close match. Press Enter to complete the Free Transform or double-click inside the Transform bounding box.

Step 17: Zoom out to fit the image on screen by pressing ⌘/Control+0. Change the blending mode back to Normal.

Now let's get rid of the broken leg, shoulder, and face, leaving only Christina's hair. The bottom of the Layers palette has several tools.

Step 18: Click on the second tool from the left to add a layer mask to hair (9.13).

| | | X: 1913.0 px | △ Y: 752.0 px | W: 100.0% | H: 100.0% | △ -10.0 ° | H: 0.0 ° | V: 0.0 ° | ⊘ ✓ |

9.12

Tip

Just as the arrow key will nudge an active layer 1 pixel for each stroke, pressing an arrow key while in Free Transform affects an image in units of 1 depending on the function selected. Holding down the Shift key and pressing an arrow key moves in units of 10.

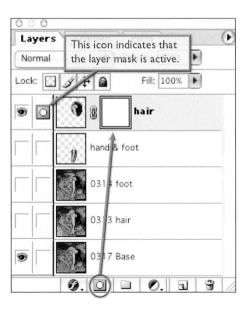

9.13

Step *19*: **Press B on the keyboard to choose the Brush tool. Press X to make black the Foreground color.**

Step *20*: **Using a soft-edged 150-pixel brush, paint over the leg and shoulder areas and around her head.**
Do not paint out any of her hair. Zoom in to 100% by pressing ⌘/Control+Option/Alt+0.

Step *21*: **Refine the mask with a smaller brush. Click on the eye icon of 0317 Base to turn it off.**
Only the areas of the hair layer not brushed are visible. It is a helpful to leave some of the background and blend it in with the brush. This avoids the helmet hair look of so many composites (9.14). Clean up any skin or background that doesn't belong. Click the Look icon of 0317 Base on and off to check your work.

Step *22*: **Select the Move tool (V) and nudge the hair layer with the down arrow until the hair meets the model's right cheek. Refine the work on the layer mask of the hair layer until a natural cheek line is achieved.**
If the skin line that blends into the shoulder doesn't quite match, don't worry; that gets fixed during retouching (9.15).

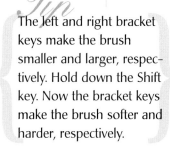

Tip
The left and right bracket keys make the brush smaller and larger, respectively. Hold down the Shift key. Now the bracket keys make the brush softer and harder, respectively.

9.14

Tip
Pressing the X key eXchanges the Foreground and Background colors. When working on a layer mask, painting with black conceals the underlying image. Press X to switch to white. Painting with white reveals the underlying image.

9.15

9.16

Okay. Now on we go to the hand and foot. The procedure to replace them is mostly the same as for the hair.

Step 23: Click in the foot & hand layer to activate it. Change the Blending Mode to Difference to see how well it lines up with the base layer.

It is important that the top of the leg is registered with the base layer. Use the Move tool (V) to nudge the layer until the leg becomes black (9.16). Change the Blending Mode back to Normal.

Step 24: Click the Add Layer Mask icon at the bottom of the Layers palette to add a layer mask to the hand & foot layer.

Press B to choose the Brush tool. Select a 60-pixel soft-edged brush. Set Black as the Foreground color.

Step 25: Brush with black around the hand and foot on the layer mask and blend the leg layer with the one beneath it. Blend in the arm and the surrounding fabric.

Click the Look icon of the foot & hand layer on and off to see whether there are any places where it doesn't blend perfectly. Look for hard sharp lines. Paint on the layer mask as needed. If something is accidentally painted out, press X on the keyboard to exchange the colors and paint it back in. Press X once again and refine the layer mask. The hand & foot layer will look similar to this figure (9.17).

> *Tip*
>
> Another way to align images is to lower the Opacity of the top layer to around 50%. The shortcut from the keyboard is to press 5 when the Move tool is selected. 1 = 10% opacity, 2 = 20%, and 5 = 50%. Pressing two number keys in rapid succession sets an in-between number. For example, 7,5 =75%.

> *Tip*
>
> D from the keyboard sets the Default colors: black and white. Black is the default Foreground color. X exchanges the Foreground color with the Background color.

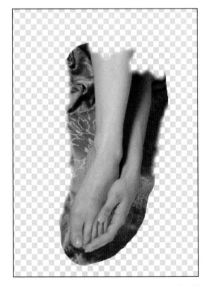

9.17

Step 26: **Zoom out to the Fit on Screen view by pressing ⌘/Control+0.**

Click the Look icons of the hair and hand & foot layers on and off several times. Look for areas at the edges of these layers that seem to jump or look out of place. Examine any you might find and refine their layer masks before continuing with the next step.

The compositing of the three frames is now completed. Indicate that by merging the visible layers onto a new layer.

Step 27: **Click the hair layer to activate it and then click the Create a New Layer icon (next to the Trash Can icon) at the bottom of the Layers palette.**

A new layer called Layer 1 appears at the top of the stack (9.18). Hold down the Option/Alt key and choose Merge Visible from the Layers palette fly-out menu. The visible layers, 0317 Base, hand & foot, and hair, are merged and copied onto Layer 1.

Step 28: **Double-click the words *Layer 1* and rename the layer *Composite*.**

This layer is the one from which we will build all the retouching in the next section of this chapter. Save the file as **2062-B-0317composite.psd**.

Wow. Photography certainly has come along way since 1888 when Kodak's motto was "Push the button — We do the rest." There are those who think that those were the good old days when someone else did the heavy lifting. Digital photography has pretty much killed the chemical darkroom and plopped the photographer in front of a computer monitor instead.

Nobody said that working with digital photographs was easy. If it were, everybody would be doing it at this level. Because it is possible to do really great finishing work, it is important that we do it. Capture on film forced us to degrade the image before it was developed. We used soft-focus filters, vignetters, and cross processing to achieve an imagined result. This means that in the name of making a photograph "pretty," we had to forego control in postproduction. For the most part we could only dream.

Now we have the tools. The control is ours. Let's get on with an exercise of this power.

Note

Some Photoshop users feather the selection before floating it so that it will blend in without using the layer mask. I am an admitted control freak and believe my eye is better that the algorithm in the program. To each her or his own.

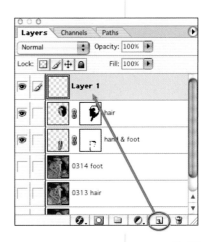

9.18

Note

The number of frames shot for this project offer many other construction possibilities. A challenge for the reader is to download the sheet of images (2062-B-03Grid.tif), print it out, and build your own version. The file 2062-B-03XX.psd has individually named layers of the sixteen images on the grid.

Strategic Retouching

Step 1: **Create a new empty layer (press ⌘/Control+Shift+N) and name it** Strategy Map.

This is the layer that maps out the work to be done in the retouching of the photograph.

Step 2: **Zoom in to 100% (press ⌘/Control+Option/Alt+0). Hold down the spacebar and drag the image until Christina's face is centered in the window.**

Step 3: **Select the Lasso tool (press L) and draw a circle around the lines under her left eye.**

The dancing ants of a selection appear. Hold down the Shift key to add to the selection. Draw under her right eye, around her forehead, and along the bridge of her nose. Circle the blemish on her chin and the one just above her beauty mark. We could remove it, but because it is a *beauty* mark — not a mole — (Christina loves it) we'll leave it alone.

Step 4: **Double-click the Foreground color to bring up the Color Picker and select a green that you like and click OK** (9.19)

Step 5: **Choose Edit➞Stroke. In the Stroke dialog box set 7 pixels as the width and click the Inside button.**

Deselect by pressing ⌘/Control+D.

Tip

Pressing F on the keyboard will fill the background with neutral gray and display the image without the window. Press F again. The background turns black and the Menu and Options bar are hidden. Press Tab to hide the toolbar and palettes. This is called *Presentation mode.* Only the image against a black background is on the screen. Press Tab again to bring the toolbar and palettes back. Press F once more to display the Menu, Options bar, and Document (image) window.

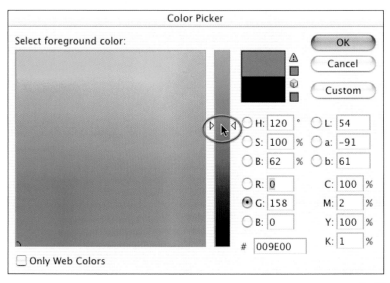

9.19

Step *6*: **Scroll around the image and circle areas with the Lasso that want retouching.**

Stroke them (9.20). I added text boxes and arrows to the Strategy Map to explain the work to be done on this image (9.21).

Step *7*: **Zoom in to 100% then scroll to center Christina's face in the window. Highlight Composite by clicking it in the Layers palette. Press ⌘/Control+J to duplicate the layer and rename it Retouch.**

All the work will be done on this layer instead of on Composite, which now serves as a backup for our work. If something gets ruined on Retouch, we can get it back. Click the eye icon next to Strategy Map off.

9.20

Note

Text boxes are helpful if the retouching is being handed off to another artist or for creating postproduction estimates for clients. They are really amazed to see all the work that goes into a final photograph.

Note

The Strategy Map is a reminder of the work to be completed. Click it on and off after finishing an area to see whether everything is finished. If an area does not blink when the eye icon and off, it has not been retouched.

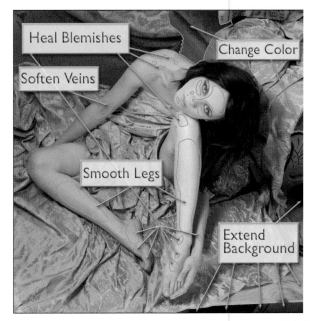

9.21

Step *8*: **Press J on the keyboard to select the Healing Brush. (Press Shift+J if you want to toggle the tool from the Patch or Color Replacement tools.)**

Choose a hard-edged 10-pixel brush from the Option bar. Make sure that Source is set to Sampled and that Aligned is not checked. Option/Alt+click to set the sample point in an area of smooth skin (9.22). Heal the blemishes by brushing over them using short strokes.

Step *9*: **Sample the area under the blush on Christina's left cheek and brush under her left eye without lifting the stylus or mouse button until the bag is completely covered.**

Lift the stylus or release the mouse button and Photoshop will heal the area. Using the same technique heal under Christina's right eye (9.23).

Step *10*: **Click the Look (eye icon) on for the Strategy Map layer and scroll over to her shoulder.**

Click Strategy Map off. Heal the blemishes using the same technique as in Step Eight.

Step *11*: **Scroll down her left arm to the vein that runs from the upper arm to the joint.**

The note on the Strategy Map is to soften the veins.

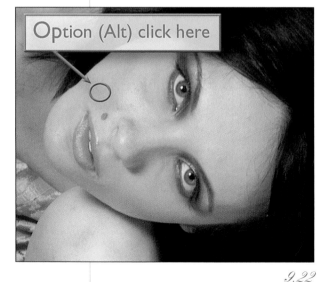

9.22

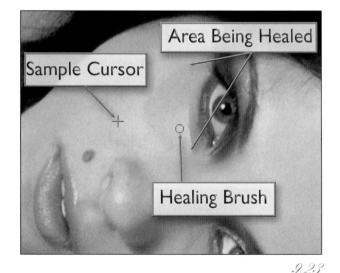

9.23

Step 12: **Press Shift+J to switch to the Patch tool.**

Be sure the Source button is selected in the Options menu.

Step 13: **Draw a selection with the Patch tool around the vein (9.24) and click inside the selection and drag it up her arm to an area of clear skin and release.**

The selection jumps back and the patch is applied. The vein is completely gone — not exactly what is called for.

Step 14: **Choose Edit➡Fade Patch Selection and drag the slider in the Fade dialog box to 34%.**

The vein is subtly revealed. Click OK. Repeat the process with the other veins on her arm.

Step 15: **Continue healing using the brush and Patch tool on the large blemishes and bruises on her right leg. Move on to the left foot and patch the shoe impressions on top of it.**

Be careful not to select right up to the edge of her hand. Heal the blemishes on her foot, hand, arm, leg, and knee. Click the Look icon (the eye) of the Retouch layer on and off to see the progress so far. Don't worry about healing the shaving stubble. That gets softened in a later step.

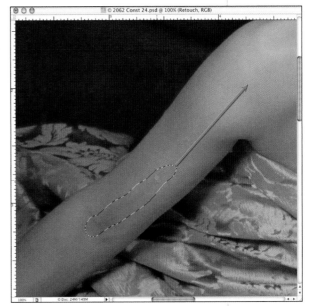

9.24

Note

The Healing Brush and the Patch tool sample areas out-side of the edge of the brush or selection. When you use the healing tools too close to an area that is a different color or tone, the sample that extends beyond where the tool indicates it is working will blend and cause a discolored result.

Tip

The keyboard shortcut for the Fade command is Shift+⌘/Control+F. This command works with most tools and filters to control the effect immediately after the fact.

Okay, this is how we soften that shaving stubble:

Step *16*: **Duplicate the Retouch layer by pressing ⌘/Control+J. Rename it Soften Legs.**

Step *17*: **Choose Filter→Blur→Gaussian Blur and set the Radius to 8 pixels. Click OK** (9.25).
The whole image becomes blurred.

Step *18*: **Choose Filter→Noise→Add Noise and set 3% as the amount.**
Set Distribution to Uniform. Select the Monochromatic check box (9.26). Click OK.

Step *19*: **Add a black layer mask by holding down the Option/Alt key and clicking on the Add Layer Mask icon at the bottom of the Layers palette.**
Everything's sharp again.

Step *20*: **Select the Brush tool (press B) and choose a soft 70-pixel brush at 100% Opacity.**

Step *21*: **Make white the Foreground color and brush over the legs, being careful to stay inside them.**
If the edges should become blurry, press X to switch to black and paint them back. Switch back to white and complete the smoothing. Yes, they do look like plastic. Wait, there's more.

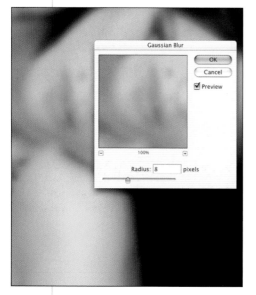

9.25

9.26

Step 22: **Change the blending mode of Soften Legs to Darken.**

"Holy razor blades, Batman! It's magic. Her legs are smooth — believably smooth." "Yes, Robin, thanks to the magic of Photoshop!" replies your ever-so-careful Batman-impersonating author.

Extending the Background

Continuing along, the last two to-do's on the Strategy Map are extending the background and changing the color of the fainting couch behind Christina.

Step 23: **Add a new layer by clicking the New Layer icon at the bottom of the Layers palette; name it** Retouch 2.

Merge Retouch and Soften Legs by holding down the Option/Alt key and choosing Merge Visible from the Layers palette fly-out menu.

Step 24: **Select the Lasso tool (press L) and draw a selection like the one here** (9.27).

Make the selection into its own layer by pressing ⌘/Control+J. Rename the layer **Extra Background**.

Step 25: **Enter the Full Screen mode by pressing F.**

See the sidebar, "Free Transform" for more information about Full Screen mode.

Note

If any layers below the Retouch layer are visible, they won't appear on the merged Retouch 2 layer. The Merge Visible command merges only what can be seen on the monitor to the new layer.

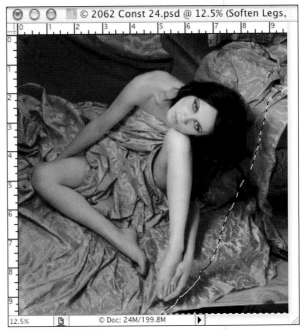

9.27

Modifying selections or layers in the Free Transform mode often means working outside the document window. Before entering Free Transform, press F on the keyboard to go into the Full Screen mode with Menu bar. You can also activate this mode from the toolbar. Access Free Transform from the Edit menu or by pressing ⌘/Control+T. Zooming using ⌘/Control++ (plus sign) or – (minus sign) is available while using Free Transform.

Free Transform

Step *26*: **Choose Edit➡Free Transform or press ⌘/Control+T.** A bounding box appears. Pull the lower-right handle diagonally toward the lower right of the screen until the fabric covers the cell phone and the plywood. Drag the upper-left handle toward the upper-left corner of the screen until the gap formed by the first drag is covered (9.28). Click the check mark in the Options bar to apply the transformation.

Step *27*: **Click the Add Layer Mask icon or choose Layer➡ Add Layer Mask➡Reveal All from the menu bar to add a white layer mask to the Extra background layer.**

Step *28*: **Select the Brush tool (B) and make a soft-edged 70-pixel brush in the Options bar.**
Set black as the Foreground color. Zoom in to 100% — ⌘/Control+Option/Alt+0. Blend the image on Extra background with Retouch 2 below it. Extending the background does double duty in this case by covering the red fabric at the right edge of the fainting couch. Minor gaps can be taken care of on the final retouching layer (9.29).

9.28

9.29

During the time around the Civil War, chaise-like lounges were placed at the top of the stairs in plantation houses. The corsets in vogue at the time were often laced so tightly that a woman wearing one would nearly faint from lack of breath by the time she reached to the top, so she had to "sit a spell." Hence the name *fainting couch*. A fainting couch is a wonderful prop when posing fashion and figure models.

Corsets, Couches, and Catching Her Breath

Scroll to the maroon fabric above Christina's shoulder. Our last step is to change the color to one more in keeping with the golden fabric.

Step 29: **Using the Pen tool, create a path around the fabric. Double-click the work path and save the path as** Path 1.

Step 30: **⌘/Control+click on Path 1 in the Paths palette to make it into a selection.**
Feather it (choose Select→Feather or press ⌘/Control+ Option/Alt+D) and set a feather radius of .3 pixels. Click OK.

Step 31: **Click Retouch 2 to activate it and make the selection into a layer by pressing ⌘/Control+J.**
Rename this layer **grayscale**.

Step 32: **Convert this layer to grayscale by choosing Image→Adjustments→Desaturate.**
Click the Lock Transparent Pixels icon in the Layers palette (9.30). Duplicate the grayscale layer (⌘/Control+J).

Step 33: **Use the Eyedropper tool (press I) to pick a golden color from the fabric. Click the grayscale copy to activate it. Rename it** multiply.

Note
If you are not familiar with the Pen tool yet, click the Paths tab in the Layers palette. ⌘/Control+click on the fainting couch to make the selection. Click back on the Layers tab to return to the Layers palette.

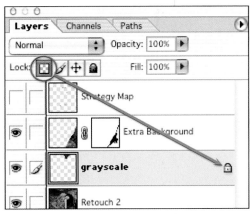

9.30

[201]

Step *34*: **Choose Edit→Fill from the menu bar.**

In the Fill dialog box, set Use: to Foreground Color, Mode: to Normal, and Opacity: to 100%. Duplicate the multiply layer. Rename the multiply copy layer **overlay**. The screen should look like this (9.31).

Step *35*: **Set the Opacity of both multiply and overlay at 50%. Choose the Move tool (press V), click the multiply layer, and then press 5 on the keyboard. Click the overlay layer and press 5 on the keyboard.** Done! Almost.

Step *36*: **Change the Blending Mode of the overlay layer to Overlay.**

Look! Some of the fabric texture is showing. Now change the Blending Mode of the multiply layer to (you guessed it) Multiply. Looking good. Click on the overlay layer. Duplicate it, and there right before your very eyes is a color change from maroon to dark gold. Cool!

Step *37*: **Click the Extra background layer to activate it. Make a new layer. (Click the New Layer icon at the bottom of the Layers palette.) Rename the layer Final.**

9.31

Step *38*: **Merge the visible layers to Final. (Hold down the Option/Alt key and choose Merge Visible from the fly-out menu on the Layers palette.) Save your work.**

Step *39*: **Zoom in to 100% (⌘/Control+Option/Alt+0) and scroll over the entire image.**

Look for any artifacts from the work that has been done. Usually all that's needed is a bit of attention from the Healing Brush or the Clone stamp. When the review is complete, save the .psd file again.

Step *40*: **Option/Alt+click on the Look (eye icon) of the layer Final.**

This turns off all the looks except the one for Final. Scroll down to the bottom of the layer stack and turn the Look icon on for the 0317 Base layer. Scroll back up to Final and click the Look icon on and off to see where this all started and just how far it has come.

Step *41*: **Flatten 2062-B-0317.psd and save it as** 2062-B-0317.tif.

This file is the one that goes to the printer or a client. Archive the .psd. It is your work product.

Note

This is the time to clean up any minor blemishes on Christina's legs. If anything's left that is bothersome, here is where the finishing touches go. It is a good idea to click the Strategy Map layer for one last look to make sure everything is, in fact, completed.

A lot of work goes into finishing a file after it has been captured. This has always been the case. The big difference is that now the work is sourced to labs, printers, and retouch artists. Eventually there will be digital labs that accept files for retouching much the way film labs do. It is important to remember that keeping the original vision intact is difficult when other vendors are in the loop.

The next chapter examines the techniques of retouching beauty photographs. We'll study methods of smoothing skin without losing texture, healing without tonal bleeds, and even making eyes the same size.

Some of the compositing and retouching techniques are easier to learn when you can watch someone do them. A companion CD-ROM with QuickTime movies and the image files is available through Software Cinema. You can watch and work along with me pausing or rewinding the movie at any time as I show you how to use Layer Masks, Free Transform, the Healing Brush, and Patch tools. For ordering information go to www.amesphoto.com/learning and then click "Chapter 9" or the "Learn More" link.

Learn More

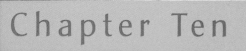
Chapter Ten

Retouching Beauty

There is certainly no absolute standard of beauty.
That precisely is what makes its pursuit so interesting.
John Kenneth Galbraith

I visited the Metropolitan Museum in New York with an eye toward looking for examples of retouching done in the past, before Adobe Photoshop, and even before photography. The purpose of the visit was to look at paintings from European portraitists and see how they painted women. I saw wondrous works that have the most incredible detail in the gowns, fabrics, and tapestries. Every thread is visible. The textures look amazingly real. I felt a subconscious urge to reach into the canvas and feel the cloth.

Retouching a Face: Part 1

Christina is our model (Elite Model Management /Atlanta). The photography is for an Atlanta makeup artist, Janeen Loriam (www.moodymakeup.com), who also has a line of skin care products and makeup. The set was ready and Christina was in place. I noticed that her left eye was smaller than her right. My first reaction was to flop the set so that her small eye would be closer to the camera, making it appear larger. Then two things came to mind: 1) This is a simple fix in Photoshop and 2) It is important *not to draw attention to a person's flaws.*

In photography of a non-model, changing the set would not be a problem. She would have no idea why I would do this and the universal reason ("the light is better") comes into play. Models on the other hand are very aware of their features. Christina knows her left eye is smaller. And I know she knows because she favors her left side *toward* the camera. It is a subtle communication.

Resizing Christina's eye is part of the upcoming project, We will go through many beauty retouching techniques that are useful in developing your own style of artistic license in portraiture.

Step *1*: **Download 2062-B Christina CU.tif from www.ames photo.com/learning and open it in Adobe Photoshop CS.**
The file has already been through the pre post production process. (Notice the © in the document header.)

Step *2*: **Zoom to 50% so that both eyes are visible.**

16-Bit Editing

One of the professional features of Photoshop CS is the ability to work in 16-bit using layers. This editing style is about producing the highest output quality. The screen captures follow the 16-bit workflow. They are of the full resolution file. The file on www.amesphoto.com/learning is provided in 16-bit format at a much lower resolution (100ppi) to make the download faster.

Step 3: Select the Measure tool under the Eyedropper icon in the toolbar and then click and drag a line from the left side of her right eye across the eyeball to the tear duct.

The Info palette shows the size across her right eye. In this case it is an inch and an eighth across. Now click and drag across the left eye using the same constraints. The result is less than an inch showing the left eye is, in fact, significantly smaller (10.1)

Step 4: Make a copy of the Background layer by pressing ⌘/Control+J and rename the layer Retouch.

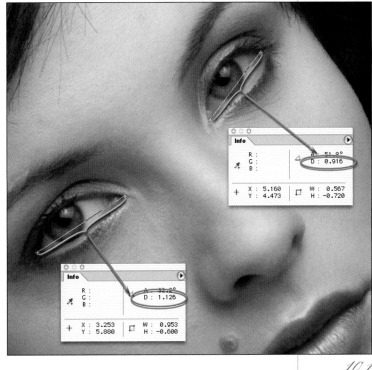

Step 5: Press L (or choose the Lasso tool from the toolbar) and draw a big selection around the left eye.

In the selection include at least half the nose and the area outside of the face to the right (10.2).

Step 6: Press ⌘/Control+J and rename this layer Left Eye.

There are two ways to do this next step. One is to enlarge the Left Eye layer well, by eye, using Free Transform until it looks right. The other is to use the right eye as a guide. The latter method is the one we'll use so that you can get a feel for the process. After you do this to several photographs, the "by-eye" method will be easy.

Step 7: Press V to select the Move tool and then press 5 to set the Left Eye layer to 50% Opacity. Drag the layer until the tear duct of Left Eye is over the left-most (as you look at the screen) edge of her right eye (10.3).

Step *8*: **Choose Edit→Free Transform or press ⌘/Control+T. Drag the anchor point over the point where the tear duct and the left edge of the right eye are aligned. Click the link icon (Maintain Aspect Ratio) in the Options bar and highlight the W field. Press the up arrow on the keyboard four times.**
The Left Eye layer enlarges from the tear duct.

Step *9*: **Now position the cursor just outside the upper-right corner handle of the bounding box. The rotate cursor appears. Click and drag clockwise until the eyeballs align** (10.4).
Check the size. They are very close. (It's okay as long as Left Eye is not larger than the right eye.)

Step *10*: **Click the check mark in the Options bar to finalize the transform or press Return/Enter.**

Step *11*: **Press ⌘/Control+Option/Alt+Z three times to undo the transform, the move, and the opacity change.**
Left Eye has returned to its original size, location, and transparency (none).

Step *12*: **Now press ⌘/Control+T to open Free Transform again. Click the Maintain Aspect Ratio link icon. Enter 104% in the W: field. Click the commit check box to apply the transform to the Left Eye layer** (10.5).

10.4

10.5

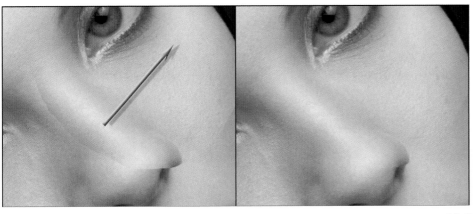

10.6

Step *13*: **Click and drag the Left Eye layer to the left until the edge on the bridge of the nose disappears** (10.6).

Step *14*: **Create a layer mask on the Left Eye layer by choosing Layer→Add Layer Mask→Reveal All or by clicking the Add Layer Mask icon at the bottom of the Layers palette** (10.7), **or by choosing Layer→Layer Mask→Reveal All from the menu.**

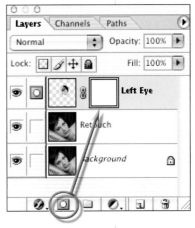

10.7

Step *15*: **View actual pixels (100%) by pressing ⌘/Control+ Option/Alt+0 (zero).**

Press B to select the Brush tool. Make it soft edged (click Shift+[(the left bracket key on the keyboard) with 100% Opacity and a size of around 100 pixels.

Step *16*: **Press D to set the default colors and paint with black (foreground color) over the cheek, edge of the face into the hair, eyebrow, and nostril to blend Left Eye with the image under it (the Retouch layer)** (10.8).

10.8

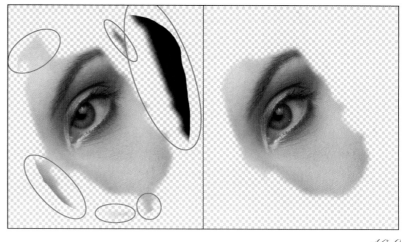

10.9

Step *17*: **Check the blending by clicking the Background and Retouch layers off.**
Look for hard edges. Continue painting on the layer mask with black until they are gone (10.9).

Step *18*: **Click the eye icon on the Retouch layer to turn it on and then click the eye icon on the Left Eye layer on and off to see what a difference 4% makes.**
This is also a check to make sure the blending is perfect. Remember that the skin texture on the Left Eye layer is 4% larger, too. You take care of that later.

Step *19*: **Save the file as 2062-B** Christina CU.psd.

Retouching a Face: Part 2

The next set of steps involves fixing the stray hair that falls under Christina's chin and across her shoulder. Later, we'll brighten her eyes, soften the skin texture and lines under her eyes, and remove the blemishes on her shoulder.

Step *1*: **Create a new layer (choose Layer➡New➡Layer, or click the Create a New Layer icon in the Layers palette) above Left Eye and name it** Retouch 2.

Step *2*: **Hold down the Option/Alt key and choose Merge Visible from the fly-out menu (arrow at the upper-right corner) of the Layers palette.**

Step *3*: **Select the Pen tool from the toolbar or press P to select it.**

Step 4: **Zoom in to 200% and draw a path along the very edge of Christina's cheekbone starting just below her left eye.**

Be sure the path is outside of the very fine hairs that show up against the dark background. Continue it along her jaw line and around her chin. Complete the path across her shoulder and up the edge of the frame and back across to the first anchor (10.10).

Step 5: **In the Paths palette, double-click Work Path.**

The Save Path dialog box opens and suggests the name *Path 2*. Click OK to accept.

Step 6: **⌘/Control+click on Path 1 (the supplied path, or Path 2 the one you created) to make it into a selection.**

Step 7: **Choose Select➡Feather and enter 1 in the Feather Radius field. Click OK.**

This selection will keep the healing away from her cheek and the tiny hairs. Without it, the healing job would look too sharp and perfect.

Step 8: **Make a new layer at the top of the layer stack and name it Heal.**

10.10

Note

The Pen tool makes the very best and most controlled selections of all the tools in Photoshop. The importance of a photographer/retoucher being strong in the use of this tool cannot be stressed enough. Yet it seems that this tool is the one that everyone works to avoid at all costs. There is a lesson on the CD for this chapter from Software Cinema that explains how to use the Pen tool to draw paths. For more information on this CD, look in the Chapter Ten section of www.amesphoto.com/learning. If you are not comfortable drawing your own paths yet, click the Path tab and it is included in the file. Its name is Path 1.

Step *9*: **Choose the Healing Brush from the toolbar and set up the Options bar as shown here** (10.11).
It is important that Use All Layers is checked.

Step *10*: **Carefully Option/Alt+click on the edge of Christina's shoulder for your sample and start healing at the edge where the loop of hair is on her shoulder** (10.12).

The point is to get rid of the loop of hair for the next step. The key to the Healing Brush in this case is to heal in strokes parallel to the shoulder line and as you go down the jaw and chin line. When you do this, one of the strands of hair might be duplicated. Don't worry. Keep going (10.13). A smaller brush using overlapping strokes works better when the healing happens. The trick is to cover the area as shown in Figure 10.13 without lifting the brush.

Note

Photoshop 7 users: The previous version of Photoshop does not allow healing to layers. Do the healing for this step on the Retouch 2 layer.

10.11

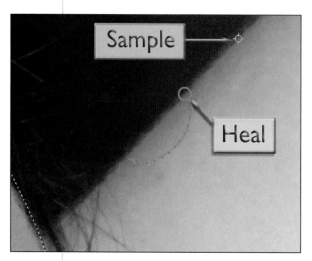

10.12

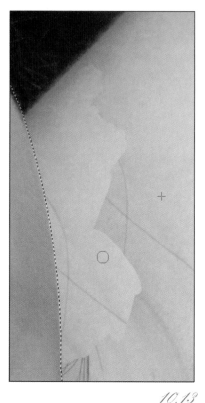

10.13

Resist the temptation to clean up the hair strands on her shoulder. We'll get those in a minute. Start from the same place on Christina's shoulder that you did in the last step and heal up into the dark area along her cheekbone. Heal enough to get the hair away from the line the shoulder makes against the background.

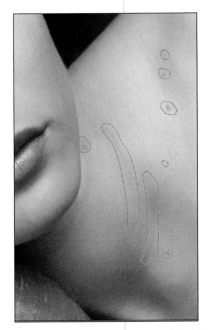

10.14

Step *11*: **Resample (Option/Alt+click) in the background and continue healing up the cheek.**
Clean up the stray hairs in the background and within the selection. You can fix hair outside the selection later.

Step *12*: **Resample the Healing Brush on the skin of her shoulder and clean up the remaining hairs from Step Eleven. Finish healing the hair along her chin.**

Step *13*: **Press ⌘/Control+H to hide the marching ants of the selection.**
Look closely along the chin line. Make sure the healing has blended and that the tones all match. If you can see a line that is out of place, resample in a similar tone and heal the area again.

As long as we're here, let's clean up the areas on her neck and shoulders, especially the lines and blemishes. There is also a scar just below the right side of her chin. I have circled them in red (10.14).

Step *14*: **Press ⌘/Control+D to deselect.**

Step *15*: **Go around Christina's head and heal any hair frizzies that annoy you.**

Note
If Photoshop won't do what you want it to do, stop trying! Often a hidden selection is keeping things from working. Go to the Select menu. If *Select* is not grayed out, a selection is active. Press ⌘/Control+D and go on with life.

Retouching a Face: Part 3

This section is concerned with bringing out the quiet simplicity and beauty of Christina's makeup by healing the small blemishes on the right side of her face. I created a map of the work to be done (10.15). The dots along her eyelid indicate that the area is to be softened, not healed completely.

Step *1*: **Make sure the Heal layer is active and that you are working in actual pixels view (100%).**
Start above her eyebrow and heal the blemishes that are outlined in the map. When it's time to heal the lines under her eyes, sample (Option/Alt+click) to sample directly below the line and heal toward the nose (10.16). The brush size is still 10 pixels. There is a separate step for softening the eyelid, so leave it out for now.

Step *2*: **Zoom in to 200% and look at the whites of the eye.**
Bloodshot? Well not really. Let's clean them up anyway.

Step *3*: **Sample in a clear part of the eye white** (10.17).
Use a fairly small hard brush and heal the blood vessels. Be subtle. Don't overdo it.

10.16

10.15

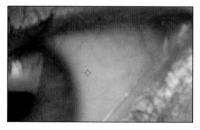

10.17

Step 4: **Sample in the eyelid below the lowest line and heal toward the tear duct using short strokes. Resample often to avoid brushing in a pattern.**

The before and after eyelid healing are illustrated here (10.18).

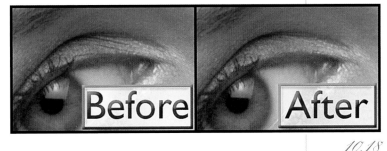

10.18

Step 5: **Now to soften the eyelid line, make a new layer and rename it** Eyelids.

This layer will be used again for the other eyelid.

Step 6: **Sample from the left and above the line in Christina's lid.**

Stroke across the eyelashes, down, and then back up to get the thickness that is shown here (10.19). Lift the pen from the tablet or unclick the mouse.

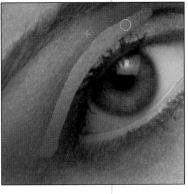

10.19

Step 7: **Now choose Edit→Fade Healing Brush or press ⌘/Control+Shift+F to open the Fade dialog box and set 35% in the Opacity field.**

Sample just above where the last strokes ended and finish healing the lid. Remember to fade the selection to around 35% as well. Click the eye icon on the Eyelids layer on and off to see the effect.

Okay, I admit it. The next two steps are totally anal retentive . . .

Step 8: **Click the Add Layer Mask icon at the bottom of the Layers palette and pick a really teeny-tiny brush (yes, it is supposed to be hyphenated; see the sidebar), say one pixel. Make Black the Foreground color.**

Step 9: **Zoom in to 300% and brush the individual eyelashes back in where they had been slightly faded by the healing step.**

Sheesh. Okay. No one will ever notice that there are 35% fewer lashes there. I'll know. And I want it right. And I know how to make it right. So I did. And now you know how to make it right, too. It feels good doesn't it?

[217]

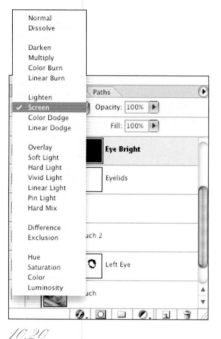

10.20

Now it's time to brighten the iris of her eye.

Step *10*: **Create a new Curves layer by clicking the Create New Adjustment Layer icon at the bottom of the Layers palette and selecting Curves from the pop-up menu.**

Step *11*: **Click OK in the Curves dialog box.**
No changes have been made. Rename the layer **Eye Bright**.

Step *12*: **Press Option/Alt+Delete/Backspace to fill the layer mask with the Foreground color (black).**

Step *13*: **Click the Blending Mode drop-down menu and set the Blending Mode to Screen** (10.20).

Tip

Screen is a blending mode that adds brightness uniformly to the layers below it. A good way to think of Screen is to imagine two slide projectors loaded with identical photographs aimed on a *screen* (cool way to remember this, huh?). One of them is on. Turn the second one on and the projected image doubles in brightness.

Noted retouching artist Rob Carr told me once that when art historians look back on the dawn of digital retouching, they would call it the era of the "too-white-eyes." As our conversation evolved, he explained that eye whites are really gray, so they bring out the eyes themselves — the true windows into the soul of the subject.

Eye Whites Are Really Gray

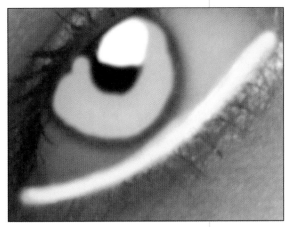

10.21

Step *14*: **Zoom into 200% and select a 10-pixel, soft-edged brush at 100% Opacity.**
Press X to exchange the colors, making the Foreground color white. Carefully brush over the catchlight in the eye.

Step *15*: **Change the brush Opacity to 50% by pressing 5 on the keyboard or using the "scrubby-slider" by dragging over the word *Opacity* in the Options bar.**
You can also use the regular slider or enter **50** in the field.

Step *16*: **Paint in the iris of Christina's eye without lifting the brush.**
This guarantees that the paint is 50%. Leave the dark band that surrounds the eyeball and the pupil alone. Brush a line along the lower lid. If you overpaint, press X to make black the Foreground color and paint the mistake away. Do *not* brighten the whites of the eyes. This figure shows the layer mask super-imposed over the eye to show the painted areas (10.21).

Step *17*: **Zoom out to 50%.**
That eye is scary-bright. Let's tone it down some.

Step *18*: **Press V to select the Move tool. Press 5 to set Eye Bright to 50%.**
That looks so much better.

This chapter has just barely gotten our feet wet in the possibilities of retouching beauty. Don't fret, though. There will be more on the subject throughout the projects to come. And there will be lots of opportunities to practice techniques like brightening eyes and removing lines. There are more than sixteen million gray tones available in an 8-bit RGB color photograph. The next chapter goes through the many methods of making color files into black and white and discusses how they work, and which ones do the job with the most control. The chapter also includes lots of step-by-step demonstrations to help you make the best black and white ever.

Chapter Eleven

Sixteen Million Shades of Gray

I know they'd never match my sweet imagination.
And everything looks worse in black and white.
"Kodachrome" by Paul Simon

Now I'm not suggesting that things look worse in black and white at all. As a matter of fact, listen to Simon and Garfunkel's performance of "Kodachrome" during their Concert in Central Park. They change *worse* to *better* — *Everything looks better in black and white.*

I believe that a good black-and-white photograph is one of the most visually sensuous art forms going. There are so many tones and relationships among them that I feel compelled to become lost in the image. A great print can be so rich I want to pull it over me as if it were a great down comforter on a brisk winter's night.

Black and white seems to be a mystery. Where are all of those cover-me-up tones hiding? How come when the film comes back from the drugstore they look flat? (Duh.) One of the all-time masters of black-and-white photography, Ansel Adams, wrote extensively about producing optimal negatives and prints. This chapter does not pretend to explore black and white anywhere near the depth that Ansel did. My goal in this chapter is to demonstrate several methods of making high-quality black-and-white images from color photographs that exist in the digital space. It doesn't matter if they were scanned from color film or if they were captured digitally. The important consideration is all the information contained in the three black-and-white channels known as RGB.

Chapter 1 explored how digital color consists of three channels of black and white, each shot through a red, green, or blue filter. To illustrate this concept even further, imagine taking three Wratten color separation filters from Kodak — a number 29 Red, a number 58 Green, and a number 47 Blue — and laying them down on a light table so that they overlap. Where red overlaps green, yellow appears. Where green overlaps blue, cyan appears. Where blue overlaps red, magenta appears. Where all three colors overlap the light is white (11.1). Russell Brown, Adobe's Senior Creative Director and author of *The Photoshop Show Starring Russell Brown*, includes a color reference when he demonstrates how black and white works. If you've ever had the opportunity to see Russell in action, you know how dynamic, passionate, and yes, crazy he is. (If you have never seen him in action, take this as a four star recommendation as a must see.)

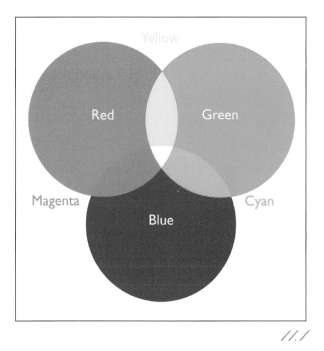

11.1

Seeing Black and White (and Shades of Gray)

There are several methods to convert an RGB image into a black and white one. Some methods are destructive — they throw away the color information. I'll discuss these methods even though I don't recommend them. The others work very well in conjunction with the practice of non-destructive Photoshop editing.

One of the most useful tests available in the darkroom to compare the degrees of exposure is the *ring around*. To conduct this test, create a series of prints varying in degrees of over- and underexposure. Process each print exactly the same, dry them, and then mount them around the "normal" print. The resulting ring around the normal print allows comparison of varying degrees of exposure. Contrast ring-around tests are also useful.

We are going to make an RGB to black-and-white conversion ring-around test to compare the results of each method. The image for this section is available in Chapter 11's folder on www.amesphoto.com/learning.

First we'll create the files for the ring around. This section shows most of the methods of converting color to black and white and what they do in the process. We'll use a photograph of Amanda, a model from the Click agency in Atlanta for this section.

Step *1*: **Open For BW.tif in Photoshop CS by double-clicking it in File Browser.**

Step *2*: **Choose Image→Duplicate. Name the file** Grayscale (11.2).

Step *3*: **Choose Image→Mode→Grayscale. When the Discard color information? dialog box appears, click OK. Save the file as** Grayscale.tif.

Step *4*: **Click the Channels tab.**

There is now only one channel: Gray. This is because all the color was removed during the conversion. You can't tone this file without first converting it back to RGB (11.3).

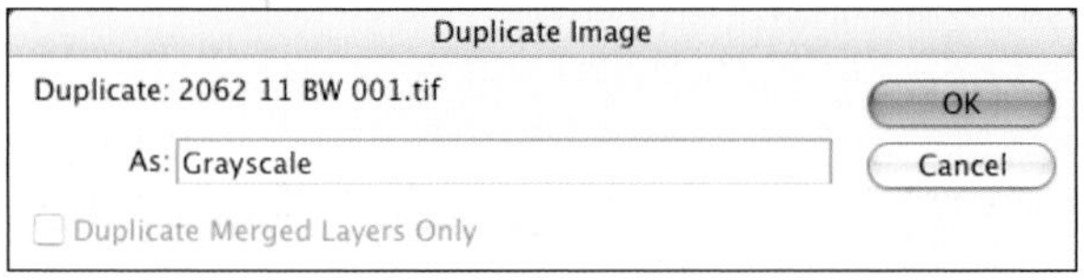

Duplicate Image
Duplicate: 2062 11 BW 001.tif   OK
As: Grayscale   Cancel
☐ Duplicate Merged Layers Only

11.2

11.3

Step 5: **Duplicate For B&W.tif again. Name it** Desaturate.

Step 6: **Choose Image➡Adjustments➡Desaturate.**
Look in the document header. This file is still in RGB. Click the Channels tab for confirmation (11.4). Save the file.

Step 7: **Look at the color circles in Desaturate.tif** (11.5).
The red, green, and blue circles have each been assigned the same pixel value. Each circle now shows the same tone of gray as the other two, including the overlapping complementary color areas.

The rest of the steps use layers and are non-destructive. The first one is kind of off-the-wall. And it has some interesting properties.

Step 8: **Duplicate For B&W.tif once again. Name it** Color Layer.
This method is kind of off-the-wall. It does have some interesting properties.

Step 9: **Click the Create a New Layer icon at the bottom of the Layers palette or press ⌘/Control+Option/ Alt+Shift+N.**

Step 10: **Press D to set the default colors. Fill the layer with either black or white or any neutral tone.**

Step 11: **Change the blending mode to Color.**
The image changes to black and white (11.6).

11.4

11.5

Note
The Desaturate command, when used in multiple layers, affects the active layer only. You can achieve the same effect by choosing Image➡Adjustments➡Hue/ Saturation or a Hue/Saturation adjustment layer and moving the Saturation slider to –100.

The color blending mode applies the hue and saturation of the layer set to Color with the luminosity (grayscale tones) of the layer below it. In this example the color has no hue or saturation so only the grayscale information of the Background layer shows. Let's look at how this can be useful for more than making color into black and white.

Step *12*: **Duplicate Layer 1 by pressing ⌘/Control+J.**

Step *13*: **Choose a 250-pixel soft-edged brush. Set a shade of green as the foreground color. Paint green on the background of Layer 2.**

The background of the image becomes green while retaining the gradations of the spotlight behind Amanda. You can reduce the intensity of green by lowering the opacity (11.7). This is useful in colorizing black-and-white photographs.

Step *14*: **Discard Layer 2 or turn off its eye icon. Save the file as** Color Layer.psd. **Flatten the image and leave it open.**

We'll use it later in this section.

Step *15*: **Make another duplicate For B&W.tif. Name it** CM RGB 33.

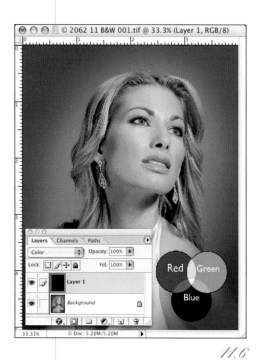

11.6

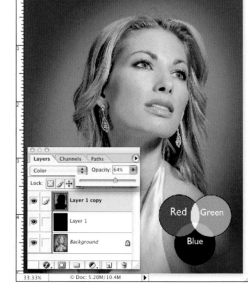

11.7

Step 16: Click the New Adjustment Layer icon at the bottom of the Layers palette and choose Channel Mixer. Enter 33% into each of the Source Channel fields. Select the Monochrome check box then click OK (11.8). Flatten the image and save the file.

The next three versions of For B&W.tif illustrate the effect of each channel individually at 100%.

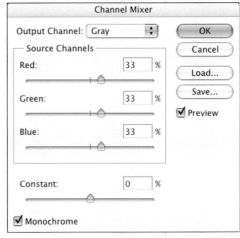

11.8

Step 17: Make three duplicates of For B&W.tif. Name them CM Red100%, CM Green100%, and CM Blue100%.

Step 18: Add a Channel Mixer adjustment layer to CM Red100%. Then leave the Red channel at 100%. Select the Monochrome check box and then click OK. Flatten and save the file.

Step 19: Activate CM Green100%. Add a new Channel Mixer layer. Enter 0 in the Red field and 100 in the Green field. Select the Monochrome check box, and then click OK. Flatten and save the file.

Step 20: Activate CM Blue 100%. Add a new Channel Mixer adjustment layer. Enter 0 in the Red field and 100 in the Blue field. Select the Monochrome check box, and then click OK. Flatten and save the file.

The three 100% versions represent the effect of black-and-white film being exposed through a red, green, or blue filter. Each color filter absorbs its color, leaving it white. This effect is demonstrated by each pure color of the filter turning completely white in the RGB circle according to which color is mixed at 100%. For example the red circle is white when the Channel Mixer is set to 100% red (11.9).

11.9

Let's make two more duplicates to represent a realistic conversion to black and white.

Step 21: **Make another duplicate of For B&W.tif. Name it** CM R 60 G 30 B 10.

Step 22: **Add a Channel Mixer layer. Set the Red field to 60, the Green field to 30, and the Blue field to 10. Select the Monochrome check box and click OK** (11.10). **Flatten the file and save it.**

This conversion is very close to Kodak's black-and-white film Plus-X Pan. We'll make one more conversion for the ring around. This one is specific to the photograph of Amanda.

Step 23: **Make one final copy of For B&W.tif. Name it** CM R 80 G 20.

Step 24: **Add a new Channel Mixer layer to the file. Set the Red field to 80 and the Green to 20. Leave the Blue at 0. Select the Monochrome check box. Click OK. Flatten and save the file.**

I have made a ring around, well, let's call it a chart, of the effects. The document header indicates the effect (11.11). Arrange the documents you created on the screen in the same order. Let's do a row-by-row breakdown.

Note

{ The guideline for using the Channel Mixer is to make certain that the channels add up to no more than 100%. }

Channel Mixer

Output Channel: Gray

— Source Channels —

Red: +60 %

Green: +30 %

Blue: +10 %

Constant: 0 %

☑ Monochrome

OK
Cancel
Load...
Save...
☑ Preview

11.10

The top row shows differences among Grayscale, Desaturate, and the Channel Mixer (RGB 33%) methods. Take a close look at the RGB circles. There is a good distribution of colors in the Grayscale image. The circles show equal amounts of gray in the Desaturate and Channel Mixer (RGB 33%) images. They look flat.

The next row shows the 100% versions of red, green, and blue. The blue channel is least attractive for people. It also contains most of the noise in a digital photo or the grain in a photo shot on film and scanned. It is easy to see that a combination of the red and green channels will yield a better black and white. Move on to row three.

The neutral filled layer in the color blending mode does a respectable job of making color into black and white. The distribution is even, including the complementary colors. Compare it to the Channel Mixer R 60, G 30, B 10. The additional amounts of red and lower amount of blue open up the image. Now look at the last image in the row; the mix of red 80 and green 20 works very well for Caucasian skin.

The best part of Channel Mixer is that it allows each black-and-white conversion to be a custom fit. I love this. Think of it. Every color photograph has all the black-and-white filter possibilities you could ever want! Mixing channels is much more satisfying than mixing chemicals in the darkroom.

11.11

Okay. Let's put this information to work.

Flashback . . . to the '60s, '70s and '80s when high-fashion, contrasting black-and-white photography was very en vogue. The skin tones were almost white if they were not blown-out completely. The images had mystical shadows. Black hair sported the most amazing detail. Eyes simply glowed. And it was all done without computers! How *was* this magic done?

Overexposure was the secret potion back in the day. Photographers added between a stop and a half to two and two-thirds stops of light to the diffused value. (See Chapter 3.) This meant that eyebrows and lips had to be applied significantly darker during makeup to record as a normal tone in the final photograph.

Fast-forward to the new millennium where overexposure still works really well on film though it's not so hot when capturing digitally. This is another example of simple postproduction wizardry. First we'll apply what we've just learned about turning color into black and white. Let's start with a full-color photograph styled and art directed by L.J. Adams of Annie Shu, a model with Elite Model Management/Atlanta (11.12).

Step 1: **Open 2062-D-0325.tif by double-clicking it in File Browser.**

The retouching on this file is already done. When doing black-and-white conversions the retouching should be done first on the color file.

11.13

Step 2: **Do a quick scan of the channels by pressing ⌘/Control+1 for Red, ⌘/Control+2 for Green, and ⌘/Control+3 for Blue** (11.13).

Once again the Red and Green channels have the better tones. Reviewing the channels is a good starting place when starting to convert photographs into black and white.

Step 3: **Return to the composite, full-color view by pressing ⌘/Control+~ (tilde).**

The skin tones are carried in the Red channel. Because Annie has naturally darker skin, we'll want to mix in more green. This step will be important, too, because we are going to open up the highlights later in this project.

Step 4: **Create a new Channel Mixer adjustment layer. Enter 60 in the Red field and 40 in the Green field. Select the Monochrome check box. Click OK. Rename the layer** R 60 G 40.

11.14

Step 5: **Make a new layer. Copy the visible layers to the new one by holding down the Option/Alt key and selecting Merge Visible from the Layer palette's fly-out menu. Name the layer** Base.

The result has good tonal range and contrast 11.14. I want to force attention to Annie's face. Moving the values of the tones in her gown lower would do just that. Now the temptation to use Curves or Levels is huge. There is another way.

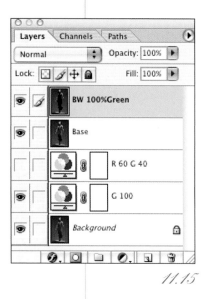

11.15

11.16

Step 6: Hide the Base and R 60 G 40 layers by clicking off their eye icons.

Alternatively, hold down the Option/Alt key and click the eye icon of the Background layer.

Step 7: Make a new Channel Mixer adjustment layer. Enter 0 in the Red field and 100 in the Green one. Select the Monochrome check box. Click OK and name the layer G 100.

Step 8: Make a new layer. Name it BW 100%Green.

Step 9: Merge the Background and G 100 layers to BW 100%Green by holding down the Option/Alt key and choosing Merge Visible from the Layers palette fly-out menu or by pressing ⌘/Control+Option/Alt+Shift+E.

Step 10: Drag BW 100%Green above Base. Click the eye icon on for Base.

The Layers palette looks like this (11.15).

Now there are several ways that the darker tones of the gown could be added to the layer below. The tried-and-true and usually my personal favorite is drawing a path, making a selection, and then adding a layer mask. Another is to add a black layer mask and paint it in with white. Of course, there are the sloppy methods, such as using the Magic Wand (keep your fingers crossed — it helps) to select the gown, and so on. In this case there is an easier way.

Step 11: Double-click the BW 100%Green thumbnail in the Layers palette.

The Layer Style dialog box opens. Look in the Additional Blending section for the Blend If drop-down menu. By default it is set to Gray. Perfect. The key to this step is in the This Layer slider.

Step 12: Click the Highlight slider. Drag it to the left until the highlight window reads 40.

The highlights on the gown from Base show through (11.16).

Step 13: Hold down the Option/Alt key. Drag the right half of the highlight slider until its window (the number right of 40) reads 195. Click OK.

So far the result of all of these steps is making the gown a non-reproducible, way too dark, gray tone. Wait, there's more.

Step *14* : **Select the Color Sampler tool from the toolbox. Hover the cursor over the gown around Annie's middle. Click to place Sampler #1.**

Note the readings in the info palette (11.17). They are all 20. At best the gown is at the threshold of printing shadow areas with detail.

Step *15* : **Lower the opacity of BW 100%Green to 70%.**

Note the shadows measured by the sampler now read 32. They will brighten up when the fashion effect is applied (11.18).

Step *16* : **Click the eye icon of BW 100%Green on and off to see how the eye now naturally falls on Annie's face (11.19).**

Step *17* : **Create a new layer above BW 100%Green. Name it B&W. Merge the visible layers to it. (See Step Nine.)**

Step *18* : **Open the Levels dialog box by choosing Image➤ Adjustments➤Levels or by pressing ⌘/Control+L. Hold down the Option/Alt key. Drag the highlight slider to the left.**

The document window goes black as the highlight slider starts to move. This is a good thing. Drag until white areas appear. Remember the area while returning the slider to its original position on the far right.

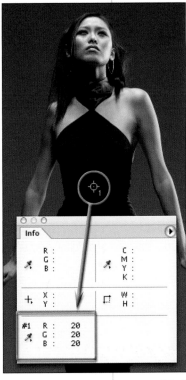

11.17

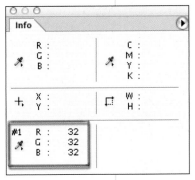

11.18

11.19

Step *19*: While watching the info palette, move the cursor around the area until it is over the area with the highest value, probably around 232. Hold down the Shift key and click to place Sampler #2. Click Cancel to close the Levels dialog box.

Step *20*: Make a new Curves adjustment layer. When the dialog box opens, click OK without making any changes. Name it Curves 1. Change the blending mode to Screen.

The entire image brightens. Most important, Annie's face takes on that sixties almost-blown-out face and very open shadows look of overexposure. Note the Info palette. The shadows are way open at 59 (Sampler #1) and the brightest highlights are at 252 (Sampler #2) (11.20). All that's left is to focus the effect.

Step *21*: Choose the Elliptical Marquee tool. Draw a selection around the inside of the photograph's frame.

Step *22*: Choose Select➡Transform Selection. Drag the side handles of the bounding box toward the center point until the selection looks like this (11.21). Select the Commit check box.

11.20

11.21

[234]

Step 23: Drag the selection up until the lower half of the selection cuts through Annie's hands (11.22). Fine-tune its position with the arrow keys.

Step 24: Inverse the selection by pressing ⌘/Control+Shift+I.

Step 25: Fill the selection with black by choosing Edit→Fill Use: Black (11.23). Press ⌘/Control+D to deselect.

That hard edge is just not elegant. Let's fix it.

Step 26: Choose Filter→Blur→Gaussian Blur to open the Gaussian Blur dialog box. Enter 130.4 pixels in the Radius field. Click OK.

Step 27: Back off the Opacity of Curves 1 to 80%.

Step 28: Make a new layer above Curves 1. Merge the visible layers to it. Rename the layer Final. Save your work.

Step 29: Option/Alt+click the eye icon of the Final layer to hide the layers under it. Click the eye icon of the Base layer. Click the eye icon of Final on and off to see the before and after (11.24).

11.22

11.24

11.23

That's pretty much it. The Curves adjustment layer set to Screen has provided variable overexposure through the opacity and the layer mask. Annie's face and shoulders are now the highest tonal values. They are guaranteed to draw the viewer's eye. The tones of her gown make an arrow shape that point the eye toward her feet. The highlights once again bring the viewer to her face.

Having Fun with Black and White

The best part of working in black and white in Photoshop is that it doesn't take hours and hours to play in the darkroom. There are no chemicals, no water, no dark . . . yes, I do occasionally play DVDs while doing postproduction. One of the best things about Photoshop is that my clothes no longer have fixer stains nor do my hands carry chemical smells. Using Photoshop is so much better, and in this section I provide a series of how-to's that include adding grain and toning photographs digitally.

ADDING GRAIN

11.25

Think about this. Film has grain. Digital does not have grain. When film was the only option, we talked incessantly about techniques for reducing the amount of grain in a photograph. Digital has no grain. So what are we talking about now? That's right. The topic on the table is how to add grain to digital files to (are you ready for this?) make them look more like film. Sheesh!

Step 1: **Open 2062-F-0293.tif by double-clicking it in File Browser.**
This file has already been retouched and converted to black and white. It is an 8-bit file (11.25).

Step 2: **Make a duplicate layer by pressing ⌘/Control+J. Name it** Base. **Click the eye icon off for the Background layer.**

Step 3: **Duplicate the Base layer. Rename it** Grain (11.26).

Step 4: **Choose Filter→Filter Gallery. Click the disclosure triangle for the Artistic filters. Click (what else?) Film Grain. Set 15 in the Grain field. Set the Highlight to 15 and leave the Intensity field at 10. Click OK.**

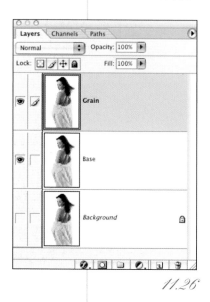

11.26

Note

The Filter Gallery is a new feature in Photoshop CS that enables you to apply multiple filters sequentially at the same time. Think of it as layers for filters. The dialog box is divided by default into three panes. On the left is the preview pane. The center pane houses the thumbnails of the available filters. The right-hand pane displays the options for each filter. Below that is the filter stack. The chosen filters are applied in the order they appear in the stack from the bottom up. Rearrange them for drastic changes in the effect. The Filter Gallery is worth hours of play. Play is the wellspring of creativity. Play well and prosper creatively!

11.27

Step 5: **Zoom in to 100% and scroll to Marie's face. Study the result of Film Grain filter on the photograph** (11.27).

It is scary grainy. A natural response to too much of anything in Photoshop is to lower the opacity.

Step 6: **Enter** 50% **in the Opacity field with the Grain layer active** (11.28).

The result is more pleasing, appearing to be that of a photograph blown up from a negative shot on Kodak's Tri-X Pan film from a 35mm camera. Let's look at some modifications.

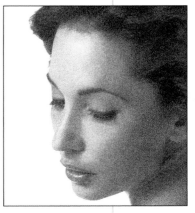

11.28

Step 7: **Duplicate Grain by pressing ⌘/Control+J. Rename the layer** Grain Blurred.

Grain on film is not sharp edged. It is sharp when it is created digitally. Let's soften it some to make it look more film-like.

Step 8: **Choose Filter➡Blur➡Gaussian Blur. Set the pixel radius to** 1.0. **Click OK. Compare the results** (11.29).

The image is softer overall due to the soft edges created by the blur. Of course there's more. Let's explore finer grain.

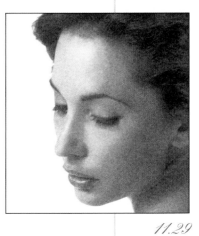

11.29

Step *9*: **Click the eye icon for Grain off. Lower the Opacity of Grain Blurred to 20%** (11.30).

This figure represents a fine grain film. There is one more subtle addition.

Step *10*: **Click the Grain layer and lower its Opacity to 20%.** Adding the sharp grain layer to the blurred one makes the structure appear subtly better. The grain effect you'll use on a printed piece will need tweaking depending on the paper you choose. Add the grain after you have sized the file for output (11.31).

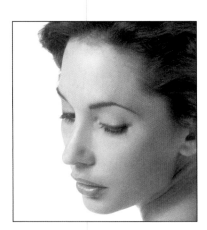

11.30

11.31

TONING PHOTOGRAPHS DIGITALLY

Traditional methods for toning photographs often required very offensive-smelling chemistry, especially if the desired result was the popular sepia-toned print. The process was very time consuming, not totally repeatable, and hard on the nose. The odor was caused by sulfur and was reminiscent of rotten eggs. Lovely.

Toning images using tools in Photoshop has improved the results by making subtle changes quickly possible, repeatable, and (whew) odor free.

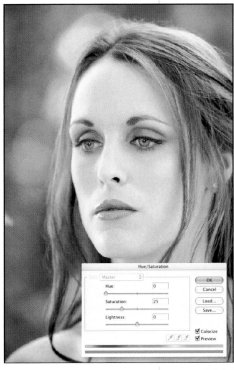

11.32

Step 1: **Double-click 2062-P-203.psd in File Browser to open the photograph of Cara in Photoshop.** The Channel Mixer layer that converts the photograph to black and white is already in the layer stack.

Step 2: **Make a new layer and merge the Background layer and Channel Mixer to their own layer. Name it** B&W.

Step 3: **B&W is highlighted. Create a new Hue/Saturation adjustment layer. Select the check box next to Colorize (the only function in Photoshop that actually does what it's named).** The default setting is a red tone (11.32).

Step 4: **Drag the Hue slider to the right until 33 appears in the field.** It's that simple. Sepia! No fuss, no muss, and best of all, no smell (11.33)!

Hue controls the color, so let's explore the other sliders. We already know that moving the Saturation slider to 0 makes the image black and white. Because the base is already black and white, we won't go there.

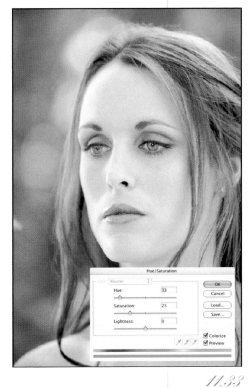

11.33

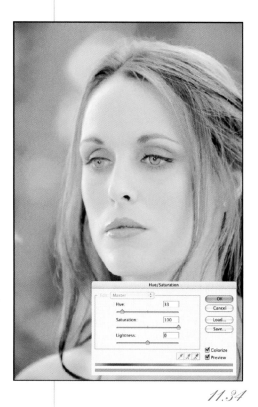

11.34

11.35

Step *5*: **Move the Saturation slider to the right until the field reads 100.**

Bright, huh? This is a great place to look for false, dare I say, "oversaturated" colors (11.34). Now for the Lightness slider — moving it all the way to 0 on the left makes the image black. Black without white isn't particularly useful. We'll go the other direction.

Step *6*: **Move the Lightness slider to the right and a reading of 80.**

When this slider reaches 100, the image is white (11.35). Save the file. Don't close it just yet. We'll use it in the following "PowerSection" for Photoshop power users. This is a great way to make an image have the ghosted-back look for use behind type or as a background for a Web site.

Another method for toning is to uses a Curves adjustment layer in place of the Hue/Saturation adjustment layer. You can also use a Curves adjustment to fine-tune the colors and contrast of the Hue/Saturation layer effect. Experiment, play, enjoy!

Faking Colors

I now want to show you a great new feature of Photoshop CS, the Photo Filter adjustment layer, and a different way to use it. The Photo Filter's purpose is to adjust the overall color of a photograph. Let's start there.

Step 1: **Open the File Browser and double-click 2062-D-0366.tif** (11.36).

Step 2: **Click the New Adjustment Layer icon at the bottom of the Layers palette and choose Photo Filter from the drop-down menu.**
The dialog box opens with the default warming filter 85B selected. Drag the Density slider to the right until it reads 40%. The image warms up. Click OK (11.37).

These two steps show the real use of the Photo Filter. It's great for adding that extra touch of color. This is the chapter on black and white and the section on faking color. We move on.

11.36

11.37

Step *3*: We won't use the Photo Filter layer again so you can either delete the Photo Filter layer or (Mr. Non-Destructive Photoshop here) click the eye icon off. Make a new Channel Mixer adjustment layer. Set the Red field to 60% and the Green field to 40%. Leave the Blue field at 0. Select the Monochrome check box. Click OK (11.38).

Step *4*: Create a new Photo Filter adjustment layer. Just for fun, drag the slider over to about 55.
Hmm . . . another way to tone a photograph (11.39). I digress.

Step *5*: From the Filter drop-down menu select Deep Red. Enter 100 into the Density field and deselect the Preserve Luminosity check box. Click OK.

Step *6*: The Power User shortcut keys come into play to merge the visible layers to a new layer – hold down ⌘/Control+Option/Alt+Shift press N and then press E. Rename the layer Red. Turn its eye icon off.

Step *7*: Double-click the Photo Filter 2 thumbnail to open it. (If you deleted the Photo Filter in Step Three, it will be Photo Filter 1.) Change the color to Deep Emerald then click OK.

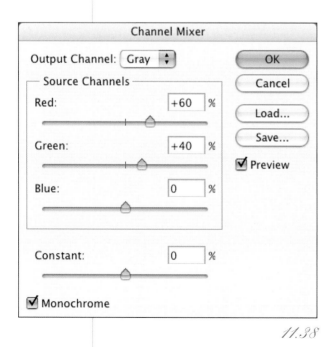

11.38

11.39

Step *8*: **Press the Power User New Layer and Merge keys (refer to Step Six). Rename the layer** Green. **Turn off the layer's eye icon.**

Step *9*: **Open the Photo Filter layer again. Change the drop-down menu to (you guessed it) Deep Blue** (11.40). **Click OK.**

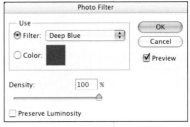

11.40

Step *10*: **Do the merge thing again. Rename the layer** Blue. **Hide the layer by clicking its eye icon off.**

Step *11*: **Hide the Photo Filter Layer.**
We'll need a black and white layer, too.

Step *12*: **Merge the remaining visible layers to one layer and name it** B&W. **Drag it above the Red layer.**

Step *13*: **Duplicate the Background layer and rename it** Color. **Drag it into position below B&W.**
The layer stack looks like this (11.41).

Step *14*: **Save the file as** BW2Color.psd.
All the preliminary layer creation is finished. We'll use them to create a step-and-repeat photograph that represents the black-and-white channels making a full-color image.

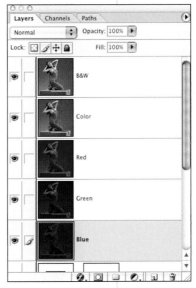

11.41

Creating the Composition

Now we will use the Marquee tool, the Move tool, and layer styles to make our work of art. The first part of the project is to make the image large enough to hold it.

Step *1*: **Choose Image→Canvas Size.**
At the top of the dialog is Current Size section. It tells us that the file is 9.653 inches high and 9.653 inches wide. The Relative check box should be selected.

Step *2*: **Enter** 10 **in the Width field. Click the center square in the left-hand column of the Anchor box. Click OK.**
The black-and-white image is on the left side. The right side of the image is white.

Step *3*: **Select the Rectangular Marquee tool. In the Options bar set the Style drop-down menu to Fixed Size. Enter** 3 in **(for inches) in the Width field, and in the Height field enter** 10 in.

Step *4*: Highlight the Red layer. Click in the image file and a 3 x 10-inch selection appears. Position it as shown here (11.42).

Step *5*: Press ⌘/Control+J to make the selection into its own layer. Drag the new red layer automatically named Layer 1 above B&W.

Step *6*: Hold down the ⌘/Control key and click Layer 1 to load its pixels as a selection. Activate the Green layer by clicking its thumbnail in the layer stack. Press ⌘/Control+J to make the selection into Layer 2. Drag it above B&W and below Layer 1.

Step *7*: Once again hold down the ⌘/Control key and click Layer 2 to load those pixels as a selection. Click the Blue layer to activate it. Hold down the ⌘/Control+J to make the selection into Layer 3. Drag the new layer above B&W and below Layer 2. The image and layer stack looks like this (11.43).

11.42

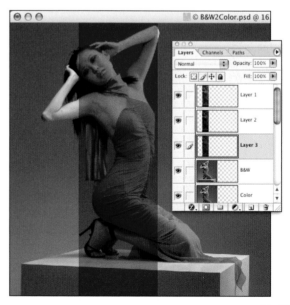

11.43

Step *8*: Select the Move tool from the toolbox. Highlight Layer 1. Start dragging the red panel to the right. After you start dragging hold down the Shift key to constrain the movement horizontally.

Step *9*: Highlight Layer 2. Drag the green layer to the right of the red one. Remember to hold down the Shift key after you start dragging. Use the arrow keys to nudge the green image right next to the red one.

11.44

Step *10*: Highlight Layer 3. Drag the blue layer to the right of the green one (11.44).

Step *11*: Highlight the Color layer. Drag it to the far right until the box Annie is kneeling on almost touches the edge of the frame. Hold down the Shift key to constrain the move horizontally (11.45).

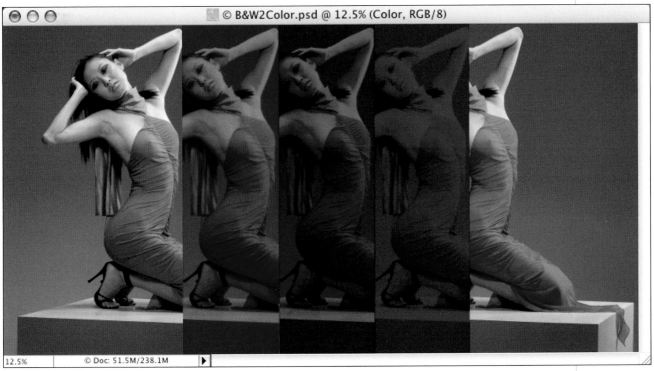

11.45

Step *12*: **Highlight B&W and link Layers 1, 2, 3 with it by clicking the box next to their eye icons. Drag all the linked layers to the left until the blue section reveals Annie's head. The left elbow on B&W will go out of the frame** (11.46).

This looks good and can look better with the application of a layer style.

Step *13*: **Double-click in the thumbnail of Layer 1 to open the Layer Styles dialog box. Select the Bevel & Emboss check box. Click the words *Bevel & Emboss* to open their specific controls. Set the following settings in the Structure section: Style = Inner Bevel, Technique = Smooth, Depth = 251, Size = 13, and Soften = 9. Click OK** (11.47).

Finally we'll duplicate the Bevel and Emboss effect to the green and blue layers.

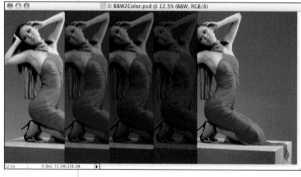

11.46

11.47

Step *14*: **In the layer stack, click the word *Effects* under Layer 1 and drag it under Layer 2. Click the newly arrived Effects under Layer 2 and drag it under Layer 3 (11.48).**

That's it. The photograph representing the stages of color from black-and-white channels is finished (11.49). In making it we have explored the Channel Mixer and Photo Filter adjustment layers, creating new images in the layer stack, and cutting them into our step-and-repeat creation.

In the next chapter, the subject is lingerie for a magazine editorial. We're shooting on location so turn the page to join me, the crew, and our model Carrie Thomas in a high-rise condominium on Atlanta's famous Peachtree Street.

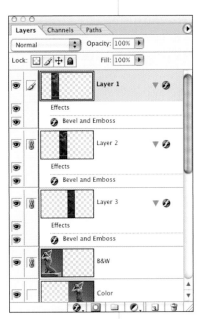

11.48

11.49

Chapter Twelve

Lingerie: A Day Being a Girl

The camera is a passport into worlds we might otherwise be denied travel.
Kevin Ames

Women fascinate me. Like many, many men, I love them, I like them, and I am an outsider in their world. Women do things that are totally understandable to other women and yet very mysterious to the men in their lives. My love of photographing women has offered a glimpse into their world. It isn't a secret one, especially to them. As a matter of surprise to me, when I asked about ironing in their underwear, every one of them said they did it, often. Why? "Because the outfit I want to wear is the one I'm ironing." Who knew?

Men don't think much about their underwear. Our choices are limited: boxers or tightey-whiteys. Women on the other hand, love lingerie. Wearing it makes them feel good, sexy, desirable, cute, fun, happy, pretty, beautiful, and more. Shopping for it does, too. One model told me that she enjoyed walking down the street knowing how beautiful she looked in her underwear even though no one else did.

Many women also love quiet, alone time. Playing piano, lounging on the sofa, putting on makeup, ironing, or dreamily watching the world through a window is somehow better in lingerie.

Over afternoon coffee, Linda Adams, a freelance art director/ stylist, and I decide to produce a "day of life in lingerie" editorial. A lot of planning goes into the actual day of shooting. Our list includes location, hair and makeup, wardrobe, styling assistant, and photographic/digital assistant.

The location is a two-bedroom, fourth-floor condo overlooking world-famous Peachtree Street in Atlanta. Carrie Thomas from the Elite Modeling Agency is the model. Janeen Loria does the makeup and hair. Cristle Grizzelle handles wardrobe. Linda picks the colors and styles to match each scene. Assistant Justin Larose and I set the lighting, camera angle, and settings. Like a movie, the editorial is not shot in sequence. The window light dictates the time each setup is photographed.

The lighting is kept simple. One flash head on a light stand, a 42-inch x 72-inch Chimera panel with reflector or a diffusion fabric, and a flag to keep flare off of the lens is the whole kit.

The entire shoot is done with a Kodak DCS-760C digital camera tethered to a Macintosh Titanium G-4 PowerBook G4 with a 30GB OWC Mercury On-The-Go FireWire drive. The external hard drive makes it possible to capture an almost unlimited number of images. Each scene is set, lit, and photographed with a GretagMacbeth ColorChecker Gray Scale Balance Card. The reference is used to set the diffused value on the camera. It is used later in postproduction for neutralizing the color.

While I am shooting, Justin watches each image as it appears on the PowerBook. He monitors the changing window light. Linda watches the take on the laptop and steps in to smooth wrinkles or adjust a prop. The team behind the camera frees me to work with Carrie on pose and expression. Their feedback is important, too. It lets us all push the work farther than is prudent when shooting film.

The shoot continues through the day and finally wraps with everyone out the door by seven o'clock. We have made over eight hundred photographs of eight scenes in ten hours. Linda and Cristle gather up the lingerie and accessories. Carrie changes into to her street clothes. Janeen packs up her makeup. Justin and I load the gear into the car. Everybody says goodbye.

Back at the studio, the raw files on the FireWire drive are renumbered in File Browser, divided into CD-sized folders in the Finder (or Windows Explorer), and burned to CDs. The ten archived discs are proofed by making JPGs from each file. A Web photo gallery is generated in Photoshop and then posted to the Web. E-mails with links go out to the team who worked on the shoot and the magazine's photo editor. It is ten o'clock. Justin and I grab a quick meal and call it a night.

Having shot with film all my life, the speed the images are ready for review amazes me. I hope I never take this for granted. I know clients will as this process becomes commonplace. For better or not we live in a want-it-right-this-second world. In the morning over coffee at Aurora (my favorite Atlanta coffeehouse), I'll review the take on my laptop and pick the photographs I like for the editorial and to use in this chapter.

The projects in this chapter concern using Photoshop to solve photographic issues that would have taken too much time to fix on location, such as overly shiny brass window handles. Sometimes the problem is degrees bigger, such as when a manufacturer sends a bustier set that is a size too small for the model. Read on . . .

This chapter explores some of the photographic techniques of Adobe Photoshop CS. It also discusses how to create strategy maps for retouching, and healing to layers. To get started, download the files for Chapter 12 from www.amesphoto.com/learning.

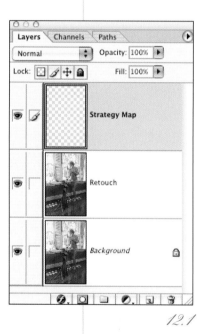

12.1

Creating the Strategy Map

Step *1*: **Click the downloaded folder in File Browser.**
When the light table populates, double-click 2062-M-0171.tif to open it. The file is in 16-bit per channel color.

Step *2*: **Duplicate the Background layer by pressing ⌘/Control+J or by choosing Image➡Duplicate Layer and click OK.**
Rename the layer **Retouch**.

Step *3*: **Create a new layer by typing ⌘/Control+Option /Alt+Shift+N or by chooseing Layer➡New➡Layer and click OK.**
Name the layer **Strategy Map** (12.1).

Step *4*: **Press B+Shift+B to select the Pencil tool, and set the pixel size to 4.**

Quality versus Speed	The work in this section is done using 16-bit files, which are twice as big as 8-bit files. The higher bit depth files provide the best quality. If the computer you are using operates a lot slower as you work through the following steps, these bigger files are probably the reason. To speed things up choose Image➡Mode➡8 Bits/ Channel. The techniques are the same.

Step 5: **Open the Swatches palette and select RGB Green** (12.2).

Step 6: **Zoom in to view actual pixels at 100% by typing ⌘/Control+Option/Alt+0 (zero) and then press the Home key.** Examine the photograph tile by tile by pressing the Page Down key on the keyboard. ⌘/Control+Page Up moves the view one tile to the right. ⌘/Control+Page Down moves it one tile to the left. You have to hold down the Fn key, too, on Mac laptops. Windows laptops vary according to manufacturer whim. As you page through the image, circle the areas to be cleaned up in green. Refer to my version of the Map and compare it with yours. They will be different. You and I are different. We don't see things the same way either. This is good. Save the file as **2062-M-0171.psd**.

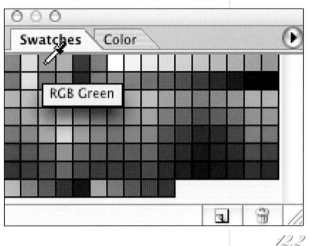

12.2

Not all photographs require massive amounts of retouching. This one is typical of the tweaks that an image receives to get it ready for output.

Step 7: **Create a new layer above Retouch and name it** Healing.

Step 8: **Press J to select the Healing brush, and on the Options bar click the Use All Layers check box.**

Step 9: **Click the eye icon next to the Strategy Map layer to hide the layer and then start at Carrie's neck and heal all the circled areas, working down her body. Use the healing brush to remove the electrical cord from the floor. We'll burn down the window sill on the left later.** Click the Strategy Map eye icon on periodically to make sure you are healing all the circled areas. Don't be concerned with the window hardware. That fix comes later. When you are finished, press ⌘/Control+S to save your work.

Tip

You can change *Copy* to *8-bit* in the Duplicate Image dialog box.

TIF and PSD

Photoshop CS's ability to work extensively in 16-bit is new and a welcome addition. Yet this new workflow offers potential problems to output vendors, service bureaus, pre-press houses, and corporate clients who might not understand what 16-bit is and how it works with previous versions of Photoshop. Very few output devices can use 16-bit files. Graphics professionals blame the file as being corrupt when it won't output. Sometimes the problem is that a 16-bit file was delivered instead of one in 8-bit. Establishing a convention of what file type carries which bit depth will be useful. In my workflow, the 16-bit TIF file generated either from Camera Raw or a camera manufacturer's software is modified in Photoshop CS in layers. When I finish the work I save the image as a Photoshop document with the same name as the original 16-bit TIF file only with the extension .psd.

I then flatten the file when the postproduction is complete and save it with the same name only as a TIF file with the .tif extension. It overwrites the original TIF file. The PSD file carries the original TIF file in its Background layer. PSD files are always working files. They have the layers. PSDs are never delivered to clients. They are work product; you might think of them as proprietary information that is your exclusive property. TIF files are always either *origination* files (the raw file is the original, remember) or *delivery* files that go to clients for output. Although TIF files *can* save layers, most of today's applications can't use them. *Never save layered files as .tifs.*

Note: The first time you save a file with layers, save it as a *Photoshop* file (.psd.) There are only two working files for each image. One is a TIF and the other is a

Restoring Shiny Hardware

The brass handle on the window and catch on the shutter are blown out in this photograph. It makes sense that reflective surfaces would do this especially when they are as strongly backlit as they are in this scene. To restore the handles and shutter catch in the final image, shooting a set of background brackets with the model out of the scene. It is a good practice to capture a background image just for its bits and pieces. An image that is "underexposed" can provide exactly the right parts for the final image. All that matters is that the camera angle is very close. Ideally, you would make a set of scene brackets every time you zoom a lens or pan the camera. This isn't practical. It breaks the flow of the shoot.

Step ⁄: **Open 2062-M-0064.tif.**
It has already been prepared for this step. This file is dimensionally the same size as 2062-M-0171.psd.

PSD. There is an exception. Some functions in Photoshop – mainly filters – do not work on 16-bit files. The workflow for these images is to finish the 16-bit editing and save the file as a .psd. From the Image menu select Duplicate Image. This duplicate will be named the same as the original file with the addition of the word *copy* before the .psd extension (12.3). Convert this file to 8-bit. The word *copy* in the name of a PSD file is the cue that it is destined to become an 8-bit image.

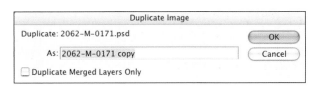

12.3

Look at this figure (12.4). The photograph on the left is 16-bit. There are three clues: one from the workflow and two from Photoshop. The workflow clue is that *copy* is not in the header. Photoshop states the color space and the bit depth of the file in the header, in this case RGB/16. The document size at the bottom left of the window is twice as big as the 8-bit file.

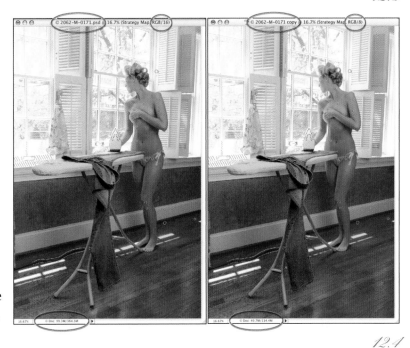

12.4

Step *2*: **Choose the Lasso tool from the toolbar or press L to select it.**

Step *3*: **Locate the handle on 0064 and draw a selection around it** (12.5).

Step *4*: **Select the Move tool from the toolbar or press V and click inside the selection.**
Hold down the Shift key and drag the selection onto 0179. It becomes a layer in 0179's stack. Rename it **Handle**.

Step *5*: **Drag the handle over the one by the iron in 0179.**
It does not exactly match.

12.5

Step *6*: Press 5 on the keyboard to lower the Handle layer's Opacity to 50% and nudge it so the upper-left corner is positioned over the blown-out version (12.6).

Step *7*: Press ⌘/Control+T to select the Free Transform tool and drag the anchor point from the center of the bounding box to the corner where both handles align (12.7).

Step *8*: Hold down the Shift key, click the lower-right hand corner handle, and drag it diagonally away from the anchor point.

The handle enlarges. Drag until it is slightly larger than the one it will replace Adjust the rotation if necessary.

Step *9*: Click the check mark in the Options bar to accept the changes or press Return/Enter.

Step *10*: Press 0 (zero) to return the Opacity of the Handle layer to 100%.

Step *11*: Create a layer mask on the Handle layer by clicking the Add Layer Mask icon at the bottom of the Layers palette or choosing Layer➡Add Layer Mask➡Reveal All.

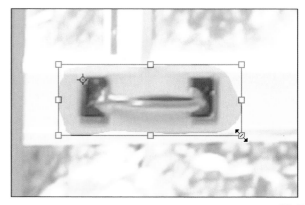

12.7

12.6

Step *12*: Press ⌘/Control++ (plus sign) to zoom in to 200% and select a soft 20-pixel brush (12.8).

Step *13*: Set the foreground color to black.
D sets the default colors of black and white. X exchanges them if needed.

12.8

Step *14*: Paint over the white paint on the Handle layer.
Leave a bit of the shadow under the handle itself. If you paint out the handle, press X to switch white to the foreground and paint it back in. Press X to go back to black. When you work on the inside edges of the handle, press the left bracket ([) key to reduce the brush size to 10-pixels (12.9).

12.9

Step *15*: Zoom out to the actual pixels view – 100%.
The handle is now too dark. Changing the opacity of the Handle layer will only make it transparent. Here's how to lighten just the handle: Click the New Adjustment Layer icon at the bottom of the Layers palette and select Curves. When the Curves dialog box appears Click OK. Rename it **Lighten Handle**.

Step *16*: Hold down the Option/Alt key and position the cursor between the Lighten Handle and Handle layers.
The nesting cursor appears.

Step *17*: Click and the Lighten Handle layer indents and a down-pointing arrow appears indicating that this layer is now grouped with Handle.
Handle is now underlined indicating it, too, is part of a group (12.10).

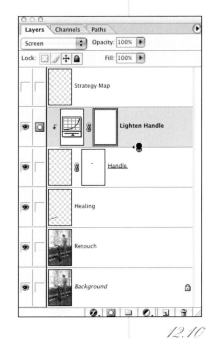

12.10

12.11

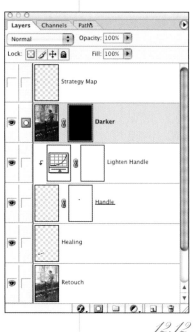

12.12

Step 18: **Change the blending mode of Lighten Handle to Screen.**

The handle is brighter and not blown out (12.11). Photographic believability is in the details!

Step 19: **Return to File Browser and double-click 2062-M-0171darker.tif to open it.**

Step 20: **Select the Move tool from the toolbox. Press the Shift key and drag 2062-M-0171darker.tif onto 2062-M-0171.psd.**

This adds the darker version above Lighten Handle in the layer stack. Name the new layer Darker.

Step 21: **Add a layer mask filled with black to Darker by pressing the Option/Alt key and clicking the Add layer mask icon at the bottom of the Layers palette (12.12).**

Step 22: **Select a 50-pixel brush with a soft edge at 100% opacity. Set white as the foreground color. Brush on Darker's layer mask and bring back the lower part of the window.**

Paint the sill back in as well. Change the brush opacity to 25%. Brush the blown out mullion back in. When the brush is at a lower opacity, each new stroke builds up paint to a total of 25%.

Step 23: **Repeat Steps Two through Twelve on the other handle. Paint in the layer mask of Darker to reduce the shine on the pull above the clasp behind Carrie's head.**

Squaring the Shot

One last thing about this photograph: It's a receding perspective caused by a low angle with the camera tilted up. Look at the windows behind Carrie. Their vertical lines are not perpendicular with the floor. That's the hard way to say: "The camera wasn't level when the photograph was made." It happens even when the camera is on a tripod as it was for all the images in this chapter. Oh well. Nobody's perfect. Especially me.

By now you have more than likely figured out that this little kind of thing can really bother me. If it doesn't make you crazy, skip this next section. On the other hand, if you want to follow along I'll quickly correct this faux pas.

Step 1: Press ⌘/Control+R on the keyboard to show the rulers and click in the vertical ruler and drag out a guide. Line it up with a mullion, one of the vertical dividers in the window pane. I have exaggerated the line by highlighting it in green.

Sure enough, the whole image is skewed clockwise (12.13).

Step 2: Double-click the Background layer.

When the New Layer dialog box appears with the name *Layer 0*, click OK.

Step 3: Make sure that the eye icon on Strategy Map is off and highlight Handle (you did fix the other handle, didn't you?) and make a new layer either by clicking the Create a New Layer icon at the bottom of the Layers palette or by choosing Layer→New→Layer. Rename the layer Final.

All the retouching is finished. And the work is finished except for this picky bit . . .

12.13

Step 4: Hold down the Option/Alt key and select Merge Visible from the Layer palette fly-out menu (12.14).

All the visible layers have been copied and merged together on the Final layer.

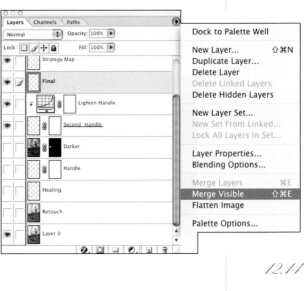

12.14

Turn the Strategy Map layer on and turn off all the other layers except Layer 0. Turn the eye icon on the Final layer on and off. If every circle in the Strategy Map layer blinks, the work is complete. If areas outside the map blink, you did extra work. Congratulations! You are becoming just like me (now is a good time to be afraid . . . very afraid). Kidding. Fix any that might have been missed.

Checking Work

[259]

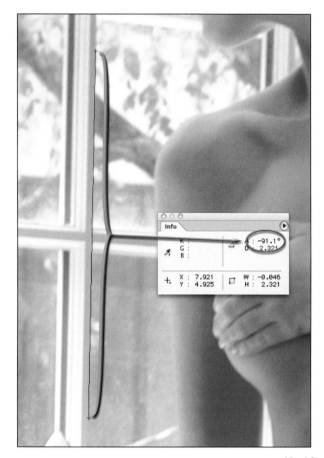

12.15

Step *5*: **Select the Measure Tool from the Eyedropper fly-out menu in the toolbar and then click and drag along the mullion in the window from Carrie's arm up to her eye** (12.15).
The Info palette reads 86°.

Step *6*: **Choose Edit➡Transform➡Rotate.**
The measurement 1.1° is automatically entered in the angle window in the Options bar. The problem is that Transform doesn't know which direction to rotate so it defaults to clockwise. The preview does, too.

Step *7*: **Enter a minus sign (-) in front of the 1.1° in the window.**
The preview corrects itself.

Step 8: **Click the Commit Transform check box or press Return/Enter.**

Take a look at the amount of rotation by Option/Alt+clicking on Final's eye icon. This hides all the layers except the active one. The transparent areas show just how "off" 1.1° is. All's right with the world except for the transparency where Final was rotated (12.16).

Step 9: **Press ⌘/Control+; (semicolon) to hide the guide.**

Final is highlighted and a brush icon appears next to the eye icon, indicating that any changes will be made to this layer.

Step 10: **Press C to select the Crop tool.**

Step 11: **Draw a cropping box around the image excluding the transparent areas. Select the Hide button in the Cropped Area section of the Options bar (12.17). Click the Commit Crop check box or press Return (Enter).**

The file looks cropped. All the information is still there.

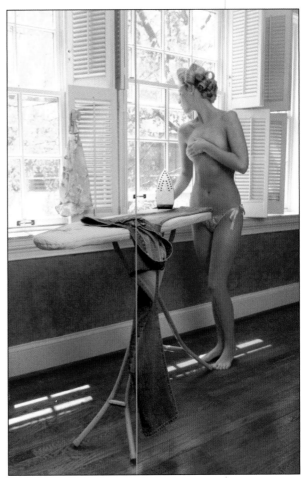

12.16

12.17

Selecting the Hide button does exactly that. It hides the cropped area from view. The entire image is still there. Click into the Move tool and highlight the Final layer. Drag it back and forth. Sure enough, there is the cropped transparency. Hide the Final layer and highlight only Layer 0. Drag it from side to side. The cropped data appears. Increase the canvas size to get all the cropped data back. Non-destructive Photoshop! Woo-Hoo!

Where Did It Go?

Creating Midday Mood Lighting

I love this next shot — even though the light of mid-afternoon clashes a bit with the mood one might imagine for this ensemble of lingerie by La Perla. The day outside wants to be darker and the room secondary to Carrie who is the center of attention.

Step 1: Open 2062-M-0642.psd from the folder of images for this chapter.

I included a retouching strategy map so you can practice using the Healing brush non-destructively. (See the previous section of this chapter.) Do all the retouching before you go on to Step Two.

Step 2: Click the Strategy Map eye icon to turn it off.

This step drops the values of the light outside and coming through the window.

Step 3: Create a new Curves adjustment layer and rename it Window.

Step 4: Make black the foreground color and then fill the Window layer mask with black by clicking Option/Alt+Delete/Backspace (12.18).

Step 5: Change Window's blending mode to Multiply.

Step 6: Duplicate the Window layer by typing ⌘/Control+J, and rename it Sofa & Floor.

Step 7: Select the Brush tool and set it to 900 pixels with a soft edge and 100% Opacity.

Step 8: Highlight the Windows layer and change the foreground color to white.

Paint from the upper-left hand corner to the right corner. The windows darken dramatically.

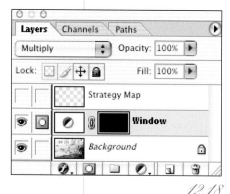

12.18

16-Bit Editing

Layers is a new feature set available in Photoshop CS. This entire section is retouched in 16-bit. This workflow assures the highest quality file is available for output. If you are working in Photoshop version 7, open 2062-M-0642.tif and convert it to 8 bits before continuing.

Step 9: Highlight the Sofa & Floor layer and change the Opacity of this layer to 50%.

Paint over the left side of the sofa and across the floor.

Step 10: Create a new layer and rename it Vignette.

Step 11: Draw an oblong circle around Carrie using the Elliptical Marquee tool.

Step 12: Choose Select➡Transform Selection.

Rotate and/or size the circle until it looks like the one shown here (12.19). Click the Commit Transform check mark or press Return/Enter (12.20).

12.19

Step 13: Option/Alt+click the Add New Layer Mask icon to add a layer mask to Vignette.

The layer mask is active. You can tell by the frame around Carrie and because the layer mask icon is displayed next to the eye icon.

Step 14: Click the layer thumbnail.

The frame moves to it and the icon next to the eye icon changes to a brush.

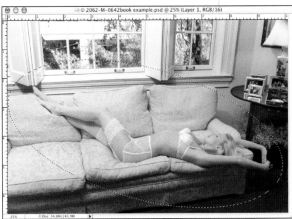

Step 15: Make black the background color and fill Vignette with black by pressing ⌘/Control+Delete/Backspace.

Carrie is *definitely* the center of attention now. Worry not, there's more . . .

12.20

Step 16: Select the Move tool (V) and press 5 on the keyboard to set Vignette's Opacity to 50%.

Step 17: Highlight the layer mask icon.

Open the Gaussian Blur dialog box (Filter➡Blur➡Gaussian Blur), set the Radius to 200 pixels, and click OK.

Step 18: The windows look artificial now. Get a 500-pixel soft brush and paint with 100% black over the shutters, windows, lampshade, wall above the table, tabletop, and molding.

The layer mask is shown here (12.21).

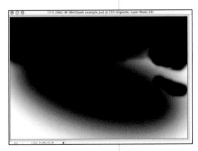

12.21

Step *19*: **Highlight Vignette's thumbnail icon and choose Filter→Noise→Add Noise.**

In the Add Noise dialog box, set the amount to 3%, the distribution to Gaussian, and make sure the Monochromatic check box is selected.

Step *20*: **Choose File→Save As and name the file** 2062-M-0642 Final.psd.

Step *21*: **Choose Image→Duplicate and click OK.**

Close 2062-M-0642 Final.psd. Flatten the copy and then select the Crop tool and crop to taste.

Step *22*: **Save the file as 2062-M-0642 Final.tif and press ⌘/Control+W to close it.**

Compare the Before (12.22), Final (12.23), and Final Cropped (12.24) versions of the image.

12.22

12.21

12.23

Beating the Wide-Angle Blues

There are times when people have to be shot with wide-angle lenses. Usually those are the times when you want to shoot the photographer, or if you are the photographer, you want to shoot the art director for picking a location that has to be shot with a wide-angle lens. (One of the best parts of writing is getting really long, run-on sentences published in a book just to make your English teachers cringe! Ah ha! Not if you have an alert editor. . . .) Shooting people this way makes them wide when they are in the foreground, as Carrie is in this photograph (12.25).

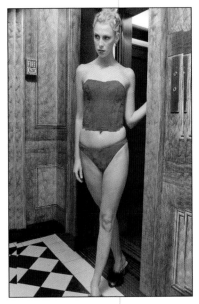

If the tiny, harshly lit location wasn't bad enough, the bustier/panty set was tiny, too. Carrie is small — though not that small. The bustier made her middle bulge. The leg holes squeezed the skin at the top of her thighs. So along with the regular retouching: healing blemishes, brightening the eyes, softening arm wrinkles, and removing hair frizzies, there is some body work to do as well.

12.25

Check out the strategy map for this project (12.26). The horizontal arrows indicate an overall compressing of the image's width. Shaping needs to be done around her middle. The red lines indicate areas where the skin has been pushed out by the panties being too small. The blue lines are wrinkles that must be smoothed.

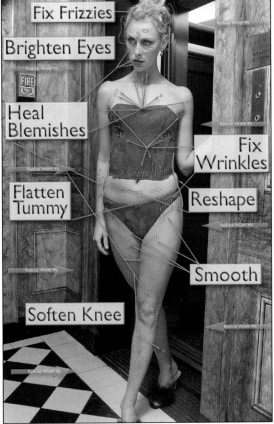

There is serious work to be done so let's get started. You already know how to do the healing work so I'll leave that up to you. Do the healing after the liquify step.

Step 1: **Open 2062-M-0764.tif.**
This 16-bit file has already been color corrected and had the USM Alias © Action run. Study the Strategy Map layer then click its eye icon off.

Step 2: **Make a copy of the Background and name it** Compressed.

Step 3: **Select the Move tool then select Free Transform by pressing ⌘/Control+T.**

Step 4: **Highlight the W field in the Options bar and enter** 91%.
The sides of the image compress toward the center.

12.26

Tip

To avoid even more confusion, highlight the Strategy Map layer and press ⌘/Control+Shift+T to run transform again. The Strategy Map now fits the Compressed layer. Click off the eye icon for Strategy Map. Highlight Compressed.

Step 5: Commit the transform and click the Background layer off to avoid the confusion of seeing the slimmer file edges repeated.

At first glance Carrie's head looks odd. Don't give it a second thought. In a minute or so it will look normal. If you don't believe me, show it to someone else. They'll comment on the outfit not the head compression.

Step 6: Duplicate the Compressed layer (⌘/Control+J) and rename it Liquify.

Step 7: Save the file.

Step 8: Duplicate 2062-M-0764.psd and rename it 2062-M-0764 8-bit.psd.

Click OK and then close 2062-M-0764.psd.

Step 9: Convert the 16-bit version to 8-bits by choosing Image→Mode→8 Bits/Channel.

Step 10: Choose Filter→Liquify

The keyboard shortcut is ⌘/Control+Shift+X.

There is preparation to do within the Liquify filter to protect areas of the image that are adjacent to the ones to be moved about.

Not in 16-Bit You Won't . . .

Photoshop CS offers a tremendously improved 16-bit workflow. Not everything is high-bit friendly in this release. The main holdout is in the Filter menu. The grayed-out choices, including Liquify, work only in 8-bit. Not to worry, Adobe has to leave something for us to look forward to. . . .

We'll use Liquify to fix the bustier-inspired bulges. This process is involved and will cover quite a few steps. It will also help familiarize you with this powerful tool. Shown here is the Liquify toolbar (12.27). While working in the Liquify filter some damage will happen in places. You'll repair these artifacts after you've applied the filter.

Liquify to Reshape

	(W) Forward Warp Tool
	(R) Reconstruct Tool
	(C) Twirl Clockwise Tool
	(P) Pucker Tool
	(B) Bloat Tool
	(O) Push Left Tool
	(M) Mirror Tool
	(T) Turbulence Tool
	(F) Freeze Mask Tool
	(D) Thaw Mask Tool
	(H) Hand Tool
	(Z) Zoom Tool

12.27

Step *11*: **Click the Zoom tool in the Liquify filter's toolbar on the left edge of the dialog box and draw a box around the area shown here (12.28) to zoom in.**

Step *12*: **Press F to activate the Freeze Mask tool.**
Select Green as the Mask color in the Options bar so that the protected areas stand out from the red bustier and panties.

Step *13*: **Select the Push Left tool (O) and starting at the hip on our right, stroke upwards using the left side of the brush to push the pixels to the left. Shape the skin back into an inward curve.**
This will take three or four strokes. Be careful not to overdo it (12.29).

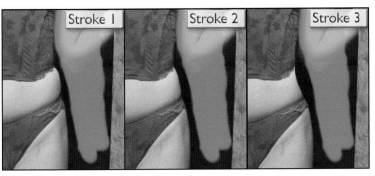

Stroke 1   Stroke 2   Stroke 3

12.29

12.28

Freeze and Thaw Mask Tools

Create, modify, and remove masks when working in the Liquify filter. The Freeze Mask tool paints a red mask that protects the area beneath it. The Thaw Mask tool removes the protection. Select the mask color via a drop-down menu in the View Options section of the control panel on the right side of the dialog box. You can hide it from view.

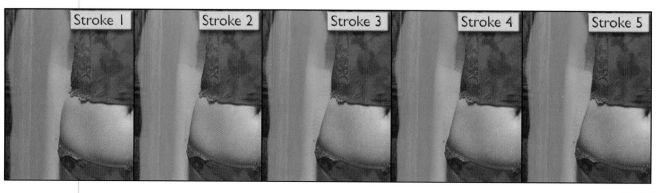

12.30

OK
Reset
Load Mesh... | Save Mesh...

Tool Options

Brush Size: 27
Brush Density: 38
Brush Pressure: 51
Brush Rate: 80
Turbulent Jitter: 50
Reconstruct Mode: Revert
☑ Stylus Pressure

Reconstruct Options

Mode: Revert
Reconstruct | Restore All

12.31

Step 14: Do the left side.

This time use a downward stroke starting above the ribcage and shaping down to the panty. Use long smooth strokes. Keep the + in the center of the brush from touching her skin (12.30).

Step 15: Zoom in to 200%. Hold down the spacebar and drag the image over to the right.

Notice the distortions around her waist and arm above the elbow.

Step 16: Press R to select the Reconstruct tool, and set the Options as shown here (12.31).

Brush along the green mask. Don't work to fix all the distortion, because you will bring back the old shape. Not good. You can get rid of the skin tone and reduce the wavy areas. If some of her skin reappears, press ⌘/Control+Z (12.32). We'll take care of the rest outside of the Liquify filter.

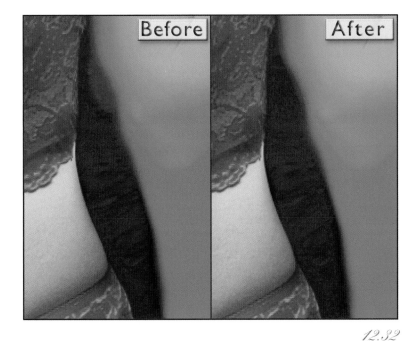

12.32

Step *17*: **Click OK to commit the changes and click the Liquify layer eye icon on and off the see how much that little bit of brushing helped.**

Now is the time to fix the Liquify induced artifacts.

Step *18*: **Zoom to 200% and scroll over the wall on the right side by Carrie's waist.**

Step *19*: **Create a new layer above Liquify and name it** Healing.

Pick the Healing brush and sample a non-wavy area. Heal close to her skin without affecting it.

Step *20*: **Scroll over to the left.**

The Push Left tool wave pattern is very apparent on her arm. Before you can do the healing you have some preparation work to do.

Step *21*: **Using the Pen tool, outline down the bustier and around the line of the panty.**

If you aren't comfortable with the Pen tool, use the path named *left arm artifacts*. It will probably need some modification to match the Liquify that you did. When the path is finished, go to the Paths palette, double-click the Work Path and save it as **Path 1** (12.33).

12.33

[**269**]

12.34

Step 22: ⌘/Control+click on the path to make it into a selection and feather the selection 2 pixels.

Now this next part is a little tricky and maybe confusing. Hang in there with me. . . .

Step 23: **Go back to the Layers palette. Click the eye icon on Liquify off and heal from Compressed to Healing over the bulge.**

The effect will look like the bulge has been covered up. After you finish, deselect then click the Liquify eye icon on. The effect looks natural. The artifacts are gone. One of the advantages to non-destructive editing is that there is always something from previous steps to copy or heal from when recovering from Liquify's artifacts (12.34).

HEALING THE TUMMY LINE

The next concern is the indentation that the panty makes in her tummy. This would not be apparent if the bustier was not pushing her tummy down as well. What is it that line anyway? It is a shadow. Remove the shadow and it's back to flat abs-ville.

Step 24: **Draw a path all the way around the panty.**

If you don't want to draw your own, look in the Paths palette. It is named Panty (duh). Make it into a selection and feather it 2 pixels.

Step 25: **Choose Select➡Inverse or choose ⌘/Control+Shift+I to inverse the selection.**

⌘/Control+H will hide it.

Step 26: **Sample the Healing brush on the light area above the shadow and heal along the panty line from one side to the other** (12.35).

Slick fix huh?

There are skin creases along the leg holes. They, too, are caused by the panty being too small. Again this is a job for the Healing brush to cover the shadows.

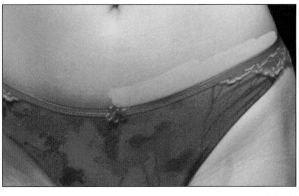

12.35

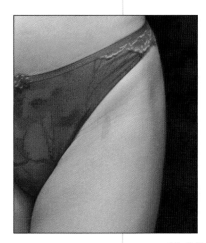

12.36

Step 27: **For the right leg, sample on the top of the thigh and heal the birthmark first** (12.36).

Then heal from the panty line away toward the hip. Don't heal the muscle dimple to the left edge of the right hip. It's pretty.

The right leg is a little more work. The light in the room is harsh, causing texture and shadow to show readily. Carrie's weight is on the right leg. There are muscle shadows that would not show under softer light. (The elevator lobby was way too small with no room for anything more that a bare bulb flash.)

Step 28: **Sample on the middle of her right thigh and heal the area above it completely** (12.37).

Lift the mouse button and view the work. Continue along the panty line. Remember this is about healing the shadows. While you are at it, heal the razor bumps along the line as well (12.38).

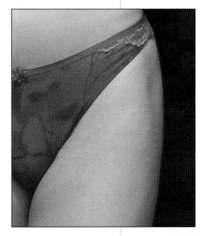

12.37

Wrinkles. It's time to heal the wrinkles. Yes, I use the Healing brush a lot. And it whips the Clone Stamp tool hands down for this sort of thing. Because you are close to the panty, heal the wrinkles along the right hip.

Step 29: **Sample just below the waistband in the area that has no pattern and heal the wrinkles.**

Resampling as you work with wrinkles to avoid healing patterns from developing is a good idea.

Step 30: **Using the same techniques, heal the wrinkles on the bustier.**

This is definitely looking better!

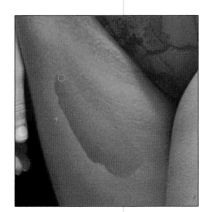

12.38

The right knee shows a lot of shadow and could do with some softening. We'll want this on its own layer.

Step *31*: **Create a new layer and name it** Heal Knee.
Sample the just above the knee and heal the wrinkles. Sample the inside of the thigh and heal the shadow along the left of the knee. Repeat for the right shadow. Heal the skin just below the kneecap. When you have finished, the knee will be almost smooth and totally unbelievable.

Step *32*: **Select the Move tool and press 5 on the keyboard to reduce the Opacity of Heal Knee to 50%.**
Play with other opacities and see which one works best for you. The example shows before and after healing and 60% of Heal Knee showing (12.39).

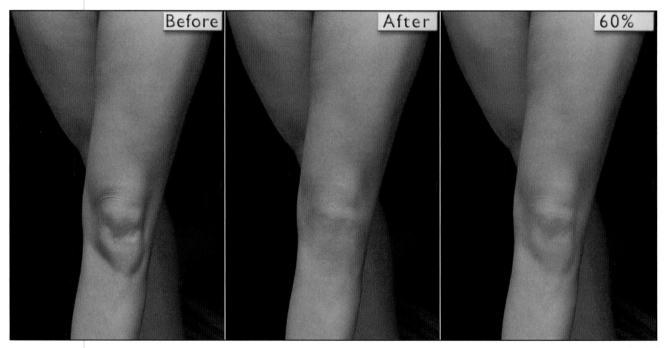

12.39

Now heal the arm wrinkles. We'll do the right arm together as a refresher.

Step 33: Highlight Healing and then pick a sample point including the edge of the bustier and heal back and forth along the wrinkle.

Step 34: Choose Edit➡Fade or press ⌘/Control+Shift+F and fade the healing to about 50%. Heal the wrinkle and bumps at the top of the arm joint, too (12.40).

PRACTICING RETOUCHING TECHNIQUES

Finish healing the blemishes and lines that are shown on the strategy map. Brighten the irises of the eyes (refer to Chapter 8), fix the smudged lipstick, and tame the flyaway hair. (Hint: Use the Clone Stamp tool when you are working close to her face. Then heal any tonal inconsistencies.) Some of these techniques might be hard to master without seeing them done. The compression, liquify, healing, and facial retouching techniques for the Wide-Angle Blues section is available on my CD, "Enhancing Beauty" from Software Cinema. Go to www.amesphoto.com/learning and click the link for this chapter to learn more. You can order from the link as well.

The editorial that these images were from was very well received. The editorial is available as a downloadable PDF if you want to see how they appeared in print. The next chapter takes us on location to continue the exploration of using Photoshop to control contrast outdoors. We also take this book's cover model, Rachel Keller, to ruins near Dublin, Ireland, digitally. Placing a model in an existing location requires planning at the camera as well as the magic provided by Photoshop CS.

12.40

Chapter Thirteen

Indoors, Outdoors

Making photographs of women in the studio is easy. It is a controlled-access environment. Outdoors is another matter entirely. The considerations range from security to weather. The light changes as the sun moves. (Okay, the earth rotates. You *know* what I mean.) There are insects and the curious who see a camera and wonder what's up. All of these factors can stress the photographer. Some of them can also stress the photography by having the potential to make the model feel uncomfortable. Here is a key to doing this kind of work: If the model feels comfortable and at ease, the photographs will reflect those feelings. The converse is also true.

First and perhaps most important, models must be comfortable in their own skin. If they aren't, there is nothing to be done to make the photo shoot successful. The next comfort level is with the crew. In shooting women particularly, care has to be exercised in the choice of the crew. Respect in everything is key. Make sure another woman is in the crew, especially if the photographer is male. Remember the whole point is to come away with great photographs.

Controlling Contrast After the Shoot

Once again lingerie is the subject. The location for the shoot is the backyard of a home in midtown Atlanta. The elevated grounds are surrounded on one side by a stone fence and dense foliage on the other. The lush greenery breaks up the backgrounds and provides privacy. Lighting is natural. Cara is the model. This setup is on a deck; the background is a stone wall. Cara is seated in a metal chair draped with her robe (13.1). The warm, dappled light breaks through the leaves of the trees. Scattered patches of sunlight are overexposing areas in the photograph. The sun on Cara's face completely overexposes her face. It makes her squint, too. The same problem is happening on her leg. This is *not* pretty at all.

The solution lies in placing a Chimera 42 x 72-inch diffusion panel between the sun (origin of light) and Cara. You can see the panel's effect by the rectangular shadow cast on Cara (13.2). The larger source of light (the diffusion

13.1

13.2

panel) is now soft and flattering. The diffused value is metered again. One f/stop of exposure is added at the camera to compensate for the density of the diffusion fabric. The additional exposure increases the brightness of the high-lights outside of the area of soft light created by the panel by one stop as well. These hotspots pull the eye away from Cara. Their brightness competes with the subject for the viewer's attention. They are the subject of this project.

The focus of this project is to use the high-bit data contained in the raw file to tone down the distracting highlights. The strategy map outlines the areas of concern for this project (13.3). You can get the files for this section from www.amesphoto.com/learning. Download the folder for Chapter 13. It contains the raw files 2062-R-014.dcr, 2062-R-073.dcr, and a .psd version with a strategy map.

13.3

Step 1: **Open the folder, 13 Cara, in File Brower. Double-click 2062-R-073.dcr to open the Camera Raw dialog box.**

The settings section shows that the image is displayed as shot. This is the out-of-the-camera untweaked file (13.4). Look at the histogram. There is a full range of highlight exposure indicated. Note the red channel has more pixels in the highlight distribution. The info display at the bottom of the dialog box shows R: 248. The comparatively high red values are accounted for by Cara's skin tone (13.5). This photograph is a little flat because the shadow side of the histogram is a little weak. The shadows are open with a lot of detail. We want the viewer to concentrate on Cara and her lingerie. Darker shadows are in order.

13.4

13.5

Step 2: **Move the shadow slider until the 6 appears in the field** (13.6).

The histogram expands to the left and the shadows darken. The reading in the info window shows that the new shadow setting will still reproduce on press.

Step 3: **Set the drop-down menus at the bottom of the Camera Raw dialog box to read: Space: Adobe RGB (1998), Size: 3032 by 2008, Depth: 8 Bits/Channel, and Resolution: 300 pixels/inch** (13.7). **Click OK.**

Step 4: **Run the USM Alias © Action from the Postproduction Actions set.**

The function key assigned in Chapter 2 is F13.

Step 5: **Choose Image➡Duplicate.**

Rename the duplicate image **2062-R-073Normal**. Close 2062-N-073.dcr. Click Don't Save.

Step 6: **Double-click 2062-R-073.dcr in File Browser to open the Camera Raw dialog box once more.**

Drag the Exposure slider to the left until the setting reads –1.50. Click OK.

Step 7: **Run the USM Alias © Action on 2062-R073.dcr.**

Step 8: **Select the Move tool and then hold down the Shift key. Drag Normal onto 2062–R-073.dcr.**

Normal appears in the layer stack as Layer 1. Rename Layer 1 Normal. Normal is highlighted. Close 2062-R-073 Normal.

Space:	Adobe RGB (1998)	Size:	3032 by 2008
Depth:	8 Bits/Channel	Resolution:	300 pixels/inch

13.7

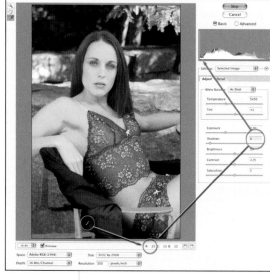

13.6

Step 9: Click the Add a Layer Mask icon at the bottom of the Layers palette (13.8).

Step 10: Select a 150-pixel soft brush and set the Opacity to 50%. Set black as the foreground color.
Refer to the retouching strategy map for the areas to darken. Zoom into 100%.

Step 11: Paint on the layer mask using continuous strokes over the too-bright highlights.
This reduces the contrast of the background, bringing the eye forward in the image to Cara. Compare the darker background on the left to the original on the right (13.9). The modified layer mask is shown here (13.10).

Step 12: Make a new layer and rename it Retouch. Hold down the Option/Alt key and choose Merge Visible from the Layers palette fly-out menu.

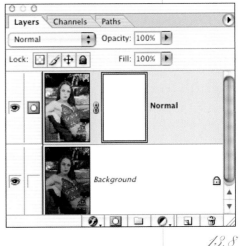

13.8

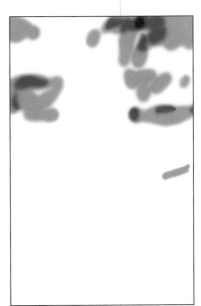

13.10

13.9

Going Further

Cara is a natural beauty. And yes, her eyes are that bright naturally. My strategy for retouching her photograph is simple and subtle. Mainly it involves cleaning up some of the textures on her face and removing flyaway hairs. The body retouch is minimal. Here's what I came up with. Make your own strategy and go for it!

The raw workflow offers postproduction options that are simply not available with camera-produced JPGs or TIFs. The high bit depth versatility gives the digital photographer options that with film could only be accomplished on location by large crews equipped with extensive light modifiers. Often photographers had to settle. Times have changed — for the better. Check out the final version of Cara from this exercise (13.11). Fabulous!

13.11

Working In Studio for On Location

Occasionally the location, the photographer, and the model can't quite be in the same place at the same time. Now as much as we would all love to hang problems on the location, it is pretty much out of the question. Travel considerations, costs, and schedules all conspire against the success of the envisioned photograph.

Successful compositing has been a holy grail dangled as an unfulfilled fruit of digital imaging. The dream has been to take any location shot at anytime of day (or night) and drop a person into it seamlessly. This is, of course, nothing more than whimsy, a fantasy or a pipe dream used to romance the promise — it isn't gonna happen anytime soon. And more than likely it will never be as easy as they (remember "them"?) would like us to believe. That's not to say it's impossible. It's just not easy.

The problem is light. All the qualities have to match in order for a composite to be believed.

Shoot the location. Then look at the photograph closely. Careful study reveals the light, color, quality, and angle (check out the shadows). Go into the studio. Match what is happening in the photograph of the location. Then the composite can work.

This section covers the process of seeing the light in an image. The location is a ruin outside of Dublin, Ireland (13.12). The sun is setting on the left side of the photograph. Open sky provides fill. The light to match is the warm directional sunlight coming from the left side.

The photographs of model, Rachel Keller from the Elite modeling agency, were made specifically for insertion into this scene. A guide print of the photograph was on set to match the lighting. A Rosco #3407 warming gel was attached to a medium Chimera Super Pro lightbank. This light coming from the left provided the orange-ish late afternoon sun effect on Rachel. It was about fifteen feet away. A large (4 x 6-foot) Chimera Super Pro lightbank was aimed from the right at 45° from the lens and 45° above to simulate fill light from an open sky. It can be argued that Rachel looks too well lit when compared to the building. I take lighting gear on location when shooting fashion to ensure the clothes and model look their best. Fashion shooting has an element of fantasy in it. In this case proper

13.12

lighting on Rachel is part of my exercising artistic license to achieve the fantasy. A fan to move her hair and dress was blowing from the left as well. An iTunes playlist by first assistant Justin "Top Forty" Larose flowed from the sound system, Rachel moved, and I made photographs. Twenty minutes and a hundred and twenty shots later we reviewed the take. We had the shot. The challenge was determining which one to use.

Nine of the favorites for the composite are shown in the figure (13.13). My pick is 2062-I-0097.tif. Download it and Irish Ruins.tif from the Chapter 13 folder on www.amesphoto.com/learning. This project consists of four sections. The first two involve retouching Rachel and removing her from the studio background. In the third section we prepare the location photograph. In the fourth section we blend the two together so that they appear seamless.

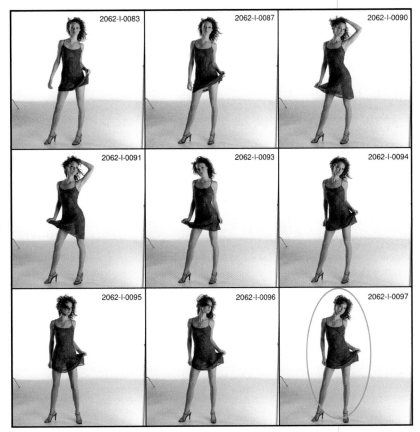

13.13

Retouching Rachel

Rachel has an Irish complexion. Her hair is naturally curly and red, her skin is pale with wonderful freckles. Some of them are large enough to draw the viewer away from her face. They have been circled on the retouching strategy map (13.14). Some lines need smoothing on her face and armpit. The skin on her legs needs some smoothing, too. All the retouching techniques have been covered in previous chapters. So the first section's step-by-step is to show the order of retouching Rachel.

Step *1*: **Open the chapter's folder in File Browser and double-click 2062-I-0097.tif to open it.**

Step *2*: **Begin on Rachel's face. Heal the lines to a new layer named Lines.**

13.14

Let's face it. The Healing brush rules for lines everywhere except under eyes with mascara on the lower lashes. The Healing brush reaches outside the brushed area shown on the screen and blends the sampled data to that under the just healed area. When a large tonal or color difference exists, that difference is included in the calculation. A dark or colored blend results. Large, dark "poor, poor, pitiful me" crying-all-night eyes appear. And they aren't pretty. Here's the fix: Zoom in to at least 200%. Draw a selection around the area to be healed (13.15); for best precision, use the Pen tool. Use the Quick Mask technique to feather the selection to the edge of the eyelashes. Heal the under-eye lines. Tah-dah! No bags (13.16)!

13.15   *13.16*

Step 3: Heal the large blemishes on Rachel's face, arms, and shoulders.

Step 4: Heal the line at her armpit. Press ⌘/Control+Shift+F to fade the healing about 50%.

Step 5: Heal blemishes and lines on her legs and feet.

Step 6: Draw a path around the skin of Rachel's legs. Outline the skin between the straps of the shoes and around the ankle bracelet (13.17). Save your path.

Of course, if you want to cut right to the next step, there is always the path named Legs already drawn and most conveniently located in the Paths palette.

Step 7: Return to the Layers palette. Make a new layer named Retouch. Merge the visible layers to it.

13.17

Of Days and Fashions Past

Fashion changes. Duh. That is its nature after all. One of these [r]evolutions is bare-legged women in dresses. There was a time before Photoshop that this was not acceptable. Pantyhose were the order of the day. Stockings made the shape of the leg, covered blemishes on the skin, and made the legs in photographs perfect.

Women in today's world are far more active. They are involved in sports, careers, and family pursuits that can and do inflict bruises, scratches, and other "unsightly" marks on their legs. Hose have been relegated to formal dress-up events.

Smooth flawless legs are still desirable, especially in photographs where they can be observed more closely than in real life. Photoshop offers the ability to smooth the skin without reverting to those "oh-so-last-millennium" hose.

Step 8: **Move to the Paths palette and ⌘/Control+click the just-created path to make it into a selection** (13.18). **Return to Layers.**

Step 9: **Feather the selection 0.5-pixels by pressing ⌘/Control+Option/Alt+D.**

Step 10: **Make the selection into its own layer by pressing ⌘/Control+J. Rename it** Legs (13.19).

13.18

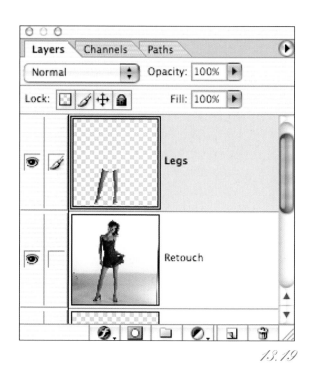

13.19

Step 11: ⌘/Control+click on the new Legs layer to activate the selection again. Choose Select➡Modify➡ Contract. Enter 5 in the pixels field in the Contract Selection dialog box. Click OK.

Step 12: Click the Lock Transparency icon.

Step 13: Press Q to enter Quick Mask mode. Choose Filter➡Blur➡Gaussian Blur. Enter 3 pixels. Click OK. The blur extends almost to the edge of the skin (13.20). Press Q and return to the normal mode. The marching ants reappear.

Step 14: Invert the selection (⌘/Control+Shift+I.) This selection extends into the skin 5 pixels from the edge over a 3-pixel feather.

Step 15: Use the Gaussian Blur dialog box to apply a 1.5-pixel blur to the selected area (13.21).

Step 16: Inverse the selection again. Blur the skin on the inside of the leg 3 pixels (13.22).

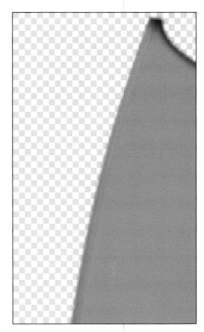

13.20

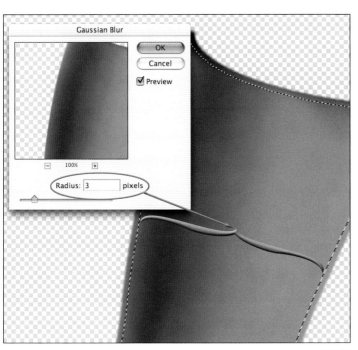

13.22

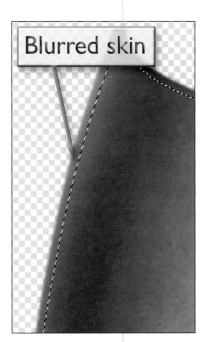

13.21

**Blur + Noise =
Nirvana**

No, not the late great Kurt Cobain's grunge band . . . great printed output without banding or posterization.

Step *17*: **Deselect (⌘/Control+D).**
The transparency is still locked on the Legs layer.

Step *18*: **Choose Filter➡Noise➡Add Noise. Enter** 1.15% **in the Amount field of the Add Noise dialog box. Click OK.**
Rachel's legs and feet look smoother without being plastic. Noise added to the blurred skin helps it retain some of skin's natural texture (13.23).

Step *19*: **Make a new layer. Rename it** Rachel. **Merge Retouch and Legs to it. Save the file as** 2062-0097.psd.

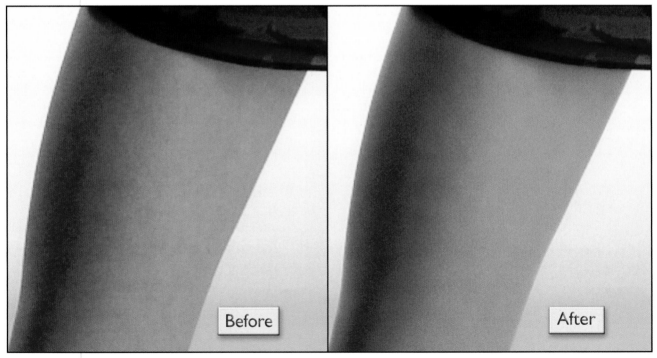

Before   After

13.23

Creating a Layer of Her Own

This next section floats Rachel and her fab red hair onto her own layer. Then she will be ready for a (digital) journey to Ireland.

Step 1: **Go to the Paths palette and select New Path from the fly-out menu. Draw a path around Rachel's body. As the path reaches her head draw it inside her hair** (13.24).

The path is shown in green for clarity. As always, should you choose not to make your own path one is provided in the Paths palette. It is named Rachel.

Step 2: **Make the path into a selection. Feather it .5 pixels.**

Step 3: **Go to the Layers palette and press ⌘/Control+J to make the selection into a layer.**

Name the layer **Rachel–hair** because some of her hair got left behind (13.25).

Step 4: **Choose the Elliptical Marquee tool. Drag a selection around Rachel's head. Highlight the Rachel layer** (13.26).

13.24

13.26

13.25

Step *5*: **Press ⌘/Control+J to make the selection into a layer. Name the layer** Hair. **Click the Hair layer and drag it above Rachel–Hair.**

Step *6*: **Click the eye icon on the Rachel layer off to hide the layer.**
Rachel appears against a transparent background (gray and white checkerboard) with a white ring around her head (13.27).

Note
{ Layers are linked to the active layer. }

Step *7*: **Link the layer Rachel–hair to the Hair layer by clicking in the box next to the eye icon of Rachel–Hair** (13.28).

Step *8*: **Open Irish Ruins.tif.**

Step *9*: **Click 2062-0097.psd. Drag this file to reveal part of Irish Ruins.tif.**

13.27

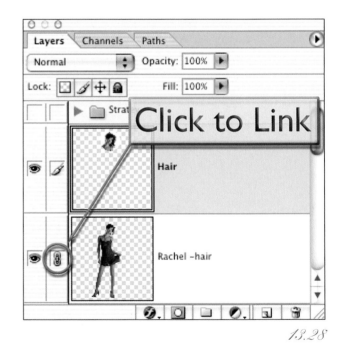

13.28

Step *10*: **Select the Move tool. Click the photograph of Rachel. Drag it into Irish Ruins.tif** (13.29).

Irish Ruins.tif's layer stack now includes the linked layers Hair and Rachel–hair. Rachel still has a white halo around her head.

The next steps are similar to bringing back Adair's hair in Chapter 8. The difference is that Rachel's hair has to blend with the colors of the background instead of 255 white. There are numbers we need to know.

Drag 2062-I-0097.tif into Irish Ruins.tif.

13.29

Step *11*: **Activate the Background layer. Open the Levels dialog box (⌘/Control+L). Hold down the Option/Alt key and move the highlight slider to the left.**

The screen starts out black. As the slider moves left a white area will appear from the posterized colors. Remember where the white appeared. Move the slider to its original position at the far right. Release the Option/Alt key. Hold down the Shift key. Click the center of the white area. A color sampler appears (13.30). Click Cancel to close the dialog box.

Note
You cannot drag linked layers into another Photoshop file from the Layers palette. Only the highlighted layer will go. Move linked layers by dragging the image from one open file to another. This technique works with linked adjustment layers, too.

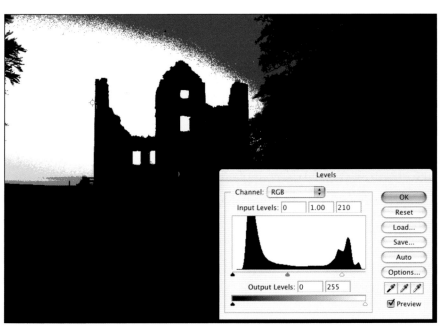

13.30

Note

The numbers from the samplers are guides for the blending sliders. The brightness is not going to exceed the highest number in the underlying layer. The shadow areas are the lowest value of the blend. The blending numbers will fall between the highest and lowest values.

Step 12: Use the Color Sampler tool to add another picker on the building to the right of Rachel's hair.
The values are displayed in the Info palette (13.31).

Step 13: Open the Layer Style dialog box by double-clicking the thumbnail of the Hair layer. Drag the Highlight slider to the left until the number above it reads around 235.

13.31

Step *14* : **Hold down the Option/Alt key. The sliders split down the middle of the triangle. Drag the left half to the left until the number on the left reads around 95** (13.32).

During this procedure, Rachel's halo blends with the layer below it (13.33). Remember, no pixels are on the Rachel–hair layer. The blend is made with the Background layer, the ruins.

Step *15* : **Hide the Background layer. Create a new layer named** Rachel. **Merge the layers Rachel–hair and Hair to it.**

Step *16* : **Show the Background layer. Hide the layers Rachel–hair and Hair. Choose Layer➡ Matting➡Remove White Matte.**

Step *17* : **Open the General Preferences dialog box by pressing ⌘/Control+K. Set the Image Interpolation to Bicubic Smoother. Click OK.**

This option is not available in older versions of Photoshop.

Tip

A 16-bit transform results in much higher quality image interpolation for both up and down sizing. The use of the appropriate Bicubic sampling method in the General Preferences dialog box improves the quality of the transform, too.

13.32

13.33

Photoshop CS sports one improved and two new interpolation modes for enlarging or reducing image size. Bicubic (Better) is the improved overall interpolation algorithm. It's great for general reducing and enlarging using 110% steps. Bicubic Smoother is for enlarging. Bicubic Sharper is designed for reducing large files that might be used on the Web, for instance. These settings are global. They affect Free Transform, Crop, and Image Size. Image Size has an override drop-down menu that defaults to the preference setting after each use.

Step 18: **Press ⌘/Control+T to open the Free Transform dialog box.**

Click the Maintain Aspect Ratio link icon in the Options bar. Enter 150% in either the W: or the H: fields. Click the Commit Transform check mark icon (13.34). Save the file as **Irish Ruins.psd**.

Creating Shallow Depth of Field

At this point in the project, the work on Rachel is pretty much complete. Some visual disconnects still exist. Closer examination reveals that while Rachel is sharper and more detailed than the background image, the background image is still too sharp. A photograph made late in the day would be shot with the lens aperture (f/stop) set almost wide open to increase the shutter speed and help freeze the model's hair. The large aperture would produce shallow depth of field. Rachel would be sharp and the ruins would be out of focus. Photoshop CS adds a new tool: the *Lens Blur filter*. It is perfect for finishing this photograph.

Note

The Lens Blur filter is an 8-bit only filter.

Step 1: **Choose Image➡Duplicate. Name the copy** Irish Ruins 8-bit.psd. **Close Irish Ruins.psd.**

In this exercise, Rachel will remain sharp, but the background will be softened from the foreground to the background. Because it will be purposely blurred, the quality of a 16-bit workflow from this point on is unnecessary.

 Photoshop File Edit Image Layer Select Filter View Window Help

X: 1545.5 px Y: 1666.0 px W: 150.0% H: 150.0% 0.0 ° H: 0.0 ° V: 0.0 ° ⊘ ✓

13.34

Step *2*: **Convert Irish Ruins 8-bit.psd to 8-bits per channel. (Choose Image➡Mode➡8 Bits/Channel.)**

Step *3*: **Drag the Hair and Rachel–hair layers to the Trashcan icon at the bottom of the Layers palette to delete them.**
Both layers were saved in the 16-bit Irish Ruins.psd.

Step *4*: **Duplicate the Background layer. Rename it** Ruins.

Step *5*: **Press ⌘/Control+R to display the rulers. Select the Move tool. Drag a guide from the horizontal ruler at the top of the document window to the horizon line in the photograph. Drag another one to the point on the vertical ruler at about 8 5/8 inches** (13.35).

Step *6*: **Click the Channels tab. Select New Channel from the fly-out menu** (13.36).
When the dialog box opens click Selected Areas in the Color Indicates section. Set the Opacity to 100%. The name can remain Alpha 1 (13.37).

Note
The original 16-bit file, Irish Ruins.psd, is available for up-rezzing if the image is required to be significantly enlarged at a later time.

13.35

New Channel

Name: Alpha 1   OK   Cancel

Color Indicates:
◯ Masked Areas
⦿ Selected Areas

Color
Opacity: 100 %

13.37

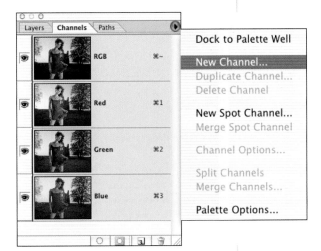

Dock to Palette Well
New Channel...
Duplicate Channel...
Delete Channel
New Spot Channel...
Merge Spot Channel
Channel Options...
Split Channels
Merge Channels...
Palette Options...

13.36

[293]

Step 7: **Set black as the foreground color and white as the background color. Select the Gradient tool. Choose the Foreground to Background icon in the drop-down menu (13.38) from the Options bar.**

Step 8: **Hold down the Shift key. Click on the bottom guide and drag to the upper one.**

A gradient appears, black in the foreground fading to gray to the upper guide, and then white above the upper guide (13.39).

Step 9: **Press ⌘/Control+; (semicolon) to hide the guides. Press ⌘/Control+~ (tilde) to return to the RGB composite in the Channels palette. Click on the Layers tab.**

Step 10: **Highlight the Ruins layer. Choose Filter➡Blur➡ Lens Blur.**

The Lens Blur dialog box opens. The preview area displays the highlighted layer, which in this case is Ruins. A rendering of the lens blur appears quickly when the Preview is set to Faster. To view a higher quality, choose More Accurate. The setting is significantly slower and yields a close version of the final effect.

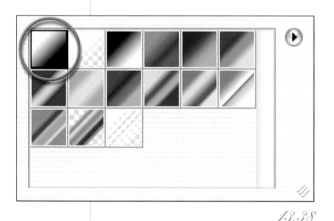

13.38

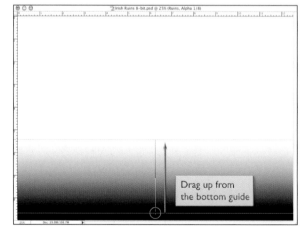

Drag up from the bottom guide

13.39

Depth Map

The new Alpha channel tells the Lens Blur filter what areas of the background are to be sharp or blurred. Black areas of the Alpha channel (0) will be sharp. As the numbers progress to 255 (white), the blur increases.

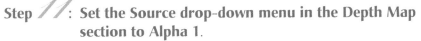

Step *11*: **Set the Source drop-down menu in the Depth Map section to Alpha 1.**
This tells Lens Blur where to apply the depth of field. The Blur Focal Distance slider is set to 0 (zero). If you wanted to reverse the effect, you would check the Invert box. The Iris section controls the actual blur effect.

Step *12*: **Set the Radius to 40.**
The Shape drop-down menu selects the number of blades of the aperture of the lens the filter will emulate. The Blade Curvature slider smoothes the aperture edges. The Rotation slider rotates the aperture.

Step *13*: **The Noise section builds the Add Noise step right into the filter. Set the Amount of noise to 3%, and select the Gaussian Distribution option and the Monochromatic check box. Click OK.**
Check the effect against the original by clicking the eye icon of Ruins on and off.

Step *14*: **Highlight the Rachel layer in the Layers palette. Select the Move tool. Drag Rachel across the background. The move is seamless** (13.40).
If the light area on Rachel's dress is not against the sky, use the Healing brush to darken it.

One result of blurring an image is the highlights become grayer. The Specular Highlights section gives them a boost. The Threshold slider controls the point where all pixels above the setting are treated as specular (mirror) highlights of the origin and/or the source of light. Brightness increases the highlights. The ruins have no specular highlights so these setting are left at 0.

13.40

[295]

Learning more about Lens Blur

The previous example scratches the surface of the Lens Blur filter. There is a lot more to it, especially when simulating depth of field. The general rule for depth of field is that one-third of the zone of focus will occur in front of the plane of focus and two-thirds happen behind it. This segment of the chapter looks deeper into the way you can use Lens Blur to mimic the way lenses work on cameras. This time Rachel gets placed in the field full length. Read on for some cool techniques with the Brush tool, too.

The project expands on the previous one using a new sample image named Rachels Field.psd. Download it from www.amesphoto.com/learning and open it in Photoshop CS.

Note

Positioning is very important in this undertaking. Once Rachel is in position, you can't move her without reapplying the Lens Blur filter. This is because the depth mask used to create the apparent depth of field is specific to Rachel and where she stands in the photograph.

Step *1*: **Select the Move tool. Drag the Rachel image to a position that works for you.**
My choice is the open sky between the tree on the left and the ruins. At the end of the job the photograph can be cropped to make the composition stronger (13.41).

Step *2*: **Rachel is too big to give you a good look at the foreground depth of field softness. Highlight her layer. Press ⌘/Control+T to enter Free Transform mode. Lock the aspect ratio of the image. Enter 90% in either the W: or H: field. Click the Commit Transform check mark (13.42).**

Step *3*: **Refine Rachel's positioning to your liking.**

13.41

Look at Rachel's feet. Only a photographer could ask a model to walk a field in high heels. Anyway, the grass would naturally cover part of her feet.

Step 4: **Make a new layer above the layer Rachel. Name it** Grass.

Step 5: **Get the Clone Stamp tool (S). Select the Use All Layers check box in the Options bar. Choose a soft 100-pixel brush** (13.43). **View actual pixels (100%). Sample (Option/Alt+click) the grass to the right of Rachel's foot** (13.44).

Step 6: **Clone grass over her right foot until it reaches just above the lower strap. Resample and clone grass over the left foot to match** (13.45).

"The devil is in the details." The quote really says it all when it comes to making composites believable. The result from Steps Five and Six is almost to the point of believability. We need to refine the result with the Clone Stamp tool and a "blades of grass" special effects brush.

13.42

13.43

13.44

13.45

Step *7*: **Click the Brushes tab in the palette well (13.46). Click the Brushes Disclosure triangle. Choose Special Effect Brushes from the drop-down menu. Click Append in the dialog box that appears.**

This step adds the special effects brushes to the palette. Scroll the brushes. Find, then click the Grass brush (13.47). Set the brush size to 40 pixels.

Step *8*: **Sample the grass and clone blades of grass along the edge of the original cloning on the Grass layer.**

Break up the lines with this technique on both shoes and the heel of the left one (13.48). Now Rachel is grounded (pun intended) by this tiny detail.

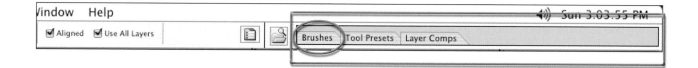

13.46

13.48

13.47

Step 9: Now build the depth map. Make a copy of the Background layer. Name it DOF. (Yet another TLA! This one means *depth of field*.)

Step 10: ⌘/Control+click on the Rachel layer to load the pixels as a selection. DOF should still be the active layer. Hold down the Option/Alt key and click the Add Layer Mask icon at the bottom of the Layers palette.

The layer mask has Rachel silhouette on it (13.49).

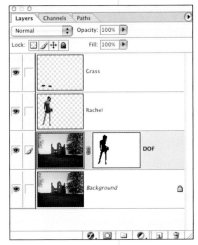

Step 11: Option/Alt+click the layer mask.

The mask is now displayed in place of the photograph. Press F to enter full screen mode.

13.49

Step 12: Pull a guide down from the top ruler and place it just below Rachel's right foot.

Step 13: Select a soft-edged 400-pixel brush. Make sure the Airbrush icon in the Options bar is inactive. Set black as the foreground color. Click once on the left below the guide.

A soft black dot appears. Move the brush icon to the right edge of the mask.

Tip

Toggle the rulers by pressing ⌘/Control+R.

Step 14: Hold down the Shift key and click and then drag the brush out of the frame (13.50). Hide the guides.

Step 15: Option/Alt+click the layer mask to bring back the normal view. Click on DOF's thumbnail to make it active.

Tip

Holding down the Shift key after clicking with a tool that uses a brush (Clone Stamp, Brush, Pencil, Healing brush, and so on) constrains the brush to a straight line connecting the first click and the Shift+click.

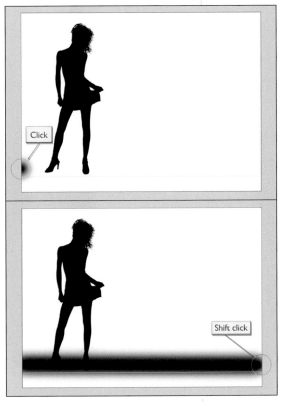

13.50

Step *16*: **Select the Lens Blur filter.**

Set the Depth Map Source to Layer Mask. The Blur Focal Distance stays at 0. Lower the Radius to 45. Everything else stays at 0. Use the standard Noise settings: 3%, Gaussian Distribution, and Monochromatic. A close look at the space Rachel will fill shows that no blur is inside the layer mask.

Step *17*: **Click OK.**

Rachel appears against a soft background and an accurately blurred foreground, too (13.51).

Step *18*: **Duplicate the file and name it** Rachel's Field Cropped.

13.51

Step *19*: **Press ⌘/Control+K to open the General Preferences dialog box. Confirm that the Image Interpolation is Bicubic (Better).**

Step *20*: **Select the Crop tool. Crop the image to your liking. Click OK. Save the file.**

This technique allows truly cool flexibility in placing a model in a new location. The key to its success is paying attention to the details of light and depth of field (13.52). The Lens Blur filter is a great new tool that makes composites even more believable. To learn more about the techniques in this section check out the section of my Software Cinema "CD Studio to Location." For more info and how to order, browse to www.amesphoto.com/learning and click "Chapter 14" or the "Learn More" link.

Locations with models actually there are lots of fun to shoot. Photoshop is used to enhance colors, occasionally change them, and of course, touch up things that can't be handled at the time of the shoot. In the next chapter we look into the glamorous world of shooting swimwear on location and how enhancement in Adobe Photoshop CS adds that "little something" to the final photographs.

13.52

Chapter Fourteen

On the Beach: Swimwear

Nature has no mercy at all. Nature says,
"I'm going to snow. If you have on a bikini and no snowshoes,
that's tough. I am going to snow anyway."
Maya Angelou

Use the Google search engine to find information on "sunshine state," and you get 1.9 million listings for Florida. The official Internet site of the Florida legislature is *Sunshine Online*. Construction companies consult *callsunshine.com* before digging up Florida's streets. So you would think that photographing swimsuits in Miami for a magazine editorial in the *sunshine* would be a no-brainer. Maya is right. Nature has *no* mercy.

Right after checking out the fabulous locations at the Sonesta Resort Key Biscayne with their publicist, Deborah Roker, the sunshine went away. Not only was the sunshine gone, it was replaced by a downpour of rain that lasted all afternoon then on through the night. The next morning dawn broke to overcast skies, a brisk chilly breeze, and the threat of more precipitation. Elite models Tia Hinton and Adelina Guerrero arrived at the hotel to be fitted with the latest swimwear by stylist Liz Lyons Powers. Assistant Justin Larose and I moved the camera, PowerBook, and lights to the beach to prepare the first setup. About an hour later the overcast sky brightened a bit. The lights were ready. Tia and Adelina arrived and we started to shoot.

A dozen frames later the rain came. Justin and I quickly broke down the gear and moved it inside as the sprinkles turned into a downpour. It was ten in the morning. Welcome to my world — professional photography and the *sunshine* state everyone. My father the fruit rancher maintained that anyone who counts on the weather for a living is crazy. Point taken.

By noon there was no sign of a break in the rain. Matthias Kammerer, the resort's general manager, graciously granted us permission to start shooting inside in the hotel's lobby. The fountain in the lobby was created by the same artist who designed the fountain at the pool. I realized that with some clever lighting and postproduction in Adobe Photoshop CS, this location would enable us to get shooting and provide visual continuity while we quietly prayed to the weather goddess for her elusive sunshine. Always have a Plan B.

Faking Sunlight

The sunshine, if any had come our way, would have been diffused a bit by the clouds. I wanted my guess of what the light might be later to match what we were doing inside. The lighting in the lobby consisted of one head and a reflector pointed into a 42 x 72-inch Chimera light panel covered with translucent fabric.

We were able to work through four setups in the lobby. Guests, front desk staff, bellmen, and the concierge all enjoyed watching the beautiful women posing in the latest swimwear.

Justin archived the raw files to CDs that evening and built out a Web Photo Gallery for review. Back in Atlanta, I reviewed the take and jotted down file numbers of shots I liked (14.1). The shape of Tia's body, her lowered chin, and smile is the winner for this suit by Luli Fama. Download the folder for Chaper 14 from www.amesphoto.com/learning to begin this exercise.

Step *1*: **Open 2062-Q-0201.dcr by double-clicking it in File Browser.**

The exposure and color balance setting have been already set for you. Rotate the file to vertical and set the bit depth to 16 Bits/Channel. Click OK. The retouching strategy map (14.2) outlines the work to be done in this project. The file 2062-Q-0201Map.psd included in the folder has the strategy layer for you to reference.

14.2

14.1

**Healing Lines
that Cross a
Shadow**

To heal lines that cross a shadow sample in the middle of the shadow (14.3) and then align the Healing brush in the center of the shadow. Heal into the shadow (14.4) and then into the highlight. The sample of the shadow is seamlessly healed along with the line.

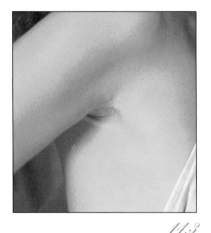

14.3

14.4

Note

All the work in Step Three has been shown in detail in previous chapters. Please refer to them for detailed step-by-step instructions.

Step 2: **Duplicate the Background layer by pressing ⌘/Control+J. Rename it Retouch.**

Step 3: **Do the retouching outlined on the strategy map, removing blemishes and softening the lines on Tia's neck and face. Heal any blemishes on her body that draw attention. Brighten her eyes.**

Look closely at the skin on Tia's hip below her bikini line. There is texture that could use smoothing.

Step 4: **Use the Pen tool to draw a path around her hip excluding the bikini, strings, and shadows. Only outline the front leg (14.5). Save your path.**

Step 5: **⌘/Control+click on Path 1 to make it into a selection.**
You can also drag Path 1 to the Load Path as Selection icon (14.6).

Step 6: **Press ⌘/Control+Option/Alt+D to open the Feather Selection dialog box and feather the selection 0.3 pixels.**

Path shown in green

14.5

Step 7: **Press ⌘/Control+J to make the selection into its own layer. Name it** Leg.

Step 8: **Click the Lock Transparent Pixels icon located under the blending modes drop-down menu in the Layers palette.**
A padlock icon appears on the right edge of the Leg layer (14.7).

14.6

Step 9: **Choose Filter➡Blur➡Gaussian Blur. Enter** 2 **pixels and click OK.**

Step 10: **Hold down the ⌘/Control key and click on the Leg layer to load its pixels as a selection.**

Step 11: **Choose Select➡Modify➡Contract, enter** 10 **pixels, and click OK** (14.8).

Step 12: **Enter Quick Mask mode by pressing Q. Open the Gaussian Blur filter dialog box. Enter 13.5 pixels and click OK** (14.9). **Press Q once more to exit Quick Mask mode.**

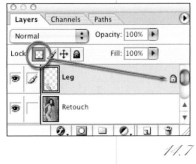

14.7

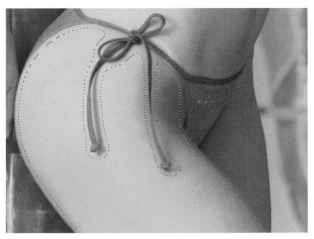

14.8

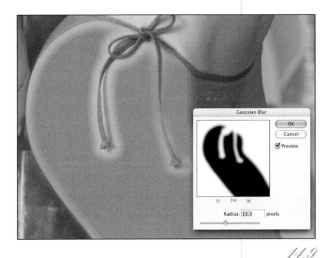

14.9

Note

By now it is my hope you are drawing your own paths. If this ultra-accurate method of making selections still escapes you or you want to move quickly through this project, one is provided in the file 2062-Q-0201Map.psd. Activate the path by clicking on Path 1. Select it with the Direct Selection tool (A) by drawing a box around it and drag it to the file you created from 2062-Q-0201.dcr. As long as the files are the same size, the path will snap into the correct position.

Step *13*: **Open the Gaussian Blur filter dialog box again. Blur the Leg layer 5.1 pixels. Press ⌘/Control+D to deselect.**

Achieving Realistic Texture

Compared to the rest of Tia's skin, the leg altered in the preceding section looks plastic and fake. We'll add some noise and use a couple of blending modes to make it look real.

Note

The Gaussian Blur filter blurs the edge of the Quick Mask, providing a visual guide to how much the edge of the selection will be softened (feathered). The blurring extends into the edges of the shadows.

Step *14*: **Choose Filter➡Noise➡Add Noise from the main menu.**

Once again we'll use 3% for the amount. This time, change the Distribution to Uniform. Select the Monochromatic check box (14.10).

Step *15*: **Choose Edit➡Fade Add Noise or press ⌘/Control+ Shift+F to open the Fade dialog box. Set the Opacity to 75% and the Mode to Luminosity (14.11).**

The result is better. It is still too smooth. Any hint of the underlying texture is gone.

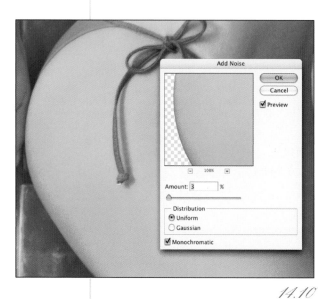

14.10

14.11

Step *16*: Duplicate the Leg layer by pressing ⌘/Control+J. Rename Leg Copy to Leg Darken. **Rename Leg to** Leg Lighten.

Step *17*: **Change the Blending mode of the Leg Lighten layer to Lighten and of the Leg Darken layer to Darken.**

Step *18*: **Set the Opacity of Leg Lighten to 60% and Leg Darken to 50%** (14.12). **Save the file as** 2062-Q-0201.psd.

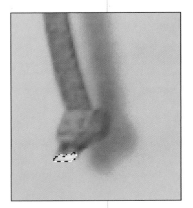

The combination of the two layers alternately lightens and darkens the textures. The Lighten layer lightens the pixels underneath it while the Darken layer does the same thing for the darker pixels. Lowering the opacity of the layers reveals varying amounts of the underlying texture. Compare the results of the skin on Tia's front leg to that on her side above the bikini. They are very similar. This is realistic enhancement.

Performing Touchups

The retouching portion is almost complete. We'll straighten out the twist on the strap on her top and get rid of the white fabric that is showing on the ends of the strings.

Step *19*: **Highlight the Retouch layer. Select the Magic Wand tool from the toolbox and set up the Options bar as shown here** (14.13).

Step *20*: **Zoom into 200%. Click the Magic Wand on the white end of the knotted string. Feather the selection** 0.3 **pixels** (14.14).

14.12

14.13

14.14

Step : **Select the Clone Stamp tool from the toolbox and sample on the wide part of the string. Using a 10-pixel brush, clone the sampled area over the selected white end.**

The selection will constrain any overcloning. Press ⌘/Control+H to hide the marching ants and check your work. Repeat for the other two string ends.

Finally we'll fix the twist in the strap on the top.

Note

If the Magic Wand selects an area outside the white, reduce the tolerance.

Step : **Draw a path around the strap where it would be if it were not twisted** (14.15).

Save the path as **Path 2** or use Path 2 from 2062-Q-0201Map.

Step *23*: **⌘/Control+click on Path 2 to load it as a selection** (14.16). **Feather the selection 1 pixel.**

Step *24*: **Use the Clone Stamp tool to sample the strap to the left of the selection by Option/Alt+clicking. Clone over the selected area.**

The selection constrains the cloning to the strap. ⌘/Control+D to deselect.

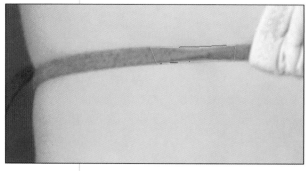

14.15

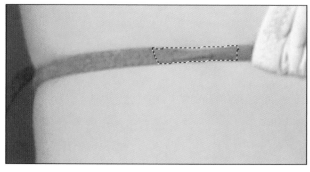

14.16

Step 25: **Make a new layer above Leg Darken. Hold down the Option/Alt key and choose Merge Visible from the Layer palette's fly-out menu. Rename the layer** Tia. **Hide all the other layers by holding down Option/Alt and clicking the eye icon on the Tia layer.**

That wraps up the retouching and enhancements to Tia. Next up, we'll take this inside photograph into the great sunshine-filled outdoors.

Getting Our Sun-Filled Shot

One of the expectations that editors have of their photographers is that they will get the shot — one way or another. Ideally everything works out on the day of the shoot. And just when did *anything* ever happen exactly as planned? While I would love to tell you that adding the beach behind Tia was always part of my plan, the truth is the idea didn't happen in Florida. I figured it out while reviewing the Web photo gallery back in the studio. If it had occurred to me during the photography, I would have put a white background behind Tia to make her hair easier to work with. Oh well. The point is that with good skills behind the camera and in front of the computer, you the photographer can make the image happen.

The three things that make this shot come together are as follows: knocking out the background, dealing with Tia's hair, and matching the focus of the replacement scene with the pillars of the fountain. We'll start with the background.

It's Pen tool time again! I can feel your excitement.

Step 1: **Use the Pen tool to draw a path around the pillars, ceiling, inside of Tia's hair, and the opening behind her. (Hint: The pillars are out of focus. Cutting the path into the out-of-focus areas is a good thing.) Save the path as** Path 3. As always, a pre-made path is available, in this case in 2062-Q-0201Map.psd. Use the technique from the previous section to move the path into place. I encourage you to make your own paths. The Pen tool is so versatile and useful it is the most powerful single tool in Photoshop (14.17).

14.17

I know you're eager to open up the background for the sky and ocean scene. Before getting onto that, later we are going to need a copy of the hair we are about to remove.

Step 2: Use the Elliptical Marquee tool to draw a circle around Tia's head, including all of her head and part of the background (14.18).

Step 3: Press ⌘/Control+J to make the selection into a separate layer. Rename it Hair. Click the eye icon off on the Hair layer.

Step 4: Click the Tia layer to activate it.

Step 5: Click the Path palette. ⌘/Control+click Path 3 to select it.

Step 6: Go back to the Layers palette, hold down the Option/Alt key, and click the Add Layer Mask icon at the bottom of the Layers palette.

The background walls and part of Tia's hair disappear to transparency. They are hidden by the layer mask (14.19). Go back to the Paths palette and click in the open area to deselect Path 3. Return to the Layers palette.

14.18

14.19

Step 7: **Open 2062-Q-0903.dcr in Camera Raw by double-clicking it in File Browser.**

We'll only use the sky and ocean as the background. The image was chosen because Elizabeth is standing to one side, offering a good portion of the background to work with.

Step 8: **At the bottom of the Camera Raw dialog box, use these settings: Space: Adobe RGB (1998), Size: 3032 by 2008, Depth: 16 Bits/Channel, Resolution: 300 pixels/inch. Prepare the Adjust tab as follows: White Balance: As Shot, Temperature: 5450, Tint: +2, Exposure: +0.40, Shadows: 14, Brightness: 50, Contrast: +27, and Saturation: 0** (14.20). **Rotate the image 90° counterclockwise.**

14.20

One more adjustment to the Camera Raw dialog box will enhance the sky and ocean.

Step 9: **Click on the Calibrate tab. Increase the Blue Saturation to +39. Click OK.**

Step 10: **Select the Move tool (V). Hold down the Shift key and drag 2062-Q-0903.dcr (the file just created from Camera Raw) on top of 2062-Q-0201.psd. Close 2062-Q-903.dcr.**

The photograph of Elizabeth is now covering Tia.

Step 11: **Enter Free Transform mode by pressing ⌘/Control+T.**

Step 12: **Control+click (right-click) inside the photograph to bring up the Free Transform context menu. Select Flip Horizontal** (14.21). **Click the Commit Transform check box.**

14.21

Step *13*: Rename Layer 1 Sea & Sky. **Click in the thumbnail and drag it just below the Tia layer** (14.22). Elizabeth is now peeking out behind Tia (14.23).

Step *14*: **Select the Move tool from the toolbox. Hold down the Shift key and drag Elizabeth behind the red column on the left.**

Step *15*: **Enter Free Transform mode again. Type in 175% in the W field and** 111% **in the H field.** Notice that Elizabeth's leg shows behind Tia's (14.24).

Step *16*: **Solve this problem by typing** 468.3 px **in the X field and** 1682.8 px **in the Y field. Click the Commit Transform check box to accept the changes.** The transformation has been done in 16 bit, meaning there will be no loss of image quality in the final file.

Step *17*: **Choose Image➡Duplicate. Rename the file 2062-Q-0201 8-bit.psd.**

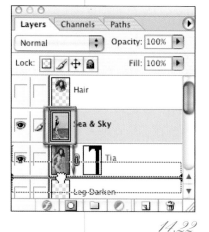

14.22

14.23

14.24

Step 18: **Choose Image➡Mode➡8 Bits/Channel. Press ⌘/Control+S to save this file. Click Save in the Save dialog box.** All the 16-bit work is finished (14.25).

Step 19: **Save and close 2062-Q-0201.psd.** This keeps all the 16-bit work intact for future use (like when the editor changes her/his mind! Note: I said *when*, not *if*!).

Fixing Tia's Hair

Tia has one of the worst cases of helmet hair going on. The next section deals with extracting her hair from the background on the Hair layer.

Step 1: **Option/Alt+click on the eye icon on the Hair layer.** This hides all the other layers. Another way of pulling hair off of a background is using the Extract filter.

Step 2: **Choose Filter➡Extract to open the Extract dialog box.**

Step 3: **Select the Zoom tool from the menu bar on the left of the dialog box. Zoom in until you can see detail in Tia's hair** (14.26).

14.25

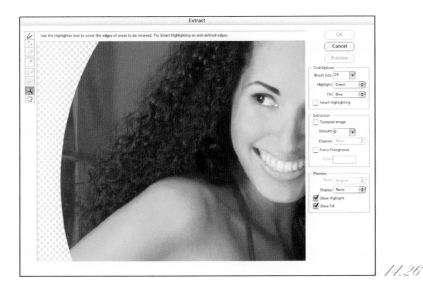

14.26

Step 4: **Choose the Highlighter tool (B). Paint green, the default color, over all the hair that extends into the background. Hold down the spacebar, and click and drag to scroll to a new section. Highlight all around the edges of Tia's hair** (14.27).

Note

The Fill tool becomes available only when an area is completely surrounded by the green highlight.

Step 5: **Choose the Fill tool (G) and click inside the highlighted area.**

It fills with blue. Click Preview.

Step 6: **Click Display in the Preview section of the dialog box. Choose Other from the drop-down menu and choose a shade of blue** (14.28).

Review the extraction. It won't look perfect. That's okay. Click OK.

14.27

14.28

Step 7: Click the eye icons of the Tia and Sea & Sky layers to reveal them. Click the layer mask thumbnail on Tia to make the layer and the layer mask active.

Step 8: Select the Brush tool with a 70-pixel soft-edged brush. Set black as the foreground color. Paint the brown background away where it showed through the layer mask (14.29).

After you modify the layer mask, the result will look like this (14.30). Tia's hair on the right side looks great. On the left it's kind of shabby. The next part of the process enhances the Hair layer. And you won't believe how simple the fix is!

Step 9: Highlight the Hair layer. Duplicate it by pressing ⌘/Control+J.

Done. Yep. It's that simple! Now we'll finesse it a little bit.

Step 10: Merge the Hair copy layer down into the Hair layer by pressing ⌘/Control+E. Add a layer mask to the Hair layer.

Step 11: Paint with black using a 30-pixel 25% hard-edged brush to hide the hair that looks too unreal.

Step 12: Make a new layer and rename it Hair Retouch.

14.29

14.30

Step *13*: Select the Clone Stamp tool. Select the Use All Layers check box in the Options bar. Option/Alt+click in a thick area of Tia's hair. With a 9-pixel soft-edged brush, fill in the areas that look thin.

Match the color selection areas with the areas being covered as closely as you can. Don't worry about subtle color differences.

Step *14*: Get the Healing brush. Select the Use All Layers check box in the Options bar. Heal any areas that are mismatched in color and texture (14.31).

Now if you are like me, and are really picky about how the hair looks, well, get over it. You and I are the only ones who know exactly what the original photograph looks like. And I'm not telling. No one will know if you keep quiet, too.

Seriously, it only has to look believable, not perfect. This is one of the secrets of working in Photoshop. Hair never looks the same as the original. There is always some loss of detail. Following is a set of six quick bonus steps for you if this is truly driving you crazy.

Step *1*: Highlight the Hair layer. Draw a selection around Tia's hair on the right (14.32).

14.31

14.32

Step 2: Make the selection into its own layer by pressing ⌘/Control+J. Rename the layer Frizzies.

Step 3: Open Free Transform (⌘/Control+T) and drag the bounding box to Tia's left side. Rotate the layer by placing the cursor just outside one of the corner handles until the rotate cursor appears. Drag the handle counter-clockwise until the hair frizzies are facing out (14.33). Click the Commit Transform check mark.

14.33

Step 4: Drag the Frizzies layer above the Hair Retouch layer.

Step 5: Select the Move tool. Drag the frizzies into place (14.34).

Step 6: Add a layer mask to the Frizzies layer and use a black soft-edged brush to blend the sharp edges into Tia's hair (14.35).

Done!

14.34

14.35

Blurring the Background

The only thing left to do is make the background a little more out of focus. The edges of the pillars are too distinct. Look at the original photograph. They are quite soft. The sharpness is a side effect of the layer mask on the Tia layer. We'll handle that first.

Usually the solution is simple. Blur the layer mask on the Tia layer and the pillars will show most of their original softness. In this project, a couple of areas must remain sharp. And there is spillover from another layer. Look at the space between Tia's arms (14.36). There is some of the wall from the Hair layer showing. It comes from making the copy of Tia's Hair too large initially. This kind of thing happens, and here's how to deal with it:

Step *1*: **Click the layer mask icon in the Hair layer to highlight the layer. With a black brush, paint out the background until only sky shows behind Tia's arm** (14.37).

Now we'll set up the layer needed to bring back some of the sharpness in Tia's arm.

14.36

14.37

Step 2: **Activate the Tia layer and copy it by pressing ⌘/Control+J.**

It is automatically named Tia copy.

Step 3: **Hold down Control and click (right-click) in the layer mask icon of the Tia copy layer to show the context menu. Choose Apply Layer Mask (14.38).**

Step 4: **Holding down the Option/Alt key, click the Add Layer Mask icon.**

A black layer mask is added to the Tia copy layer. Next we'll blur the layer mask to bring back the softness of the original.

Step 5: **Highlight the Tia layer and click the layer mask. Choose Filter➡Blur➡Gaussian Blur and set a 5.1 pixel radius in the Gaussian Blur dialog box and click OK.**

Step 6: **Activate the Tia copy layer by clicking its layer mask icon. Zoom in to 100% and scroll to the sky revealed behind Tia's arms.**

Step 7: **Select the Brush tool from the toolbox. Make the brush 30 pixels in size and soft edged. Set the foreground color to white. Paint over Tia's arms using the soft edge of the brush to blend the out-of-focus pillar into the sharpness of her arm.**

Step 8: **Scroll down to her leg. Paint along the edge of her leg and bring back the sharpness (14.39).**

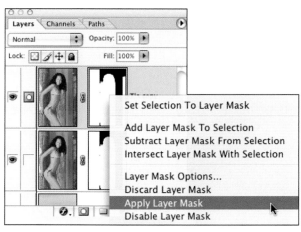

14.38

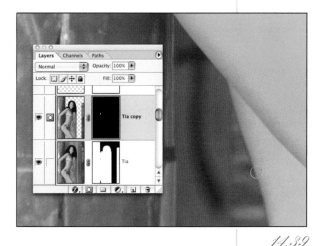

14.39

Varying the Depth of Field

There is simply too much foreground-to-horizon detail in the ocean. In a photograph such as the one of Tia, the ocean would continue to get softer as it falls off towards the horizon line. The sky is fine. After all, what is sharp about a sky? This is a job for the Lens Blur filter, which enables you to vary the depth of field.

As always some setup is required before you apply the filter for the effect.

Step 1: **Click the Gradient tool icon in the toolbox (G). Press D to set the default colors with black as the foreground color.**

Step 2: **Click the Channels tab. Click the Create New Channel icon. Click the RGB channel eye icon to show the image.**
It appears in shades of red (14.40).

Step 3: **Click at the horizon line, hold down the Shift key, and drag the gradient from the horizon line to the bottom of the frame (14.41).**
The Shift key constrains the gradient to being parallel to the horizon (14.42). Hide the Alpha 1 channel by clicking its eye icon off. Click the RGB channel.

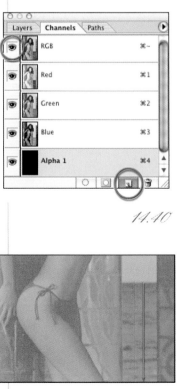

14.40

14.41

14.42

Step 4: Return to the Layers palette and click Sea & Sky. Choose Filter➤Blur➤Lens Blur to open the Lens Blur dialog box. The preview reveals the previous transforms to the layer.

Step 5: Set the Depth Map source to Alpha 1, the channel with the gradient on it. Set the Blur Focal Distance to 255. In the Iris section choose Hexagon (6) as the Shape. Set the Radius to 86. In the Noise section set the Amount at 3, the Distribution to Gaussian, and select the Monochromatic check box. Click OK.

Step 6: Make a new layer named Final and merge the visible layers to it by pressing ⌘/Control+Option/Alt+Shift+E (14.43). **Save the file as** 2062-Q-0201 8-bit.psd.

14.43

That's it. We have successfully moved a photograph made in the lobby of a hotel out into the sunshine. Now I admit that while making sunshine with Photoshop is not nearly as much fun as actually shooting outside, it has its place. The editor never saw the original and is convinced that she actually saw this scene when she did a media tour of the property a week after the shoot.

A PDF of the editorial as it appeared in *Jezebel* magazine is available on www.amesphoto.com/learning. Click "Chapter 14" or the "Learn More" link. This project is also featured on my CD *Studio to Location* from Software Cinema.

14.44

14.45

14.46

14.47

Some of the other suits from the indoor shoot are shown here (14.44, 14.46). They, too, went through the process of *making sunshine* for publication (14.45, 14.47).

Shooting Later That Same Day

By two o'clock, the rain finally stopped. The sky finally cleared, bringing Florida's claim to fame to center stage. After a quick lunch we moved to the pool. Don't worry about the models swimming right after eating — I was the one in the water for this series. As you can see from the shot of me in the pool with the camera, the sun was falling with that wonderful late afternoon directional quality that carries so much magic (14.48). It meant, too, that the wall behind the models would be in the shade, lit by the open sky behind me. The sun is coming from the left. A reflector fabric on a 42 x 72-inch panel by Chimera Lighting is bouncing the sun onto the girls, opening up the shadows by lowering the contrast (14.49). The sunlight is hitting Tia and Adelina directly. The highlights on the side of Tia's face and on Adelina's suit and torso are burned out completely. The readings in these areas are 255 across the board. The contrast of the situation is too high to capture either with digital or on film. Cutting the exposure would have killed any detail in the shadows.

We controlled the highlights by placing another panel with diffusion fabric to soften the sun coming from the right. The diffusion panel reduces the amount of direct sun so much that the bounce panel on the left side becomes the primary source of light (14.50).

This series of poolside photographs shows the light as it was without manipulation other than the normal Levels or Curves adjustment. When the weather cooperates, not all photographs have to have the huge interventions that the sky replacement project entailed. This page from the editorial shows both the front and rear views of the suit (14.51). The water in the lower-right-hand corner of the image provides an ideal space for type.

Photograph courtesy of Bruce, the dentist from Ohio.

14.48

14.49

14.50

14.51

14.52

14.51

14.53

As the sun moved lower towards the western horizon, which is artificially high due to surrounding high-rise buildings, we moved our location to the beach. Elite model Elizabeth Suttle had arrived to be fitted during the session at the pool. Justin and I shot Elizabeth in a black diva one-piece suit (14.52) while Tia and Adelina changed into new suits by Huit (14.53). Rotating models this way allowed us to shoot six outfits before sunset. We completed all twelve suits in a single day of shooting. Despite the rain, we completed the shoot a half day early.

Shooting at Sunset

With the sun (which has finally dipped below the horizon) behind the camera, we have maybe fifteen minutes of shooting left. Here, Adelina sports a Dolce & Gabbana bikini and a mesh top from Lulu K (14.54). This image was made with available light. There was no fill flash. Here is a simple method for brightening the foreground. Again the high-bit depth capture of raw files proves most useful.

Step 1: **Double-click 2062-Q-1233.dcr in File Browser to open it in the Camera Raw dialog box. Rotate the file if necessary.**

This version is the background. The settings are designed to enhance the colors of the ocean and the sunset.

Step 2: **Reduce the exposure setting to −0.50 and increase the shadows to 13.** Leave Contrast and Saturation at their defaults (14.55).

Step 3: **Click the Calibrate tab. Set the Shadow tint to +10, the Red Saturation to +23, the Blue Hue to +19, and the Blue Saturation to +40. Click OK.** The Calibration tab allows us to apply color changes to the linear data of a raw file. These changes are more robust than those made downstream using Hue/Saturation adjustment. Any modification that you can make in Camera Raw will yield a superior result to edits made in 8 or 16 bit.

14.55

Step 4: **Save the file as** 2062-Q-1233.psd. **Leave it open in Photoshop** (14.56).

Step 5: **Once again double-click 2062-Q-1233.dcr in File Browser to open Camera Raw's dialog box. Again rotate the file if necessary,**

Step 6: **Begin by choosing Camera Default in the Settings drop-down menu.**

Step 7: **Bump the Exposure slider up to +1.50. Move the Shadows slider to 8. Again, leave Contrast and Saturation at their default settings. Click OK** (14.57).

Exposure	+1.50
Shadows	8
Brightness	50
Contrast	+25
Saturation	0

14.57

14.56

14.58

Step 8: **Choose the Move tool from the toolbox. Hold down the Shift key and drag 2062-Q-1233.dcr onto 2062-Q-1233.psd. Close 2062-Q-1233.dcr without saving it** (14.58).

Step 9: **Rename Layer 1** Adelina.

Step 10: **Use the Pen tool to draw a path around Adelina. Click the Paths tab. Double-click Work Path to access the Save Path dialog box. Click OK to accept Path 1. Study the figure** (14.59) **for the details on outlining her hair.**

If you are drawing your own path on this exercise, first of all, congratulations! Second, don't draw it to modify Adelina's shape. You can do that on your own later.

Note

If your Macintosh is running under OSX Panther (version 10.3), the keyboard shortcut for Feather Selection has been reserved for the operating system. It is the shortcut to hide/reveal the Dock. You can get it back by opening Keyboard & Mouse in System Preferences in the Dock. Click the Keyboard Shortcut chicklet. Uncheck the Automatically hide and show the Dock check box (14.60).

14.59

14.60

As we reach the end of the last project in the book, I'm sure you've noticed that a lot of the techniques are similar to the point of being redundant. Actually the differences while slight, offer great finesse over the final result. Choosing the best method to apply in a given situation works only when you have seen many differing ways of doing the same job. Hair has been moved from one background to another at least four distinct ways in the projects in this book alone. Redundancy with differences is a good thing.

The Department of Redundancy Department

Step 11: ⌘/Control+click on Path 1 to load it as a selection.

Step 12: Open the Feather Selection dialog box by pressing ⌘/Control+Option/Alt+D. Enter 1 pixel. Click OK.

Step 13: Click the Add Layer Mask icon at the bottom of the Layer palette.
Bang! Adelina jumps off of the background (14.61).

As usual when a photograph has hair in it, more work is required.

Step 14: Click the Brush tool in the toolbox. Make it 20 pixels in diameter, soft edged, and set the Opacity at 75%. Make black the foreground color. Paint over the edges of Adelina's hair and in toward her face.

The increased exposure makes her hair look almost gray. The key to this technique is not to lift the mouse button or the pen from the tablet. A pressure-sensitive tablet makes easy work of this step (14.62).

14.61

14.62

Refining the Layer Mask

Not even the Pen tool can cut a perfect mask around her entire figure. Subtle work on the layer mask blends in telltale ghost lines (14.63).

Step 15: **Zoom in to 200%. Increase the size of the brush to 40 pixels. The edge is still soft. Black remains the Foreground color. Make the opacity 100%. Use just the edge of the brush to blend in the matte lines by painting in the background areas up to Adelina** (14.64).

Step 16: **Now finish removing the matte lines around Adelina. Zoom back to full frame.**
To my eye she is too bright. This is good.

Step 17: **Lower the Opacity of the Adelina layer to 70%.**
Everything blends. It's all good (14.65).

Step 18: **Merge your work to a new layer named** Final.
If the hot spots in the sunset bother you, use the Healing brush to paint them down. You can also remove the channel marker above her head to the right. Add any retouching you would like to Adelina. Finish up the work and save your file.

> **Note**
> It's okay to paint black into Adelina's body when the matte line is too small to work with the 40-pixel brush. Press X to make the foreground color white and paint the lighter tone back in (14.64).

14.63

14.64

A day of photography on location is challenging, hectic and, as you have seen, richly rewarding. We all had a great time making these images. The magazine was pleased with the work and ran the editorial just as this book was coming off the press. A location shoot produces more than photographs; it makes memories for all involved. Here is one of my favorites.

The award for *Who-Had-The-Most-Fun-On-The-Shoot* goes to my assistant, Justin Larose (14.66). Look at his grin. Can you blame him? He's right in the middle of Tia, Adelina, and Elizabeth!

Well, that's about it. We've worked through a lot of different projects together. Following this chapter is an appendix and, frankly, it's important. It is a list of the people who made the photographs possible: the models, makeup artists, assistants, and stylists. Take a moment to read these credits. Without these people and their contributions this book would not have happened. (If you're curious there is also a list of the gear used to make the photographs: the cameras, lenses, lighting equipment, computers, monitors, color management tools, and such.)

Let me know what worked for you in the book. More importantly tell me what didn't. My e-mail address is kevin@amesphoto.com. I look forward to hearing from you.

Last and most certainly not close to least, thanks for buying this book and for spending your valuable time working with the most popular subject in the history of photography to learn about Photoshop, its most fascinating tool.

14.66

14.65

Appendix A
Resources

Photoshop CS: The Art of Photographing Women was written on an Apple Macintosh G-4 Titanium PowerBook with Microsoft Word for Mac. The photographs and illustrations were produced on Apple Macintosh G-4 and G-5 computers using Adobe Photoshop CS. Colors were proofed on a Fuji Pictrography 4500 and in PDF format. The book was produced electronically in Indianapolis, Indiana, with QuarkXpress 4.11 on Apple Macintosh G-4. The typeface families used are Adobe Garamond, Christiana, and Courier.

Professional Assistance

A photo shoot includes a lot of people. Talent agents help with casting the models. The models work hard to help bring concepts to life. Stylists pull clothes and props, then dress the models and prepare the set as well. Hair and makeup artists bring out the natural beauty that the camera records. Assistants make sure everything is at the photographer's fingertips without being asked. These are the professionals who have made the photographs in *Photoshop CS: The Art of Photographing Women* happen. If you are working on location in Atlanta, I recommend them.

THE MODELS

Amanda Daniels, Click Models of Atlanta

Tiffany Dupont, Elite/Atlanta and CED Talent/Los Angeles

Marie Friemann

Adelina Guerrero, Elite/Miami

Jennifer Hendrickson, Elite/Atlanta

Tia Hinton, Elite/Atlanta

Adair Howell, Elite/Atlanta

Rachel Keller, Elite/Atlanta

Amy Lucas, Houghton Talent

Mary Beth Montgomery, Elite/Atlanta

Cara Orten

Christina Parfene, Elite/Atlanta

Laura Phillips, Elite/Atlanta

Mindy Samus

Annie Shu, Elite/Atlanta

Elizabeth Shuttle, Elite/Miami

Carrie Thomas, Elite/Atlanta

Ava Ward, Click Models of Atlanta

Valerie White, Click Models of Atlanta

HAIR AND MAKEUP

Fawn Green for M.A.C, Click Models of Atlanta

Brian Keller, Click Models of Atlanta/Carter Barnes

Janeen Loria, CREWS (www.moodymakeup.com)

Paige Schneider, CREWS

Nicole Sohn, CREWS

Tony & Guy, Atlanta

STYLISTS

L.J. Adams, CREWS (linda@dlancystreet.com)

Christa Levet, CREWS

Jamiya Williams

STYLING ASSISTANTS

Cristle Grizzelle

LaTara Jester

Lakisha Minter

Jamiya Williams

PHOTOGRAPHIC ASSISTANT

Justin Larose (404-808-2381)

Clothing and props

In Atlanta: Almanac, Atlanta Beach, Bob Ellis, Intimacy, Jeffery, L'Asia, Luna, Bano Italian Design, The PropMistress

In New York: Sanyo

Resources

CREWS, Shirlene Brooks; 877-504-6880; shrilene@crewsinc.net; www.crewsinc.net

Elite Atlanta, 1701 Peachtree Street NW, Suite 210, Atlanta, GA 30309; 404-872-7444 (contact Lois Thigpen at loisthigpen@eliteatlanta.com)

Click Models of Atlanta, Inc., 79 Poplar Street, Suite B, Atlanta, GA 30303; 404-688-9700

Cunningham, Escot, Dipene Talent Agency, 10635 Santa Monica Blvd., Suite 135, Los Angeles, CA 90025; 310-475-7573; www.cedtalent.com (contact Leslie Cascales at lcascales@cedtalent.com)

Professional Photographic Resources, 667 Eleventh Street, Atlanta, GA 30318; 404-885-1885; www.ppratlanta.com

Showcase Photographics, 2323 Cheshire Bridge Road, Atlanta, GA 30324; 404-325-7676; www.showcaseinc.com

Photo Barn, 4400 Business Park Court, Lilburn, GA 30047; 770-921-9500; www.photobarn.com

Professional Photographers of America, 229 Peachtree Street N.E., Suite 2200, Atlanta, GA 30303; 404-522-8600; www.ppa.com

National Association of Photoshop Professionals, 333 Douglas Road East, Oldsmar, FL 34677; 813-433-5000; www.photoshopuser.com

Houghton Talent, 919 Collier Road, N.W., Atlanta, GA 30318; 404-603-9454 (contact Mystie Buice at mystie@houghtontalent.com)

Gear

There is a tradition in photography books that the equipment used to make the photographs be listed with each image along with the exposure information. Those using Adobe Photoshop CS can find the exposure information in File Browser under the Metadata tab for each of the sample files you downloaded from www.amesphoto.com/learning. The cameras, lenses, supports, and lighting equipment used in creating the photographs that appear in *Photoshop CS: The Art of Photographing Women* are listed here:

CAMERAS, CAMERA SUPPORTS, AND LENSES

Canon 1Ds with 28-70mm f/2.8, 85mm f/1.8 Canon EF lenses (www.canoneos.com)

Foveon Studio Camera with 17-35mm f/2.8, 28-70mm f/2.8 Canon EF lenses (www.foveon.com)

Kodak/Nikon F-5 DCS-760C with 17-35mm f/2.8D, 28-70mm f/2.8D, and 80-200mm f/2.8D AFS Nikkor lenses (www.kodak.com)

Leaf DCBII mounted on a Fuji GX680II with 80mm and 135mm Fujinon lenses (www.leafamerica.com; www.fujifilm.com)

Sigma SD9 and SD10 cameras with 15-30mm f/3.5-4.5, 20-40mm f/2.8, Sigma DG and 70-200 mm f/2.8 Sigma APO and 180mm f/2.8 Sigma Macro APO lenses (www.sigmaphoto.com)

CAMERA SUPPORTS

Foba Studio Stand (www.sinarbron.com)

Gitzo Studex 1320 and Studex 1509 tripods (www.bogenphoto.com)

LIGHTING STUDIO

Matthews Studio Equipment: C Light Stands, Grip Heads, Grip Arms, Mafer and Matthellini Clamps, Flags, Scrims, and Cookies

Norman: 2000D, P4000, PH4000 power packs, LH2000 and LH2400 flash heads with reflectors including 22" (beauty dish) with grid spot, 16" and 10"

Chimera Super Pro II medium and large soft boxes, large strip light with fabric grids

72" x42" light panels with diffusion, white reflective and black fabric panels

LIGHTING LOCATION

Chimera: Super Pro II medium soft boxes 72" x42" light panels with diffusion, white reflective and black fabric panels

Comet CX244 and CL1250 power packs

Comet CL-24II flash heads

Lowel Light: Omni Stands, KS Stands, Full Pole

Matthews Studio Equipment: C Light Stands, Grip Heads, Grip Arms, Mafer and Mathellini Clamps

LIGHTING RESOURCES

Chimera Lighting (www.chimeralighting.com)

Lowel-Light Manufacturing (www.lowel.com)

Matthews Studio Equipment (www.msegrip.com)

Norman Electronic Flash (www.bookendzdocks.com)

DIGITAL IMAGING

Apple Macintosh Computers (www.apple.com)

G-5 Dual 2 GHz processor with 4.5GB RAM

G-4 Dual 1.42 GHz processor with 2GB RAM

G-4 Titanium PowerBook 1GHz processor with 1GB RAM

Other World Computing FireWire 400, 800, and On The Go external drives (www.macsales.com)

SOFTWARE

Adobe Photoshop CS (www.adobe.com)

Cumulus 6.0 (www.canto.com)

Portfolilo 6.0 (www.extensis.com)

iView Media Pro (www.iview-multimedia.com)

MONITORS

Barco Reference Calibrator

Apple Cinema Display (www.apple.com)

LaCie Electron Blue IV (www.lacie.com)

Radius Press View

GRAPHICS TABLETS

Wacom Cintiq 18

Wacom Intuos 2 Platinum 6 x 8 (www.wacom.com)

PRINTERS

Epson 900, 1270, and 7600 (Ultrachrome Inkset) (www.epson.com)

Fuji Pictrography 3000 (www.fujifilm.com)

COLOR MANAGEMENT

A to Z Color Consulting (www.atozcolor.com/prod.html)

GretagMacbeth Eye One Publish (www.i1color.com)

WEB SITE PROGRAMMING

Dynamic Page (www.DynamicPage.com)

SOUNDTRACK

It takes an awful lot of music to write a book. I convert my CDs to MP3 format and play them back with Apple's iTunes. Music helps with inspiration and the rhythms make the typing faster. The bands and artists whose music contributed both to the writing of this book in no particular order are:

The Ataris, The Chevelles, Weezer, Foo Fighters, Blink 182, Nirvana, The Knack, The Beatles, Pink Floyd, Led Zeppelin, Three Doors Down, Train, Jimmy Eat World, Jean Michael Jarre, Tenacious D, Keith Jarrett, R.E.M., U2, The Rolling Stones, Steppenwolf, Joan Jett, Pat Benatar, Placebo, Poe, The Police, Portishead, Morphine, Cocteau Twins, Red Hot Chili Peppers, Rickie Lee Jones, Sister Hazel, Bare Naked Ladies, Collective Soul, Guster, Smashing Pumpkins, Pearl Jam, Zwan, Yes, Styx, Queen, No Doubt, Cake, Cardigans, Garbage, Chicago, Chumbawamba, Coldplay, Counting Crows, Sheryl Crowe, David Bowie, Dire Straits, Mark Knopfler, Dirty Vegas, Eminem, Cream, Fuel, Filter, Gorillaz, The Laura Glyda Band, The RZA, Heart, Hole, James, The James Gang, Jane's Addiction, The Violent Femmes, John Mayer, Angie Aparo, The Lemonheads, Live, Massive Attack, Madonna, Natalie Imbruglia, Prodigy, Radiohead, Tal Bachman, Stone Temple Pilots, The Thorns, Van Morrison, Wyclef Jean, Pink, and Warren Zevon. We miss you Warren.

Appendix B

Photoshop CS Shortcuts and Tools

Many shortcut keys are available in Adobe Photoshop CS. So many that if you want to set up your own shortcut keys using the command, Edit➡Keyboard Shortcuts, you'll find there are not a lot of keys left to use. The point is that you don't have to know them all. Here are the ones I use all the time and ones you might, too.

Menu Shortcuts

Save File	⌘/Control+S
Save File As	⌘/Control+Shift+S
Close File	⌘/Control+W
Close All Open Files	⌘/Control+Option/Alt+W
Levels	⌘/Control+L
Repeat Previous Levels Settings	⌘/Control+Option/Alt+L
Curves	⌘/Control+M
Repeat Previous Curves Settings	⌘/Control+Option/Alt+M
Invert	⌘/Control+I
New Document	⌘/Control+N

Layers

New Layer with New Layer dialog box	⌘/Control+Shift+N
New Layer	⌘/Control+Option/Alt+Shift+N
Merge Down	⌘/Control+E
Merge Visible Layers	⌘/Control+Shift+E
Merge Visible Layers to Active Layer	⌘/Control+Option/Alt+Shift+E
Copy a Selection to a New Layer	⌘/Control+J
Cut a Selection and Paste to a New Layer	⌘/Control+Shift+J
Cycle Forward Through Blending Modes (in the Move tool)	Shift key++ (plus sign)

continued

Layers (continued)

Cycle Backward Through Blending Modes (in the Move tool)	Shift key+– (minus sign)
Layer Opacity (in the Move tool)	Press keyboard numeral 1 for 10%, 2 for 20%, 3 for 30%, and so on. Press 0 for 100%. Press two keys in rapid succession for in-between numbers (for example, 24 = 24%).

Selections

Select All	⌘/Control+A
Deselect	⌘/Control+D
Feather Selection	⌘/Control+Option/Alt+D
Inverse Selection	⌘/Control+Shift+I
Hide Selection	⌘/Control+H
Luminosity Selection from RGB Composite	⌘/Control+Option/Alt+~ (tilde key)
Luminosity Selection from Red Channel	⌘/Control+Option/Alt+1
Luminosity Selection from Green Channel	⌘/Control+Option/Alt+2
Luminosity Selection from Blue Channel	⌘/Control+Option/Alt+3
Brush Edge Harder	Shift+] (hardens 25% per stroke)

Tools

V	Move tool
M	Marquee tools
L	Lasso tools
W	Magic Wand
C	Crop tool
J	Healing, Patch, and Color Replacement tools
B	Brush and Pencil tools
S	Clone and Pattern Stamp tools
G	Gradient and Paint Bucket tools
A	Path and Direct Selection tools
P	Pen Tool and Freeform Pen tool
T	Type tool
U	Shape tools
I	Eye Dropper, Color Sampler, and Measure tools
Q	Quick Mask mode
F	Full Screen with Menu Bar (gray background), Full Screen (black background), Standard (Document window)
Brush Size	[or] (left and right bracket keys)
Brush Edge Softer	Shift+[(softens 25% per stroke)

I have not listed all the tools in the toolbox as shortcuts because there are some destructive tools that I never use. (For example, I never use the Eraser tool.) Also, knowing every single keyboard shortcut is not necessary.

In addition, there is a cool way to customize tool selection. Photoshop's default requires holding down the Shift key and presssing the tool's letter to cycle through the nested options. L+Shift+L cycles from the Lasso tool to the Polygonal Lasso tool, for example. If you go to the General Preferences pane by pressing ⌘/Control+K, and *uncheck* the Use Shift Key for Tool Switch box, pressing the letter M and then M again moves between Rectangular and Elliptical Marquee tools. This is a huge timesaver.

Index

T

U

Download the Project Files

All of the files used in *Photoshop CS: The Art of Photographing Women* are available as free downloads from www.ames photo.com/learning. Other tips, techniques, ideas, extras, and new projects will be posted from time to time making your investment in this book even more valuable. Comments, observations, and questions are welcome. Email us at learning@amesphoto.com.